COLLECTED PLAYS
2009 – 2017

ALLAN KOLSKI HORWITZ

Paardeberg
Arts Trust

First published in 2017
by the Paardeberg Arts Trust and Botsotso
Box 30952, Braamfontein, 2017
botsotso@artslink.co.za
www.botsotso.org.za

© in the text – Allan Kolski Horwitz 2017

Cover image by Pierre Lagarde

ISBN   978-0-9947081-0-6

The Pump Room was previously published by Botsotso in 2010

Comrade Babble was first published in the anthology *Against the Tide* in 2014

Photographs of *Jerico* © Sanmari Marais (State Theatre)

NATIONAL ARTS COUNCIL
OF SOUTH AFRICA

The author would like to express his great appreciation to the National Arts Council of South Africa for its continuing assistance. This support has been vital in enabling these plays to reach the stage.

CONTENTS

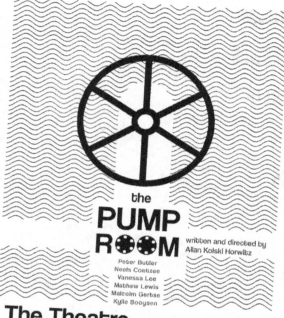

THE PUMP ROOM

Allan Kolski Horwitz

PETER and MIKE (Johannesburg production)

LOMBARD and MUMSIE (Johannesburg production)

LEWIS and ELS (Cape Town production)

ELS, LOMBARD and MUMSIE (Cape Town production)

Program notes

Force creates pressure and pressure creates counter- pressure. The result? A blowout.

The Pump Room is a drama about the intersection of the criminal and political worlds, the sexual and the ideological. It is a play about the South African reality of the late 1990s, but one which applies to many other societies that have experienced epochs in their history when, after a long period of oppression, a new period struggles to resolve the past and deal with fresh challenges.

The central event is the murder of a 'postman' carrying drugs. Over several hours on a hot summer's night, the consequences of this action cause a number of interconnected people to meet in the pump room of a public swimming pool in Cape Town. These disparate characters play out the tensions and contradictions of their pasts and presents, and a complex web of relationships emerges.

One of the key elements is the renewed confrontation between Peter, a middle-aged pump room worker (but one-time actor and political activist), with Mike and Lombard, former Apartheid agents who had previously detained and tortured him. This history dogs them. The time of both revolutionary political activism and of state terrorism is over – the cease fire of 1994 has come into place and they are all now involved in an underworld of drug dealing [and taking] and are desperately, if paradoxically, trying to restore some balance to their lives.

Other characters are Lewis, Peter's pump room assistant who is both a dealer and an informer; Elsie, Lewis's girlfriend, a domestic worker; and Mumsie, also a domestic worker and occasional prostitute, who is connected to both Peter and Lombard, but in very different, conflicting ways. An off-stage but integral character is Sandra [whose photograph in the form of a poster dominates the pump room], Peter's ex-comrade and lover. Sandra was a white woman from a privileged Afrikaner background who had joined an underground resistance group and was detained and tortured with him; her subsequent exile to Canada and success as an actress is a source of both pride and pain for Peter who has never stopped loving her and has never stopped condemning her for abandoning him.

In structural terms the first three acts introduce the characters and set out the outlines of the action; the last two clarify and explain their identities and relationships and provide a solution to the initial mystery: who 'robbed' the 'postman' and why?

In *The Pump Room* I have tried to merge soap opera and the classic Greek dramas that relentlessly expose the consequences of both arrogance and weakness. In physical terms the set represents such strongly contrasted psychological states: the pump room itself is very sparse and dimly lit, a confined and smelly space [to parallel the prison cell in which Peter was once detained]; the outside section, a moon-lit promenade with railings facing the ocean is, though in stage terms much smaller than the pump room, a space that enables the characters to divulge more intimate and details of their emotions and thoughts. Throughout the play, the audial elements [the sound of filters in the pump room, the ebb and flow of ocean waves] form counterpoints to the human noise of conversation and verbal challenge.

South African protest theatre has a rich history, but today's issues are in many ways more complex than those of the Apartheid period and their exploration requires a subtler, more poetic and sometimes humorous approach. I hope this play contributes to the evolution of a new dramatic approach and style to deal with these changed circumstances.

~~

The first performance of THE PUMP ROOM took place at the Windybrow Theatre, Johannesburg on 24 July 2009 with the following cast:

PETER	A Coloured man in his forties	Shane de Kock
LEWIS	A Coloured man in his twenties	Decklan Palmer
MIKE	A white man in his thirties	Leeroy Duke
LOMBARD	A white man in his forties	Ben Horowitz
ELSIE	A Coloured woman in her twenties	Lecurtia Booysens
MUMSIE	A Coloured woman in her forties	Nicole Hendricks

A second production was staged in April 2011 at Theatre in the District, Cape Town with the following cast:

PETER	Peter Butler
LEWIS	Malcom Geertse
MIKE	Mathew Lewis
LOMBARD	Neels Coetzee
ELSIE	Kylie Booysen
MUMSIE	Vanessa Lee

Both productions were directed by Allan Kolski Horwitz.

SETTING

The action takes place on a hot summer evening in the basement pump room of a public swimming pool in Sea Point, Cape Town, and in an outside area fronting onto the ocean.

The pump room floor covers three quarters of the stage. It is filled with a number of chairs and a table [on which are placed a bottle of wine and several glasses], a control panel and, at rear stage left, a sluice-wheel. A large poster of an intelligent and attractive woman [Sandra] is stuck prominently to the rear wall.

On one side of the pump room is a short ladder that leads up to a small platform. Leading off this platform is a single door through which all entrances and exits are made. This platform serves as both an entrance hall to the pump room and as an outside space – a section of the pool area running alongside the ocean. The platform rails thus also become the outside promenade rails.

A full moon illuminates the scenes that take place on the promenade. For these outside scenes a cloth drawing of a full moon can be draped over the door which leads onto the landing. Between scenes, during blackouts, either the crashing of waves or the hum/grinding of machinery is heard.

ACT 1	Ten o'clock at night
ACT 11	Later that night
ACT 111	Even later
ACT 1V	Much later
ACT V	Just before dawn

ACT I

Scene 1

The pump room. While the audience is taking their seats, they see PETER on stage. He is alone and is busy fixing machine parts, moving tools around and generally work-ing quietly. At one point he stops to read the newspaper, and drinks wine. The hum of machinery is heard intermittently. Soon after the house lights dim, there is a knock at the door.

LEWIS: Piet! [PETER *goes up onto the landing and unlocks the door.*]

PETER: Ha, you're early. You're nice and fucking early. [LEWIS *enters but remains on the landing; takes an overall out of a bag and starts putting it on over his pants. PETER walks back down into the pump room.*] Where you been, Lewis? It's almost ten o'clock. Where the hell have you been? You know what we've got to do. [*Slight pause.*] And where's my screwdriver? The blue one. Where did you put it? [*LEWIS ignores him, opens the door and leaves.*] Go on, run. "Get thee to a nun-nery . . ." Ja, run . . . He can never be straight. Bloody parasite. Where's my damn blue screwdriver? [*Picks up the bottle of wine on the table, fills a glass, drinks; addresses the woman in the poster.*] Day after day, what's new? Day after fucking day . . . These fools! They want everything, I hope they lose everything. That should be the law of the universe? But who's going to believe that? You fight a fight, you fight hard, you think you know where it's going . . . [*The door swings open. LEWIS is holding a blue screwdriver in one hand.*] Ah! You always come right in the end. Pass it here. (*LEWIS remains on the landing.*] Come on down already. We got work, and the future, goddammit, is in your hands. Imagine, it's almost the turn of the century, no, a fucking new millenium, and it's in your bloody hands! That's a fine state of affairs, hey, my boy? And lock the door. There cra-zies out there.

LEWIS: Give me a break, man.

PETER: You one of them now, Lewis? Why you so late? You running away? Why you doing this? You know we got to start the pumps soon.

LEWIS: It's been a hell of a day.

PETER: Why you so late?

LEWIS: I had to sort something out, a family problem. [*Slight pause.*] Jesus, look at your eyes – you been suiping again? [*Descends into the pump room.*]

PETER: And you? You're not messing around anymore, are you? No, Lewis's got a lekker plan to save his arse. Who you fooling? The day's not over. Remember that. [*Leaves his chair and starts working on a switch on the control panel.*] Talk, man, there's got to be trust. I'm getting soft on you. And after how many years of your nonsense?

LEWIS: [*Walks up to PETER.*] Listen, you still owe me. I need that five hundred.

PETER: Five?

LEWIS: That's right, my man. Five.

PETER: You'll get it. You'll get every last cent, Lewis.

LEWIS: I need it, man.

PETER: What's the rush? Go get the bucks from your other boss.

LEWIS: I can't do that, man. You know I want to get out.

PETER: You do, hey?

LEWIS: Ja.

PETER: What a pity.

LEWIS: Shut up! I need the bucks now.

PETER: Right now. Why?

LEWIS: Just look at your bladdy eyes . . .

PETER: Stop talking about my eyes and think about your backside while you still got something to sit on.

LEWIS: Piss off, man.

PETER: I don't like supporting fools.

LEWIS: I've done you more than a few.

PETER: What?

LEWIS: Favours.

PETER: Favours? You done me favours? Ha! [*Pause.*] I can't pay you now.

LEWIS: I need those bucks. I want to get out.

PETER: Who can believe you?

LEWIS: I've told them already.

PETER: And what did they say?

LEWIS: You know what they say.

PETER: So why all this nonsense?

LEWIS: Because I want to get out.

PETER: Then go.

LEWIS: I need my bucks.

PETER: Ok, tomorrow. Any particular way you'd like them – baked, stewed, boiled, fried . . .

LEWIS: I want them tonight.

PETER: I'm not running away, Lewis. Long before you rolled this way I was here minding my business.

LEWIS: Ja, that's no lie – you've been minding your business.

PETER: Hey, give me my screwdriver. There's a loose connection and we've got to empty the pools.

The sound of filters is heard.

LEWIS: These bladdy pools . . .

PETER: You told them you're pulling out so they said, "Go on, old chap. Walk away you're free, you're a free agent, Enjoy the rest of your life." Ja, enjoy it. [*Pause.*] Now tell me, where's George? No one's seen him for days.

LEWIS: Why you worried about George? He can look after himself.

PETER: When did you last see him?

LEWIS: Ag, fok George, man. [*Pause.*] Jesus, Piet . . . someone . . . they moered the postman. You hear me? Someone foking moered the postman!

PETER: Where's George?

LEWIS: They got him in the toilets by the station. There by Retreat, while he was waiting for a train. They steeked him and they got the bags.

PETER: Give me the screwdriver.

LEWIS: Didn't you hear me?

PETER: Pass the fucking screwdriver.

LEWIS: They got both bags. [*Pause.*] Shit, what can I do now?

PETER: You know what you got to do. We've got to empty the pools. That's what we've got to do. There's too much dirt, Lewis. It's a big job. The gemors is rising to the surface.

LEWIS: [*Holds the screwdriver to* PETER's *throat.*] What should I do?

PETER: [*Taking the screwdriver from* LEWIS.] You want my advice or an instruction?

LEWIS: [*Quietly.*] This was the last time. I'm not lying, Piet. I told them I'm getting out.

PETER: You go with people like that and now you complain.

LEWIS: I'm sick. My stomach, man . . . This was my last time. I told you. [*Pause.*] Elsie wants me out.

PETER: Elsie? Since when do you care what she thinks? [*Pause.*] That delivery boy was coming to you, so what will they do? [*He stabs at* LEWIS *with the screwdriver*]. They'll just sit back and say, "What a pity. We lost two bags. So what, we didn't really need them, did we?" If I was you, klonkie, I'd get out of here. And fast. [*Slight pause.*] Dammit! Where's George?

LEWIS: I'm not messing with anybody, man. But now they gonna think I was up to something.

PETER: They must have been surprised, hey – after all these years.

LEWIS: Jesus, Piet, he was taking the bags to Els's place. She's been waiting for him.

PETER: What! You using her in this business! If anyone gets to her that stupid girl will talk so fast they won't have to take off her panties to loosen her tongue. How long she been doing your business?

LEWIS: She does what I tell her.

PETER: Really?

LEWIS: And if she doesn't, she knows all about it.

PETER: And what if that's too late? Hey, but that's what you deserve.

LEWIS: What do I deserve? Who knows what I deserve?

PETER A lekker sweet pudding, my friend. What's called a just dessert. [*Sharply.*] The cops been there yet?

LEWIS: How should I know?

PETER: What if they arrive at her little hokkie? What then, my friend?

LEWIS: What shit you talking? She wasn't at the station. She was waiting for him in her room.

PETER: So you want to take a chance? Go ahead my boy, go ahead.

LEWIS: [*Pause*] No wait, you're right. Why take a chance? I'm going to fetch her. Just for a few hours, let her stay here, just for a few hours while I sort this out.

PETER: Here! That stupid little girl doesn't come through that door, Lewis. That's my door.

LEWIS: Just in case, man.

PETER: She doesn't come through that door. I don't want no cops here. I don't want no ex-cops here.

LEWIS: Let her stay while I sort something out.

PETER: No, Lewis! I've been in their hands before.

LEWIS: That was different, man. What they got to do with you now? [*Slight pause.*] They cut his throat in the fucking toilet. [*Pause.*] Whenever there's pressure you go over the top.

PETER: The only pressure I handle is in these pumps.

LEWIS: I got to find out who done this and get the bags before they get to Els.

PETER: Once I was prepared to take chances, big chances, but not for your non-sense.

There is a sharp knock on the door. There is a second sharp knock.

MIKE'S VOICE: Lewis!

PETER and LEWIS stand frozen. The buzzing of the filters is heard.

MIKE'S VOICE: Lewis! You there? Open up, man. Lewis! It's late!

PETER: Who's that?

MIKE'S VOICE: Open, my friend! You'll soon see.

PETER: Who are you?

LOMBARD'S VOICE: You forgotten so soon? Think. Think hard, mister Pieter.

PETER: What the hell! Lewis, what is this?

LEWIS: I've got nothing to do with this.

PETER: Don't talk nonsense.

MIKE'S VOICE: Open up, Lewis!

PETER: They know nothing but they come looking. [*The door is kicked.*] Shit, now I'm going to teach you a lesson. Alright, let them in.

LOMBARD'S VOICE: Where you, dammit?

PETER: Go and fetch her and bring her here! At least for now we keep her away from trouble.

LOMBARD'S VOICE: You fucking deaf? [*The door is again kicked.*]

LEWIS: Hey, Piet . . .

PETER: Tell them you're going to get something, keep them quiet with a promise. While you're gone, I'll handle them. I know how to keep these stooges amused.

LEWIS: Hey, broer, I'll never forget this . . . [*He calls out.*] I'm coming.

LOMBARD'S VOICE: You're coming? Good, Lewis. That's good.

LEWIS: I'll never forget this.

MIKE'S VOICE: Hurry up already

LOMBARD'S VOICE: [*Kicking the door again.*] Maak oop, jou . . .

LEWIS: [*To* PETER.] I won't forget this, broer.

LEWIS walks to the ladder, begins climbing, unlocks the door.
MIKE and LOMBARD enter. They face LEWIS on the platform.

MIKE: Jesus, where've you been? We've been waiting since two o'clock. Why didn't you come? Where's our stuff?

LEWIS: I've been working on the pumps, man.

LOMBARD: Wait till we start working on you! Where you been? Why didn't you phone, you little shit!

LEWIS: I've been here all the time. Where else would I be?

LOMBARD: I can think of a lot of places, you rubbish.

12

MIKE: That's no lie.

LOMBARD: Ha! And look who's here.

PETER: Gentlemen, we believe in the welcoming hand, especially for old friends. Don't we, Lewis? Come down from on high, sit. [*Gestures to the chairs.*] Coffee? Something stronger?

PETER lifts a bottle of brandy, pours two shots into cups as MIKE, LOMBARD and LEWIS climb down into the pump room.

LOMBARD: Ja, ja. Why not? Just for old time's sake. [*Picks up a cup, turns to MIKE.*] I suppose you don't want, hey? [*Quickly swallows then finishes the contents of the second cup as well.*] Ag, that was good. Loosen things up, hey? Just getting up in the morning is a big bladdy headache. You know, just here, just here, man. [*Touches his temple.*] This doctor tunes me I'm all tense. I just laughed. I'm just bladdy bored, man. [*Turns to* LEWIS.] So, you got what we came for?

LEWIS: [*To* MIKE.] We got to talk. Come outside.

LOMBARD: What? Talk here.

LEWIS: [*To* MIKE.] Come.

LOMBARD: Talk here, man.

LEWIS: [*To* MIKE.] It won't take long. Just you and me.

LOMBARD: What's the fucking secret? Talk here.

MIKE: [*To* LOMBARD.] Easy . . . I'll go out. I won't be long.

LOMBARD: Better not be. Sort out the little shit.

PETER: Another shot? [*Refills the cup.*]

LEWIS and MIKE exit.

LOMBARD: Well, well, Mister Big Shot Revolutionary – so here you are.

PETER: Ja, it's been too cosy for words and I haven't been here alone. Lewis hasn't had a chance to go out but now he can fetch you something. He likes to oblige – just like his seniors, his betters.

LOMBARD: [*Walks up to the poster.*] Like someone else I used to know. So she's still your number one. You're the faithful type, hey? How did you manage it in the first place? You need a lot of bucks to get near women like this. Very lekker. Good taste. But where's she now? Any idea?

PETER: Lewis doesn't have far to go. Ja, none of us have far to go.

LOMBARD: You didn't answer my question . . . and we don't have much time.

PETER: You've got time. You've always had plenty of time for me.

LOMBARD: For you, yes. But not for this hole. This place stinks, man. What gives? The chemicals? The other shit? I got no time for this fucking hole.

The sound of filters is heard.

PETER: The chemicals are off site, my friend. Anyway, what's your problem? You usually land up inside the holes you like.

The landing door opens. MIKE and LEWIS re-enter. MIKE walks down the steps into the pump room. LEWIS remains on the landing.

LEWIS: I'm going, Piet. Just need to get something. [*To LOMBARD.*] Meneer, I'll see what I can do. But I can't promise.

LOMBARD: What you mean you can't promise?

PETER: Don't worry – you'll get what you need. [*Slight pause.*] Hey, Lewis, I thought these are your bosom pals. After all, they're here in terms of the Law for the Preservation of Neighbourly Relations.

LEWIS: [*Gesturing to MIKE.*] He'll tell you why.

LOMBARD: He will, will he?

MIKE: [*To LOMBARD.*] Relax. Everything's under control.

LOMBARD: You've never been able to control a fucking thing! Not even this bastard. Not even him. [*To LEWIS.*] Go. Better get something fast.

LEWIS: Ok, I'm off. Check you later. [*Exits.*]

LOMBARD: You never could stop talking kak once you started.

PETER: I'm just doing my dance, man. I'm banging my drum.

LOMBARD: Go and bang something else for a change.

PETER: Bang, bang . . . ah, that reminds me. I've got to fetch a hammer, there's a broken connection and there's an inspection tomorrow . . . you know, once the pools are empty. I won't be long. [*Moves to the ladder.*]

LOMBARD: [*To PETER.*] No, wait! You just stay here and pomp.

MIKE: Easy, man. He's not going to disappear.

LOMBARD: Not half he won't.

14

MIKE: Lewis will be back in half an hour.

LOMBARD: Ok, go. But don't think you can take your time. And that pal of yours better be quick.

PETER: Come on, you've got me covered – as always. I'm just going to the store-room, man. It's not far. There's no tv but check the dials. They flash lekker. Must say, it makes a change to walk out before you. I like this. I like walking out with the two of you still inside. [*Exits.*]

The sound of filters is heard.

LOMBARD: So this is what his fortress looks like. . . He's looking old, hey?

MIKE: Ja, he looks wiped.

LOMBARD: Still as cocky as ever. He's got a fucking nerve sticking Sandra up like this.

MIKE: Must have been taken in their early days. It's a good shot. Intense but re-laxed. [*Pause.*] Shit, you went too far there. You went way too far, Mr Lombard.

LOMBARD: Don't Mister Lombard, me. What the hell did you do that was so al-right? Don't lay it all on me.

MIKE: She's famous now.

LOMBARD: You didn't know how to handle her, hey. You just folded in front of those big tits. But where the goeters, man? Why doesn't he have it here?

MIKE: He said his connection didn't pitch, this 'postman', ek se.

LOMBARD: What do you mean he didn't pitch? We've never had a problem before. Why now? I wonder who the hell is messing around? Who's in on this? Fucking coolies? The Nigerians? Our friend playing games? I don't like this. I mean, as soon as we come in, he tries to slide out like a vuilgat.

MIKE: He's served his purpose over the years.

LOMBARD: But we're not finished with him yet. Not yet.

MIKE: Give him this chance.

LOMBARD: He's a dief, man.

MIKE: Just like someone else I know. [*Pause.*] How can you send people to me like that? What have got in your head? When I'm at work, there are always people around. Do you want me to get kicked out of there as well?

LOMBARD: I thought I was doing you a favour, man. You're always complaining about not having enough cash.

MIKE: But why send them when I'm on duty, when I'm running around? I'm busy there, man. I'm out in the open.

LOMBARD: Ok, then, ok. No more fucking favours from me. I'll tell them to los you. No one needs you that bad.

MIKE: And who needs you? [*Lifts the bottle to pour himself a drink.*]

LOMBARD: You'll be surprised. [*Pause.*] Shit, your hands are trembling.

MIKE: Fuck off. You know who's a thief? Your pal Combrinck, he's the dief . . . How much does he give you for a handgun? He's more of a vark than our friend here, he robs you blind.

LOMBARD: I don't let Combrink rob me. As for this Lewis, I'll sort him out tonight.

Filters vibrate.

MIKE: Sounds like a tidal wave.

LOMBARD: You going mal again, man. These hotnots starting to get you down? [*Filters grind again.*] OK, Doctor Michael . . . sounds like a fucking tidal wave.

Blackout. The filters vibrate.

Scene 2

A section of railing running alongside a promenade facing the ocean. LEWIS and PE-TER are standing side by side under the full moon. The sound of waves is heard.

LEWIS: Sometimes you meet people at the right time. I mean, after you meet them, things go right with them, with others. But sometimes you meet people and you know that sooner or later, even if it seems ok, things are going to blow up. You know the stars aren't smiling. You know there's a skeef eye looking at whatever you're doing, checking how to trip you up, a skeef eye that doesn't move – even when the jokers hands are tight round your windpipe. I mean some dik and frisky hand round your neck but the moon doesn't drop a tear; it comes and goes together with that skeef eye that has no tears to spare.

PETER: You invited them, Lewis. After all this time you invited them to stop by – a little chat, a little business. You're mad, Lewis. You've broken the most impor-tant rule, the one that kept things going. Why, Lewis? Why now? And where's George? Where is he? Don't tell me about your postman. That's none of my business. [LEWIS *does not respond.*] Ok, I'll deal with them. I'll handle them. Just get that Lombard something. He's red in the eye and he's looking for excuses. Don't disappoint him, Lewis, because if you do, you'll have too much on your plate.

LEWIS: Who says the postman is none of your business? And George, why you going on about George? He's my blood, not yours. He's my blood!

Blackout. The sound of waves rises in volume.

Scene 3

The pump room. Sound of filters. The door opens; PETER enters, closes the door.

PETER: [*In a falsetto.*] How did you gentlemen get in here in the first place? To what do we owe the honour? [*Climbs down the ladder.*]

LOMBARD: Don't play dumb. That line didn't work too well last time either.

PETER: Really? But you can't be the best judge of that. Anyway, let's get closer to home. Lewis usually works outside. I'm still training him for the pumps. He does nightshift with me twice a week, but he won't learn. He just won't get down to it. [*Slight pause.*] In an hour or two we're going to empty the pools. And then, where's everyone going to swim? Some of us don't have quiet lagoons protected by breakwaters. And one day these sea walls won't be able to keep out the tide. Force creates pressure, and pressure creates counter-pressure. [*To* MIKE.] Now what do you know about pressure? Any signs of a blowout?

MIKE: I'm at a private clinic, it's been three years now. Got a lekker fat package from your new government so why not leave, hey?

PETER: Ja, you always looked more like an ambulance driver than a doctor. There, on the edge of the precipice, studying Theories of Stress – theories seasoned with vomit.

MIKE: The only downside is that I sometimes have to clean bedpans.

PETER: Mental or otherwise? You're a lucky man, Mr. Professor. And as always you're still dedicated to the sick and suffering – you don't mind getting your hands dirty if it's for a good cause.

LOMBARD: Ja, he really cares, man. He listens.

PETER: Even while we were screaming, he took notes.

LOMBARD: He gets inside. He gets to the bottom.

MIKE: It could have been worse, Peter. It could have been someone who had no feeling for you at all, a real animal. You know who else was around.

LOMBARD: [*Gesturing to the poster.*] She's the only killer here – your little actress. [*A cell phone rings. PETER makes no attempt to answer. It rings several times. The sound of the pumps is heard.*] Answer it or I will. Go on, talk!

PETER: [*Slowly taking the phone out of his pocket.*] I'm busy. [*Slight pause.*] Talk louder, There's too much noise. [*Slight pause.*] No, come. [*Pause.*] Come together, it's ok. [*Pause.*] Who's here? Only a few ouens who want to mix business with pleasure. [*Pause.*] See you soon . . . sweetheart.

LOMBARD: Oh . . . did I hear, sweetheart?

PETER: [*Puts the phone back in his pocket.*] Just a close friend.

LOMBARD: Impossible.

MIKE: As close as us?

PETER: No more impossible than you coming here tonight.

MIKE: What if we'd come before? Let's say five years ago.

PETER: I know this phone is bugged. You've bugged every phone I've ever had.

MIKE: Ag, that's all history.

PETER: My phones have been bugged from the day I got out and who else would want to do that?

MIKE: We're also out. We've been out for almost as long as you've been here.

PETER: I've kept my side of things. I'm just living like a rat in a sewer . . .

LOMBARD: Ah, this is really a history lesson! Hey, tell me more about sweetheart. Remember your mistake? You've got to learn to WATCH your step. Then you've got to learn to KEEP IN STEP. And maybe then you won't fall over your piepie like you used to. And now there's more kak.

PETER: Ja, there's always something to test you. And in the end, there are just two types of people – those who survive . . . and those who don't.

Blackout. Sound of filters.

ACT II

Scene 1

The pump room. The stage is in darkness.

ELSIE'S VOICE: Jesus, man, I don't remember it being so far. And that's the first and last time I jump over the rails.

LEWIS'S VOICE: Lovey, your memory has always been shit. I bet you don't even remember the first time I pulled down your pants.

ELSIE'S VOICE: Where's your manners?

MUMSIE'S VOICE: Oh, tell us about it, Lewis! She never likes to talk about such things.

LEWIS'S VOICE: Not half she doesn't.

MUMSIE'S VOICE: She only likes to talk about boring things. Like how much money you take from her.

LEWIS'S VOICE: I bring her presents every week.

ELSIE'S VOICE: That's a good one.

LEWIS: [*Opens the door, enters and stands on the landing.*] Hey, why's the light off? Where have they gone?

MUMSIE'S VOICE: Stop talking to yourself, man. Hit the switch. This party's died on us.

LEWIS: Piet! Hey, Piet!

ELSIE'S VOICE: They're just sleeping it off, man. Put the lights on.

LEWIS: I don't like this.

MUMSIE'S VOICE: And what did you expect – fireworks? I know your friends. All talk and no action.

LEWIS: I don't like it.

ELSIE and MUMSIE enter; LEWIS is carrying a bag with bottles of wine. They stand beside LEWIS on the landing.

ELSIE: God, you're the limit. [*Fumbles for the light switch.*]

LEWIS: Wait, don't touch it yet.

ELSIE: Why you acting like somebody's running on your shadow?

SHE flicks the switch. The light goes on. The pump room is as it was but LOMBARD is lying sprawled on the floor at the far end; he is partially hidden by the table.

MUMSIE: Look! Another one for the graveyard.

ELSIE: Yo, he looks bad.

LEWIS: What?

ELSIE: Man, there's someone out there on his ear!

MUMSIE: There! Behind that table.

LEWIS: Mike!

He hands MUMSIE the bag, jumps down the stairs and runs to the prostrate figure. MUMSIE and ELSIE remain on the landing. LEWIS turns LOMBARD over.

LEWIS: Ag, him!

LOMBARD moans; opens his eyes.

ELSIE: Who did you expect?

LEWIS: (*To LOMBARD.*) What happened? Where are they?

MUMSIE: Give him a chance to wake up, man. Looks like he's had a rough evening.

LEWIS: Where've they gone?

LOMBARD: They pulled out on me.

LEWIS: Was anyone else here?

LOMBARD: What you talking about, man? We were waiting for you.

ELSIE: This one of your friends, Lewis? Why don't you make the introductions?

LEWIS: When did they leave?

LOMBARD: How would I know?

MUMSIE: Maybe they went for a swim. Your pal, Piet, he's not so big, hey, Lewis? He can fit in the baby pool. [*She suddenly sees and recognizes* LOMBARD, *is visibly shocked and turns away. To* ELSIE] I knew this would be a waste of time. Maybe we should go, darling?

LEWIS: Shut up, already. Do you think I wanted to bring you along?

ELSIE: Leave her alone, man. Go calm down outside. Maybe you'll find your Piet laying on his backside dreaming of pension time.

MUMSIE: I'm going, give me the wine.

LEWIS: No stay. You can have the bag. [*To LOMBARD.*] Hang on. I'm going to find Piet.

LOMBARD: Where the goeters? I can't wait forever. [*Sees the two women; looks drunkenly at MUMSIE.*] Aha . . . you have brought me something . . . what a surprise! What more can a man want?

LEWIS: Ja, you see . . . ag, don't worry, Ill sort you out, my man.

ELSIE: [*To MUMSIE.*] You know him?

MUMSIE: Are you mal? How would I know this wreck?

LOMBARD: So you don't know me? Are you sure, sweetie? Ok, be shy. [*To LEWIS.*] Hey, don't you have a little something on you?

LEWIS: [*Climbing onto the landing.*] I'm on my way to sort you out. [*To ELSIE and MUMSIE.*] Look after him. I won't be long. [*Kisses ELSIE.*]

ELSIE: What! You leaving us alone here?

MUMSIE: Aren't you going to give me a goodbye kiss, you bastard?

LEWIS: Lock it.

MUMSIE: You promised us a good time. And this is a fucking joke.

LEWIS: Keep your mouth shut. Go down already.

MUMSIE: Voetsek already.

LOMBARD: [*As LEWIS exits.*] Hey, watch out for werewolves! There's a full moon.

MUMSIE: Those are vampires, you moegoe.

ELSIE and MUMSIE climb down into the pump room. MUMSIE takes the bottles out of the bag, places them on the table, then opens one of them.

MUMSIE: [*To ELSIE*] Are there any more cups?

ELSIE: Ja, these look real dirty.

MUMSIE: [*Looking around.*] We should have brought some ourselves. These men can't be trusted with something as simple as this.

ELSIE: Wait! Here some. [*Picks up several polystyrene cups from next to the control panel.*] New ones too.

LOMBARD: You see, ladies. we're organized. There are no werewolves here.

MUMSIE: No, you're like vampires. And this one up here. I know about monsters. Vampires dress smart. [*Stands beside the poster and addresses it.*] They're rich. They live in enormous bladdy houses with cooks and drivers and garden boys. They always talk nice but in the end they suck you dry. But werewolves, they're ordinary mense, they look like you and me. You know, street-sweepers or people who work in a bank. And they're completely normal, except at full moon. Then they go hairy and everything.

LOMBARD: Don't knock the vampires. Some of them are poor ous. They just don't have enough bucks for booze at the end of the month.

ELSIE: I know someone who doesn't know when it's the start or the end of the month.

MUMSIE: Never mind him. What about your bladdy boss? He's always uitgesuip. Man, he's really something with that bladdy boep. One day he'll squash tjou on the kitchen table, nogal.

ELSIE: I'll skop him somewhere he'll never forget.

MUMSIE: Ja! This Lady takes kak from no-one – except from you-know-who.

LOMBARD: Let me work this out.

MUMSIE: I look after her. Who else do we have in the world? We're such poor girls.

LOMBARD: Ja, poor in pocket but lekker rich in personality. [*Looks suggestively at* MUMSIE.] You two are real women – not like this one, hey? [*Turning to the poster.*] Not a spoilt brat.

ELSIE: Who the hell is she?

LOMBARD: Don't you know?

ELSIE: Ag, I can't remember. [*To MUMSIE*] What did Piet tell us?

MUMSIE: Some bladdy actress . . .

LOMBARD: [*To ELSIE*] Don't worry about her now. I mean, you and Lewis look like a pair of regular lovebirds, but don't tell me you don't have other boy-friends.

ELSIE: I got no time to run around.

LOMBARD: Liefling, you shouldn't let that Lewis tell you what you can do. You're a lekker stuk. There's lots of guys who'll jump at the chance.

ELSIE: Can't say I've noticed.

LOMBARD: Ag, don't be modest. And, Christ, who do you choose?

ELSIE: We get on ok.

MUMSIE: Don't listen to her. She talks different when we're alone.

LOMBARD: You women, you stick up for your boyfriends even when they mess you around.

ELSIE: You got a girl?

LOMBARD: Ja. [*Smiles at MUMSIE.*] I got a girl.

MUMSIE: You talk so nice, who can refuse you. [*Gestures towards ELSIE.*] You like this one, hey. [*Pause.*] All God gave me was a big mouth.

LOMBARD: And you certainly make the most of it! But it's good you like to please a man that way.

ELSIE: I don't like to hear rude stuff like that.

LOMBARD: You call that rude? Then let me tell you something else.

MUMSIE: Don't start, that's not what we came for. [*Pours herself a drink.*]

LOMBARD: Listen, I didn't mean to be rude.

ELSIE: What did you mean to be? Who do you think we are?

MUMSIE: [*Pours ELSIE a cup of wine.*] Here, take a sluk. Don't worry. He was only playing the fool.

LOMBARD: Ja, I was only playing the fool. You know, being a domkop. Like, I went to this kaffie at lunchtime for a sandwich. Toasted ham and cheese. Girl gives it to me. She writes the price on the packet. I take it to this Jihad ou at the till and he tunes me it's R10,50 when on the packet it's written R7,95.

MUMSIE: Ja, they rip you off all the time, if you give them a chance.

ELSIE: I don't trust a bladdy soul. I don't care who or what.

LOMBARD: Me, too, my darling. But then I'm paid not to trust anybody. I'm in the security business.

ELSIE: That's a good job. I keep telling Lewis he must go for something like that. This pump job's no good. The pays shit. He's been making the same fucking money for years now.

LOMBARD: Lewis makes enough in other ways.

ELSIE: Ja, maybe he does, but I don't see it. No, man, you all have your good time, but if there's any trouble afterwards, we don't hear from you so easy.

LOMBARD: Nonsense! When I came out the army, I was seeing this Malay chick for a while and when she got preggies, I even paid half the abortion. *(Winks at MUMSIE, then grabs ELSIE and tries to kiss her on the mouth; she turns away and he manages to just touch her cheek.)* Give me a kiss!

ELSIE: What do you think you're doing?

LOMBARD: Come on, man. What's a bit of a . . .

ELSIE: If Lewis walked in, he'd kill me. And you.

LOMBARD: Don't worry about him. He's still outside. They're all having a lekker skyf, they've forgotten about us.

He tries to put his arm around her; she pushes him away.

ELSIE: Stop it! You'll spoil my dress.

LOMBARD: How long you been with Lewis?

ELSIE: Six years now.

LOMBARD: That's a long time.

ELSIE: I only walked out on him once.

MUMSIE: I don't give anyone a second chance.

LOMBARD: Yes, you do. You give them seconds and thirds and fourths, and then. . .

ELSIE: He just doesn't think. He doesn't know what it is to sit down and work something out. Ja, last time the cops got him he only did one year but next time he'll get . . .

LOMBARD: Only one year! That's a bladdy joke.

ELSIE: Even ten minutes is too long, hey?

MUMSIE: Even one minute is too long.

ELSIE: You know the man didn't come today. We got nothing. Not that I mind that rubbish not coming round. They mos come at two, three o'clock in the morning, banging on my door. They piss against the walls. I told Lewis a thousand times I can't take it anymore, they must go get their boom somewhere else, but you think he listens?

LOMBARD: Yes, I know the bastard's got nothing. But he told us he can make a plan.

MUMSIE: You told me he was going to leave that business.

ELSIE: He promised.

LOMBARD: He'd better not be lying.

MUMSIE: Ag, who can believe him? He needs a flame-thrower to get through his dik skull.

ELSIE: But it's a problem. He must have a way to make extra. He makes peanuts here, and he's got people to look after.

MUMSIE: Oh, come on, lovey! You don't believe he's sending money to Mossel Bay? He doesn't look after one sister, never mind four.

ELSIE: What you talking about? I met one of them two years ago. She came for New Year with her little boy. A beautiful little boy. He was very light-skinned.

MUMSIE: Ag, that was someone he met in the street and gave R5 to make a monkey out of you. I hope he doesn't think he can make a baboon out of me.

LOMBARD: [*Starts climbing the ladder.*] I've got to take a piss, ladies. I'll check you just now. Then we can go to my place. I've got plenty of brandy and coke. [*Opens the door.*] Think about it. [*Smiles at MUMSIE.*] Especially you, my sweetheart. [*Waves to ELSIE.*] Actually, maybe you the one, liefling. [*Exits.*]

MUMSIE: [*Pouring herself a shot.*] Yes, girl, you got yourself a new admirer.

ELSIE: No, he was checking you. Anyway, that dronkgat . . . fok him. He won't get it that easy.

MUMSIE: Don't you like him?

ELSIE: I'm not that hard up yet. He wants to take a drive up the mountain, he can do it alone.

MUMSIE: [*Slight pause.*] So . . . has George been coming round?

ELSIE: Sh . . .

MUMSIE: What do you see in that George? He's so quiet. He never says a word.

ELSIE: What I like about him is that he always takes it slow. Lewis mos grabs me whether I feel like it or not.

MUMSIE: Sometimes that's nice, though.

ELSIE: Maybe for you. He mustn't take me for granted.

MUMSIE: Anyway, sweetie, those quiet ones can be dangerous. You never know what they thinking.

LEWIS: [*From off-stage.*] Elsie! Els!

ELSIE: What does he want now? Typical. He can't come in and talk proper.

LEWIS: [*Opening the door.*] Elsie, come out, man! I'm waiting.

ELSIE: Don't scream. I'm coming.

LEWIS: Hurry up!

MUMSIE: [*To* LEWIS.] Leave the door open. It's so stale in here.

LEWIS: I can't find them. They got me worried.

ELSIE: Let's go take a walk on the beachfront.

LEWIS: You, the only place you're going from here is back to your hokkie. Ag, come on, Els. I need a favour, darling.

ELSIE: No! No favours.

LEWIS: Don't make me mad at you.

ELSIE: What you want?

LEWIS: Come outside.

ELSIE: Not till you tell me.

LEWIS: You've got one minute. I'll be at the end of the corridor. [*Shuts the door.*]

ELSIE: Shit, I feel like just leaving him and going back to Grabouw. I can't fight him anymore.

MUMSIE: What would you do back there? You going to live off your ma?

ELSIE: I'll go back to the apple factories. I was a sorter when I was a girl.

MUMSIE: Not for me, darling. I want to live in the BIG city.

ELSIE: You call this living? No, there's too much grief.

She climbs the ladder, reaches the landing.

MUMSIE: Come on, Els! Don't take it so serious. You know what he's like. So what if he's full of shit. You smaak him and that's what counts. The Lord didn't think to make it easy for people to be happy.

ELSIE: Be happy! [*Gyrates her hips as she says this. Exits*]

MUMSIE: Bye, bye!

She remains seated, drinks more wine, then, at first quite softly, almost mournfully, begins singing 'Strangers in the Night'. She rises, dances, sings several lines, stops in front of the poster of Sandra, stares at it.

Damn you!

Blackout. Filters vibrate.

Scene 2

The promenade railing, facing the ocean. The sound of waves.

ELSIE'S VOICE: Jissus, it's good to get out of that bladdy pump room. How do you stand the smell? And it's so small!

LEWIS'S VOICE: Ag, you get used to anything. I mean, it's a job.

ELSIE *and* LEWIS *walk into view. They are illuminated by the full moon.*

They stand at the rails; LEWIS puts his arm around her.

ELSIE: It's nice out here. These waves an all. Hey ... [*Pointing.*] What those lights over there?

LEWIS: Where?

ELSIE: There, man – past the island, that whole bunch of lights.

LEWIS: Those? Those are too big for a trawler, must be one of these moerse tankers. Plenty round here. They out there on the water for weeks, then they come in for refreshments.

ELSIE: Ja, very fresh – like chicken breyani and ...

LEWIS: Come on, Els, don't be dof! They come for koeksusters and that Mumsie of yours.

ELSIE: [*Laughs.*] Hey, don't talk like that. Where do you think that ship's going?

LEWIS: America.

ELSIE: Why America?

LEWIS: With so many lights can't be headed for some dorp over here. That ship's big time, man.

ELSIE: Like you? [*Turns away from him.*] Lewis, what's up with you tonight? You come drag me away from tv. Where's this party? Why bring me to see a dronk Boer laying on the floor?

LEWIS: Ag, don't take any notice of him. [*Slight pause.*] Ja, sorry, lovey. Things are a bietjie mal right now. I know I been . . .

ELSIE: Talk straight, man. Tell me what's going on.

LEWIS: What can I say . . .

ELSIE: Shit, say something, anything! After I lost that baby you also didn't say nothing, and you didn't help me. I just lay there by myself in hospital. And now it's the same thing.

LEWIS: That's a lie! I came to the hospital.

ELSIE: Ja, that's all you did. And you only came once.

LEWIS: Els, that was bladdy months ago.

ELSIE: Well, we got another chance.

LEWIS: What you mean?

ELSIE: We got another chance.

LEWIS: [*Slight pause.*] You got another kid!

ELSIE: Ja.

LEWIS: How long you known?

ELSIE: Three months.

LEWIS: Shit, why didn't you tell me straight away? You think I don't need to know this?

ELSIE: I just couldn't talk to you, you been too far from me.

LEWIS: Nonsense. Am I some kind of blind, deaf and dumb man?

ELSIE: I hope it's a girl. The doctor told me the dead one was a girl.

LEWIS: Maybe it was. I mean, who knows . . . it wasn't anything yet. Ag, forget it, Els. It wasn't your fault.

ELSIE: No, it wasn't my fault.

LEWIS: And it wasn't my fault either.

ELSIE: Specially not yours.

LEWIS: Let's just . . . hey, what's the fuss, that kid's gone, Els.

ELSIE: You never wanted kids. You never wanted Basil.

LEWIS: That's a lie. I never said a wrong word against Basil. He's my boy as well. I never said a wrong word against him though you fucked him up.

ELSIE: While I fucked him up where were you? What did you do for him?

LEWIS: What do you mean? I fixed him up at my sister. I gave her bucks for chow. You didn't pay a bladdy cent for him.

ELSIE: No?

LEWIS: All you did was take him some fucking stale cake from your madam. Imagine, bladdy stale cake.

ELSIE: What? And the shirts, and the pants, and the . . . You know how much love I took him. Why do you pretend you did enough? Let me tell you, things got so bad with you never being around he used to call George 'daddy'.

LEWIS: What's wrong with that? Why shouldn't he? I asked George to check on him. Why shouldn't my brother check on him? He did a lot for Basil. [*Pause.*] I don't want to fight with you. You did your best and so did I. Anyway, right now I got no time for such things. There's . . .

ELSIE: No time, hey? Well, listen to this. Last night I had a dream. I'm out in the veld – there's just sand and dried out bossies. Standing next to me is an old woman whom I don't know but I have this feeling of respect for her. And this woman and me, we have these packs of dogs. Hers are tame and trained, but mine are wild. And these dogs start fighting. You know, biting and scratching each other. And I can't believe it – not one of her dogs is hurt. The fighting goes on and on, and mine are killed off, vrek, man – one by one. I can't believe it. How come her tame dogs moer mine? In the end I've got one last dog, and he's all covered with sores and things. But the old woman looks at him and tells me he must also die. She says all my wild dogs must be killed even the ones that look old and finished. Slag them all – you can't take a chance. But I check this old dog and I can't see why he must die. He's no danger to no one. And I reckon that if I can save him, he'll love me forever. But when I see her ready to strike him, I think, ja, she's right. No wild dog can ever be trusted. And then I think – if only I had the guts to do the job myself.

LEWIS: So she kills him?

ELSIE: Ja, I know she'll do it but I woke up before she does.

Blackout. Sound of waves rises in volume.

ACT III

Scene 1

MUMSIE is in the pump room. She stands to the side of the poster. Sound of waves merges into that of the filters.

MIKE'S VOICE: There's so much spray in the air. It'll be high tide soon.

*PETER opens the door. He and MIKE enter and stand on the landing.
They are both quite tipsy.*

PETER: Let the waves build and clean out the tidal pools – the muck, the rubbish, the old and the new. The lot.

MIKE: You speak like the damned.

PETER: No, I'm trying to escape my damnation. I'm more like a drowning man. I mean, who can stay afloat when the tide keeps running against you? I did what I could.

MIKE: [*Produces a paper bag from his pocket, opens the bottle inside it, takes a sip, and passes it to PETER.*] Here, to keep you afloat.

PETER: Aha, a little bag with something for everyone. That's very social. Specially for those who've proven their re-lia-bi-li-ty. [*Takes a sip.*] This stuff's always thicker than water.

MIKE: A real boost for those who've shown they've got what it takes.

PETER: What about those who know how to give?

MIKE: Give? Give what? You only knew how to give what you shouldn't.

MUMSIE: [*Who has been standing quietly next to the poster watching them.*] Gentlemen, welcome. I was getting lonely. There's no music – just these farting machines.

30

MIKE: Ah, good evening! How could we have missed you? You also a star? [*Points at the poster.*] Now there's a mega-star in all her glory. Isn't that so, Mister Peter?

MUMSIE: [*To PETER.*] What do you say, darling? Isn't little me as hot as that madam?

MIKE: [*To PETER but gesturing towards MUMSIE.*] This your new lady?

PETER: I don't know her – at least, not all of her.

MIKE: You hear that? He doesn't know you – you don't feature in the fight against international imperialism.

MUMSIE: International what . . .?

MIKE: Imperialism, my beauty. You know the bosses, the big ones. The ones who send armies and salesmen and priests all over the world to gobble it up. You know, the lahnies. Your Mister Peter, he's a hero in the struggle against these bastards. But he says you don't feature. Youse not po-li-ti-cal.

MUMSIE: I don't know about such things but I know you. Every time Piet talks to me, he talks about you. He's got such good memories of the old times. Now tell me, are you coming down or should I join you up there where the air is lekker sweet and pure.

MIKE: [*Jumps from the landing.*] I'm Michael. [*Takes her hand; kisses it.*]

MUMSIE: [*Putting on a different voice.*] I'm Elsie. [*Performs a mock curtsey; MIKE continues kissing her hand.*] That's enough, darling. [*Disengages from him.*] This old man taking care of you? Of course, he is. Then why doesn't he take care of me? I've had such a long wait. I'm all thirsty and hot and bothered.

MIKE: Who bothered you?

PETER: Who else but the ghosts of your ancestors . . .

MUMSIE: [*To PETER.*] Hey, come down. This party's begging to happen. [*PETER steps down, she takes his hand; they face MIKE.*] Peter and Elsie, till death us do part.

MIKE: Lovey, you'll go on forever but he's already fading.

MUMSIE: No! Not Piet. He's a real bladdy veteran.

PETER: Ja, a veteran of women's two faces.

MUMSIE: [*To PETER.*] Do you remember the last party we had? Remember, we sang a duet. [*Starts singing 'Strangers in the Night'; PETER joins in for a few bars.*]

MIKE: You aren't Elsie.

MUMSIE: You don't recognize me 'cause I changed my hairstyle.

MIKE: Maybe you changed your nose as well. But let me tell you, it wasn't a good idea.

MUMSIE: It's just that you don't like change – small change, any change. But what's wrong with a bit of a nose job? A bit of a shake up.

PETER: Change, by all means. Just don't change sides.

MIKE: And what would you know about that? [*To MUMSIE.*] You look the type who stays true no matter what. But you aren't Elsie. So who the hell are you?

MUMSIE: I'm an angel.

MIKE: [*Gestures towards the poster.*] No, that's the heavenly body. [*To PETER.*] Wasn't that her award-winning role? Special mention in the Hall of Fame. Now who was her leading man? Somehow slips my mind. I wonder why.

PETER: It's an old black and white drama you won't see again. [*To MUMSIE.*] Where's Lewis?

MUMSIE: Outside, man, with Elsie. They're doing this. [*Screws up her lips as if kissing.*]

MIKE: I knew you weren't Elsie.

PETER: [*In a falsetto voice.*] I knows her better than master knows her. Don't I, liefling?

MUMSIE: Maybe you do, jou donder.

MIKE: Jesus, who the hell are you?

MUMSIE: Okay. . . I'm Mumsie.

MIKE: Ah, I've heard about you. You and Elsie work in the same block of flats. Your room's next to hers, and you've got a peephole.

MUMSIE: Do I look like a spy?

MIKE: And what else? You study her and Lewis and take notes. Afterwards you give advice on how to solve their problems. I mean they're not a passionate, caring couple like you and your master what's-his-name . . . You work for a government official, don't you? A very high-up officer in a special service, an expert.

MUMSIE: That's for bladdy sure. He could have been one of your old bosses. At least his kids are grown up. No babysitting for me.

MIKE: So you can go joling.

MUMSIE: I'm young enough to have a good time.

PETER: Ja, but will you stay young enough to give a good time? God help us when God's servants get depressed. That's when things really start sinking. God doesn't like us answering back or asking too many questions and definitely not about the Order of Things. When we get a little swollen-headed, he shrinks us down to size with a bit of solitary confinement. You see, he likes us raucous, but not after-hours when he's taking a snooze. Hey, we really are slipping. Dammit, where's that blue screwdriver?

MUMSIE: There, under your eyes.

MIKE: Like everything else, my friend.

MUMSIE: [*Handing him the screwdriver which has been lying on the table.*] Come on, Peter, that's how close it is.

MIKE: Too close for comfort?

MUMSIE: What's wrong with a bit of comfort, man? I like my madam's flat. You either get to work on time or you don't. You either do the job or they fire you. And then you either drink your bottle quietly or you smash it over some bastard's head.

There is a muffled knock at the door.

PETER: Ha ha! Now who could that be? [*To MIKE.*] Go up and check who it is.

MIKE: Me? Why me?

PETER: Go.

MIKE: Don't talk nonsense.

There is another muffled sound.

PETER: Go, Mister Shrink. Go welcome your buddies.

MIKE: Stuff you.

MUMSIE: You two, stop your kak. (*Starts climbing the ladder.*)

MIKE: Hey, don't fall.

MUMSIE: What you talking about? I'm fine, man. I'm steady as any drunken hotnot.

PETER: Ask who it is.

MUMSIE: [*Reaching the door.*] Hello!

PETER: Don't open the door till they answer.

MIKE: Open the door!

MUMSIE: [*Opening the door.*] Jeez, I told you, man, there's no one. [*Closes the door.*]

PETER: Don't be stupid!

MUMSIE: There's no one out there, man, we're alone. Maybe a tidal wave's gone and washed the rest of them away.

MIKE: Low tide, baby. Try another one.

LOMBARD pushes the door open; he walks in, stands on the landing.

MUMSIE: Hey, how long you been here, Mister Trekboer? You still searching for a resting place?

LOMBARD: [*To MIKE.*] You left me, you cunt. Where you been? (*Pushes past MUMSIE, staggers down the ladder. MUMSIE follows him.*)

PETER: Power failure. We had to go out and check the mains.

LOMBARD: And that was a reason to just fucking leave me.

MIKE: You flaked out, pal – as usual.

LOMBARD: Don't talk shit – we know who's the flake.

MUMSIE: You do?

MIKE: Just give him a fat joint and a ripe chick and he'll wag his little tail.

LOMBARD: Why don't you give me a good wave, too?

PETER: You! You're a surfer?

LOMBARD: Shit, when you're out there, man, no one can touch you. [*To MUMSIE.*] Sweetie, don't worry, I'll look after you when that joker's gone. [*Points to PETER.*]

MIKE: [*To LOMBARD.*] You won't be the only one to look after her.

LOMBARD: Ja, for sure. There'll be quite a line. Including you.

MIKE: [*Looking at MUMSIE.*] Definitely.

MUMSIE: Don't look at me like that.

LOMBARD: Don't worry, man. He's not a problem. He's a pussy cat. (*Grabs MUMSIE; tries to kiss her. The filters are heard.*)

MUMSIE: [*Pushing him away.*] Fok jou.

LOMBARD: Of course, baby. I think you're so fucking juicy I want you right now.

MUMSIE: Tell him to shut up.

PETER: Why? You don't like what the big cock's got to say?

LOMBARD: Don't you want to fuck her as well?

He lunges at MUMSIE, grabs her and holds her by the neck while at the same time fondling her breasts. She screams but freezes. MIKE and PETER rush forward and grapple with LOMBARD. MUMSIE bites LOMBARD's hand. He yells and releases her.

PETER: Nothing's changed with you, hey?

LOMBARD: Fuck you! [*To MIKE.*] What you protecting her for? [*To MUMSIE.*] And you bitch – you bite me, I'll show you. Ja, I'll show you. You've forgotten who I am? [*As he pounds the table, there is a dimming of the lights.*]

LOMBARD: Late, when I've tried everything else, when I'm tired of the TV and the bars, tired of trying to pick up some uptight white woman, I go to find her. Up and down, I drive up and down. I track her down the main road and the beach-front. I imagine unbuttoning her blouse. I change gears. Up and down. I try to find her.

Blackout. Sound of the filters merges into that of the waves.

Scene 2

Sound of waves. LEWIS and ELSIE are still outside facing the ocean; they lean against the rails.

LEWIS: Wild dogs . . . so that's what you dream about? And me? You don't dream about your Lewis?

ELSIE: Of course, I dream about you.

LEWIS: Nay, lovey, you just have these nightmares.

ELSIE: That's right. That last bladdy old dog, you know whose face was on him?

LEWIS: Ag, don't go backwards, Els. Me, I'm too pretty for those dogs. Like I said, I'm sorry. I know I give you a hard time, but 'strues God, I don't mean it. [*Pause.*] Just smell the salt. Hey, I like it when these waves get woes.

ELSIE: The way these bladdy waves are smashing around, it's like what I'm feeling inside, man.

LEWIS: Don't go on now.

ELSIE: I knew there was no party. You just up to your old tricks.

LEWIS: Christ, you're like an old woman these days. Mumsie don't sit and moan all the time.

ELSIE: Ja, she gets out and about. You want me to follow her? [*Pause.*] Now tell me, how long you expect me to do your business? I mean, what do you give me?

LEWIS: What do I give you? I'm getting out even though I need those extra bucks. You know that.

ELSIE: How many times you said that? You put me on your cross. How many times?

LEWIS: This is it, Els.

ELSIE: You twist me round your little finger. You twist me like a lucky packet ring.

LEWIS: Els, I swear it.

ELSIE: If I knew then what I know now, you would never have touched me.

LEWIS: You know what Piet says, "No orders – no one to give orders, no one to take orders." I never give you orders. I give you other things. You couldn't even buy yourself a new dress.

ELSIE: Don't talk to me about money again.

LEWIS: How can I make more? You know I don't like to work for bosses.

ELSIE: Ja, Lewis, of course not. You've got no bosses! [*Pause.*] So what happened to the man? I was waiting. Why didn't he come last night?

LEWIS: I got a call. There's been a problem. [*Slight pause.*] Someone steeked him and took the bags.

ELSIE: Steeked him? Ag, come on.

LEWIS: I'm serious, Els. They got him at Retreat, at the station. They took the bags. They foking steeked him. Now I've got these Boere on my arse. We got to find the bags.

ELSIE: I don't believe you. You just want to forget about the baby.

LEWIS: The bags are gone, man. That's why I came to fetch you.

ELSIE: Why didn't you talk at my room?

LEWIS: I couldn't talk in front of Mumsie.

ELSIE: We've got a child, Lewis, and another one on the way. Why do you think I'm always crying?

LEWIS: I came to fetch you. I didn't want to leave you alone.

ELSIE: I've had enough.

LEWIS: This is it, I swear, Els.

ELSIE: [*Shouting.*] I can't take it.

LEWIS: [*Tries to put his arm around her.*] Stop it! You've got to handle this.

ELSIE: I don't have to – that's what I'm learning. I don't have to take your nonsense. And I haven't.

LEWIS: What do you mean you haven't? What you been doing?

ELSIE: I'm looking after Basil and myself. That's all.

LEWIS: And me? Where am I?

ELSIE: Jesus, Lewis . . .

LEWIS: Dammit, they've come here and we got to find something for them.

ELSIE: Who's they? That dronk who wants to naai any woman he can lay his hands on?

LEWIS: Piet promised to sort them out, but now he's gone and I can't find him. [*Slight pause.*] Ag, maybe the best thing will be to get out, to get out of here till things cool down.

ELSIE: You can't jus leave! What about me?

LEWIS: What else can I do? We got nothing and they need the bags bad.

ELSIE: You jus running! And where's George? Have you seen him this week?

LEWIS: Don't play with me, hey. Don't try and switch me on and off. Why you asking after George? [*Pause.*] What about the postman? Who told them? Who, Els? Who knew when he was coming? Where he was going? Who knew which train he was on? Which station? Who knew what he had in the bags? [*Grabs her.*] Who, Els? [*Pushes her backwards.*] Talk now or you may not have another chance. [*Grabs her again.*] You think I don't know what you and George were doing?

ELSIE: [*Breaking free.*] What's this? You think I was sleeping with George? You mad, man. And if you leave me to deal with these bosses of yours, I tell you I'm going to the cops. I'm not going to pay for your kak. The cops, you hear me? I'm going to the cops.

Lewis grabs her round the neck. They scuffle.

Blackout. Sound of waves.

ACT IV

Scene 1

PETER, MIKE and LOMBARD are seated in the pump room facing the audience. MUMSIE is on the landing. They look straight ahead and speak as if to themselves or to a third party; when they answer each other it is still in an off hand way almost talking past each other.

MUMSIE: We came along the beachfront. Usually I like to walk on the Main Road by the shops but tonight we took a walk by the water.

LOMBARD: Who was walking on the waves?

MUMSIE: There were these skollies eating ice cream – the gangs with stockings on their heads.

LOMBARD: Ja, the Mambas, the Good Time Boys, the Apaches, the New Yorkers.

MUMSIE: I like to walk down by the shops. I saw a sweet little dress, no frills, all black with a bow on the back.

PETER: Something to make your madam jealous.

LOMBARD: Something to show off your tits.

MIKE: I remember the sea sparkling all over the bay, out near The Island far, far down the coast. I was standing in front of a flowerbed near Marais Road and looking, just staring at these flowers. Man, you should have seen how they were breathing – opening and closing, opening and closing . . . [*To PETER.*] Have you ever taken acid?

PETER: [*Walking to the poster.*] I've got my own drugs to get me out of here.

MUMSIE: I don't like going on the beach – you get sand in your shoes. [*Pointing to the poster.*] She never gets sand in her shoes.

PETER: It was only after a year that we became lovers. She made the first move.

MIKE: You played it safe.

LOMBARD: You have to be careful with a princess – you can be charged with rape if she doesn't like what you offer.

MUMSIE: [*To PETER.*] And what did you have to offer?

PETER: We went walking in the dunes near Saldanha. It was grey and windy. We spent the night in her father's holiday house. After that, when we got back to Cape Town, I moved in with her.

LOMBARD: Free board and lodging on account of a groot slang.

PETER: But she wanted a new experience so we moved to my place – on the 'other' side. She stood out but she liked the danger. She wouldn't understand that sometimes a rose isn't a rose.

MIKE: [*Stands.*] With acid you go so deep into the real world – who wants to come back to this fake mess?

PETER: Sometimes a rose isn't sweet enough. Not even a Cassandra-rose to take away the stench of blocked drains and garbage.

MIKE: A drama school romance! You were also an actor. Why couldn't you act as if you didn't notice the rich girl slumming it for 'The Struggle'? That would have been a role worthy of your talent.

PETER: [*Returns to his chair.*] Her parents lived in Tulbagh. Her father was a lawyer, a deacon in the church, a Broederbonder. A real . . .

LOMBARD: Boer, just like me, hey? But you know, I don't skeem you're the type to live with anyone.

MIKE: Even though you once bagged a White princess.

MUMSIE: And where's she now? You still eat slap chips all the time. Nothing's changed. What could change? You've got stains on your overall.

MIKE: You've got fish-bones in your teeth. And no buttons on your shirts.

MUMSIE: You can't get her out of your mind so you choose to sleep in a cold bed.

PETER: I couldn't carry on as if the stage was more real than the shit I was living in.

LOMBARD: With a tray on your lap?

PETER: [*To MUMSIE.*] Why you still so interested in her?

MUMSIE: True love is what I'm all about.

LOMBARD: That's why you like it when the cars pull up. Even when they move on and go round the block you don't mind because you know they'll come back.

When they go round, they come back. You like it when they roll down their windows.

MIKE: I saw you play Hamlet . . . some church hall in Athlone. You added lots of lines, tried to make him a man of action.

LOMBARD: You like doing business.

MUMSIE: You like playing Superman.

MIKE: When we took you in for questioning, you were very good, credible. It took time to break that down.

PETER: I took her to meetings, introduced her to people. I tried to draw her in but it was just a moral thing for her, cake not bread.

MUMSIE: I hate your car, the pink dancer holding a rugby ball hanging from the rear-view mirror.

MIKE: I also saw you in 'Lower Depths', that Russian play. You played the most depraved character, the one who turns into a saint.

PETER: It's always the same with you people – you come from your world, you can always go back to it, and you do.

MIKE: She played opposite you in 'The Seagull'.

MUMSIE: As soon as I get into your car your hands are all over me. You look like those types who just want to touch. They usually don't pay.

MIKE: She played with conviction, she dominated the stage.

PETER: We discussed what revolution meant but she went back to her fantasies, left me for her holidays in London and Mauritius.

MUMSIE: You don't see who's here for you.

LOMBARD: I also thought you were a bladdy good actor. But you know, an act is an act. It starts and it finishes. And then what? Sooner or later, what comes down? Ja, tell us, what comes down?

PETER: [*Walks to the poster.*] She would read me Genesis. We'd go to Saunders Rocks at night with a bottle of wine. Funny, the people ignored us even though it was a 'Whites Only' beach.

MUMSIE: Because it was too dark for them to see you're a Bushie.

LOMBARD: The curtain. Yes, my china, the fucking curtain – that's what comes down.

MUMSIE: [*To MIKE.*] Was he really an actor?

LOMBARD: The first few days were the best – he played the part of a mampara, and he did very well. Then he played the part of a zombie and it was even better. By the time he got to the part of Smart Alec, he was Oscar material. That's why I stopped the gentle persuasion and got down to business.

MUMSIE: I remember you driving around. I would always try to get out of sight.

PETER: I joined the Underground on the evening of the first day of rehearsing 'The Tempest'. I did the impossible – I played the master and the slave. You caught me in Mannenberg, at my brother's place, seven years later. [*Returns to his chair.*]

LOMBARD: Tell the truth, poppie. I became your steady. You got to look forward to your . . .

MIKE: Your brother. If only he had known what it is to be your keeper.

PETER: When I joined, I couldn't carry on living with her. I couldn't tell her, I couldn't explain. We never went back to Saunders Rocks. We started going to Cape Point, to that beach with the wrecked oil rig.

MIKE: [*Stands.*] Did you seriously think you could overthrow the government? [*Walks to the poster.*]

PETER: I carried on playing Caliban, dreaming of Ariel, playing myself as actor. I told you Boere nothing of importance.

LOMBARD: Ja, ja . . . but you told us where you buried the grenades, you told us where Fredericks was, where Khumalo was, where Davids was. You told us where the machine-pistols were hidden, and the pamphlet bombs.

MIKE: [*Stands behind PETER.*] Why are you lying about her? She was a very determined, motivated woman who sacrificed so much for your cause. She helped you with everything. Why do you still lie to yourself? [*Pause.*] She recruited you. [*Walks back to the poster.*]

LOMBARD: She was your commander.

MUMSIE: [*Pointing at LOMBARD.*] You always smell of dagga.

PETER: She left for Canada while I had to sit for six years.

MIKE: Lying as usual – you sat for four. After doing your deal.

LOMBARD: Don't make him a hero. He only did two.

PETER: It was six! Dammit, she betrayed me and everyone else.

MIKE: Would you have felt better if she had been imprisoned with you?

PETER: You gave her an exit permit and a free ticket for turning State's evidence.

MIKE: Who got the ball rolling? Who first said, 'No, no, please, I've had enough!'

LOMBARD: 'No, no, please, I've had enough!'

MIKE: She was so much stronger than you.

PETER: [*Walks to the poster.*] What I can't get out of my mind was the night before you caught her. We'd had a full day, training, preparing for an action. We were lying in my room. I was holding her, one hand cradling her head, the other pressing her body against mine. There was nothing more I could want. I lay there in the dark holding this woman. I lay there feeling . . . I felt.

LOMBARD: Stop this 'feeling' nonsense . . . you were always soft in the head. [*To MUMSIE.*] Hey . . . [*Stands.*] Come outside, my skat. Need to put those lovely lips of yours to work. Come! [*She does not respond.*] Come!

MUMSIE: [*Slight pause.*] Alright. [*To PETER.*] If the one who should save me, won't, what else can I do?

LOMBARD and MUMSIE climb the ladder onto the landing while PETER and MIKE remain staring at each other with the poster between them.

MIKE: Totsiens, ou pal. Treat the lady gently.

PETER: Ja, treat her the way you would your mother. Treat her like your mother.

Blackout. Sound of the filters.

Scene 2

The railing along the ocean; sound of waves.

LOMBARD'S VOICE: Come, my sweetheart. Jesus, I need this fresh air.

MUMSIE'S VOICE: That place is real bad. Like a bladdy cell.

They walk into view. She stands at the railing overlooking the waves. LOMBARD is behind her. After some moments he tries to embrace her, but she turns away.

LOMBARD: Why did you come out with me if you don't want me to touch you?

MUMSIE: Touch? [*Shakes her head.*] But who says I don't want to talk?

LOMBARD: You know why I wanted you alone. Why play games now? Come here! [*She doesn't move.*] Hell, you're stubborn.

MUMSIE: [*Turns and faces him; speaks quietly, deliberately.*] I learnt to be stubborn a long time ago. It was after a police raid, outside Worcester, on a farm. I was four years old. They came to bulldoze the pondoks. You Boere said no more squatters. So your father came to break down what my father slaved for, while he drank . . . and drank . . . and lost me.

LOMBARD: My father was on the railways. He pegged when I was ten. He died of TB. We had no bladdy money either. He was a signalman.

MUMSIE: Ja, what signal did he give when he threw petrol over our mattress? When he smashed our plates, when he ripped up the bags with tea, and sugar and beans . . .

LOMBARD: Stop talking shit – my old man wasn't a cop.

MUMSIE: Well, your uncle was there and your second cousin, and your sister was at home making supper for them after their hard day's work.

LOMBARD: Hey, I don't want to fight with you.

MUMSIE: No, you just want to fuck me – for nothing.

LOMBARD: I pay.

MUMSIE: How?

LOMBARD: I give you my precious time.

MUMSIE: Jesus.

LOMBARD: Why you so hardegat? When you get like this, you start to look ugly.

MUMSIE: And what you do isn't ugly?

LOMBARD: My darling, you come with me because you want to.

MUMSIE: You've got a nerve!

LOMBARD: I've always treated you nice.

MUMSIE: Are you saying you talk nice?

LOMBARD: [*Pause.*] Why you hanging with Piet?

MUMSIE: That's none of your business.

LOMBARD: What can he give you? He's just a wreck, man.

MUMSIE: Leave him alone.

LOMBARD: Why don't you? You can see what he's up to.

MUMSIE: He isn't up to anything.

LOMBARD: That's just it. He can't do anything for you. He's just using you like he uses everyone else.

MUMSIE: Like who?

LOMBARD: Take a guess.

MUMSIE: Don't waste my time.

LOMBARD: Ok, don't listen, but by the time you see I'm serious, I may not be able to help you. [*She does not move.*] You really can't see what he's doing? [*Pause.*] Dammit, where the bags? Where's he put them?

MUMSIE: If I ever needed your help, what would you do? Would you fix me up?

LOMBARD: Where are the bags?

MUMSIE: You wouldn't help me.

LOMBARD: Just tell me where the bags are?

MUMSIE: I don't know what you're talking about.

LOMBARD: I'll get you a flat.

MUMSIE: A flat! Where? Here in Sea Point? You won't get me a flat. You just want a bit of chocolate every now and again.

LOMBARD: Where would you like a flat?

MUMSIE: Buy me a house.

LOMBARD: Where the bags?

MUMSIE: The only bags I know about are the ones under your eyes.

LOMBARD: Why you making life difficult? Come here.

MUMSIE: No.

LOMBARD: Come here, my pop.

MUMSIE: If I say 'no', then its no.

LOMBARD: And if I say 'yes' then it's fucking well yes. And just to prove a point. *(Takes out a gun.)*

MUMSIE: You don't frighten me with that.

LOMBARD: And if it's up against your . . .

MUMSIE: You always try that. Don't be so bladdy dom.

LOMBARD: And what was the result when it was all the way up?

MUMSIE: You forgotten, big boy?

LOMBARD: No, but you have. [*Rams the gun under her chin.*] Remember now?

MUMSIE: Take it easy. [*Puts an arm round him.*] It's very easy, sweetie. You can make me happy tonight. Trouble is you've had too much to drink.

LOMBARD: No, I'm not drunk. I'm not drunk enough. Let's go down to the beach. Let's go make music before we go back to that stinking hole.

LOMBARD and MUMSIE exit.

Blackout. Sound of waves.

Scene 3

PETER and MIKE are in the pump room, standing on either side of the poster.

PETER: Where's he taken her?

MIKE: Not far. He won't wait long. Lombard's got an appetite tonight.

PETER: If he hurts her . . .

MIKE: It's something else he wants.

PETER: I know how he enjoys himself. [*Walks back to a chair; sits.*]

MIKE: Not like you, hey. Not refined and gentle. Come to think of it, Sandra didn't like not having a shower. No toothpaste, no shampoo. After two months she couldn't take it. I must say she did smell bad. Very sophisticated method. We got everything we needed – full marks with no marks. [*Pause.*] She only talked, I mean really talked, the second time. I mean, the second time we wouldn't let her have a shower. And even then I was surprised. I mean usually they crack quickly the second time, they start to itch sooner, but she held out for weeks.

PETER: Lombard mustn't think he can just use Mumsie as he likes. He mustn't harm her.

MIKE: But didn't you do that to her a few nights ago? Right here, under that wheel. Lewis told me all about it. He was watching, standing all quiet up on the landing.

PETER: Lewis sees lots of things – in his head.

MIKE: And what's in your head these days? Sandra got her ticket and flew off and now we read all about her. We read in the papers how she makes one movie after another. She's really done well for herself, hasn't she? [*Pointing to the poster.*] She looks so confident. I remember that look. It's a pity we had to take it off her face. But then she's learnt to put it on again – not like you.

PETER: What are you going to do with Lewis?

MIKE: Sandra's done better than any of us.

PETER: If he doesn't come back in ten minutes, I'm starting the pumps.

MIKE: Your tapes make interesting listening, they're used by students – case studies of self-deceit.

PETER: I'm going to start the pumps.

MIKE: When did you take that photo of her? You could sell it now, hey. Make a packet.

PETER: I didn't tell you where we hid the explosives, or the mines. I didn't tell you lots of things.

MIKE: Lombard would have broken every bone in your body if it wasn't for me.

PETER: The pools need cleaning.

MIKE: Once she started talking, she talked quite fluently, I mean, she made sense from the start. Not like your rambling, jumping around from one thing to the next.

PETER: I can't remember your rank, but you weren't higher than a captain. You were just a child but you caused enough damage following the others around.

MIKE: It took a while to get used to the cells – the lights, the smells. The other shit. But I did.

PETER: Ja, of course you did, Doctor. You started to feel quite at home.

MIKE: On tape you sounded so confused, one contradiction after another. We got hours of you.

PETER: How could she leave the country like that? She once said all power is a fraud. And all opposition to power sooner or later becomes corrupted. [*Addressing the poster.*] Did you have to prove it yourself?

MIKE: You've done nothing for ten years but sit in this hole.

PETER: [*Still facing the poster.*] You shouted me down when I said that no matter the result it's better to have power than not to have it.

MIKE: Your tapes are a fucking mess – but we got what we wanted.

PETER: Then what's your case?

MIKE: Work that out for yourself. And maybe tonight is the perfect opportunity. [*Exits.*]

Blackout. Sound of the filters.

Scene 4

Outside by the promenade railing, ELSIE, seemingly lifeless, is propped against LEWIS. He buries his head in her breasts.

LOMBARD'S VOICE: Lay her down. Leave her. She's stopped breathing.

LEWIS: No, no, she's still breathing. She's warm.

LOMBARD'S VOICE: It's over, Lewis. Leave her.

LEWIS: She's still warm.

LOMBARD'S VOICE: Where the bags?

LEWIS: Jesus, what have I done?

LOMBARD'S VOICE: Hey, stop the play acting! Leave that to Piet. You had it in for her, my friend. Ja, whose kid was she carrying? Yours? George's? The postman's? Whose kid, Lewis? What a fucking mess . . .

LEWIS: I didn't mean it to end up like this.

LOMBARD'S VOICE: You don't mean anything, Lewis.

LEWIS: I opened the door. He was on top of her. She didn't see me, she was so lus for him. I just stood there.

MIKE'S VOICE: Stop it Lewis! Stop these lies!

LOMBARDS VOICE: Like fuck you just stood there! How many times did you steek him? How many times!

LEWIS: I just stood there while he finished inside her.

MIKE'S VOICE: Who finished inside her, Lewis? Who?

LOMBARD'S VOICE: You slit his throat, didn't you, Lewis? You slit it round then you opened his guts.

LEWIS: He was pomping her.

MIKE'S VOICE: Don't talk rubbish. Don't blame her. She was true to you, Lewis. She was your woman. You better find a better reason for losing your head.

LOMBARD'S VOICE: You covered her with his blood.

LEWIS: [Crying.] I went there to save her!

MIKE'S VOICE: Enough already! Stop your games.

LEWIS: I didn't touch him. I let him leave – I was quiet.

LOMBARD'S VOICE: All those nights you were out, she was with him. All those nights you were building your stash.

LEWIS: She's still warm. [Buries his head against her]. She's breathing, man.

MIKE'S VOICE: You've messed up, Lewis. But it's not all bad. You've also been a good boy. All these years you told us every move that Mr Peter made.

LOMBARD'S VOICE: Ja, you've done a very good job. The captain was pleased. You could even say he was satisfied. But where the fucking bags? Come clear, man-netjie. Where the bags? Why you playing games with us?

LEWIS: I don't know nothing.

MIKE'S VOICE: Really? Who took out your postman?

LEWIS: [Clutching ELSIE.] Are you dead, my baby? Are you dead? [ELSIE moves slightly.] You see she's alive, she's alive!

MIKE'S VOICE: You had the moon in your eyes.

LOMBARD'S VOICE: You had a rush in your head.

LEWIS: There was a black cloud.

LOMBARD'S VOICE: Keep talking, Lewis. Talk.

LEWIS: She didn't want me no more. She didn't want to stand by me. She said the waves was too high.

MIKE'S VOICE: They are high, Lewis. They're higher than any of us.

LEWIS: I said, fuck it – you won't take me for a ride.

MIKE'S VOICE: For Chrissake! Stop this nonsense!

LEWIS: No, woman gonna make a fool of me.

MIKE'S VOICE: You caused her too much grief, Lewis. You broke her heart.

LOMBARD'S VOICE: Now we gonna break your back, klonkie.

LEWIS: She was crying.

MIKE'S VOICE: How could you do this? She was pregnant with your child.

LEWIS: She was giving it to every prick she could find.

LOMBARD'S VOICE: No, Lewis – she only gave it to George.

MIKE'S VOICE: Stop it, man! This is cheap nonsense.

LEWIS: How could she say she would go to the cops? How? [*Sound of waves rises then subsides.*] Damn all of you! I'm not going to go down! I'm going to sort you all out!

Blackout. Sound of waves.

ACT V

Scene 1

PETER is in the pump room working on the control panel.

PETER: Ha! This connection . . . always a problem, but now I got you, we're ready for action, aren't we, you devil?

MUMSIE opens the door, enters, and stands on the platform.

PETER: Ah . . . how did it go?

MUMSIE: Sweet. He eats out of my hand, the little boertjie.

PETER: Is that all he eats out of?

MUMSIE: He tried to get me talking about you.

PETER: And you did.

MUMSIE: No. [*Pause.*] Shit, he forgets everything once he gets hard. He gave me a fright though. [*Walks down from the platform.*]

PETER: You can handle him.

MUMSIE: He could have gone further. He could have killed me.

PETER: No, he's not that mad.

MUMSIE: He's not? Look what he did to you!

PETER: That was different because he wanted something very different. I was their prisoner. Yes, every day was different then. And you knew, even at your lowest point you knew why you were living. It wasn't a blur like now. [*Pause.*] Of course you know what he wants from you . . . .

The pump room door opens, but not wide enough for anyone to be seen. Neither PETER nor MUMSIE notice.

MUMSIE: Don't talk about me! [*Points at the poster.*] You still can't get her out of your mind.

PETER: Stop!

MUMSIE: The days were different because of her!

PETER: Lay off, Mumsie!

MUMSIE: And that's why you still keep her right up there to feast your eyes.

PETER: I told you from the start what she means to me. Why can't you accept that? [*Pause.*] They caught her first. They got her by chance at a roadblock. But the way they break you, isn't by chance. She told them where I was. Can you blame her? It took them three months of solitary to get that out of her. This Lombard, he was something else. [*Pause.*] Are the bags in your room?

MUMSIE: They're in the flat in a cupboard under old washing. No one will find them.

PETER: Are you mad? Doesn't madam go sniffing around?

MUMSIE: She's too busy yapping on the phone.

PETER: I can't believe this! Move them first thing in the morning.

MUMSIE: [*Laughing.*] Don't worry! They're in my room, darling.

PETER: Is this the truth now? [*Slight pause.*] Go bring one here now. We've got to give these bastards something.

MUMSIE: [*Pulling a face.*] Pieter's just a bangbroek. Ag, you just want all the stuff here, don't you? You trust no one.

PETER: Get going already! [*Tapping the side of her head*]. Brains? No, they're here. [*Fondling her buttocks.*] Ja, definitely. Just here.

PETER takes her head in his hands as if to kiss her. While he does this, the door opens wide enough for LOMBARD to be seen. He stands quietly, observing them.

MUMSIE: You can rely on me alright, but what if I'm just one more of your cock ups? [*She moves away.*] You don't know how scared I was when I recognized him on the station platform. He didn't move when I sat next to him and the bags. I told him he had beautiful eyes. You should have seen him blush. You should have seen him when I put my hand on his, and then under his jacket. By the time the train came, he was sweating. I licked his ear and he couldn't move. [*Pause.*] It was horrible.

PETER: [*Takes her in his arms again.*] You've done well. I wasn't sure if you'd have the guts. [*Kisses her.*] Now go get the bag.

MUMSIE: [*Moving away from him.*] I can't go on my own. That mad dog is some-where outside.

PETER: He's too drunk to catch you or anything else. He's a joke now.

MUMSIE: Don't say one thing then another.

LOMBARD: [*Pushing the door wide open and stepping forward onto the landing.*] She's right, Piet. So you think I'm a joke? You think I'm finished. I'll show you a joker, Mister Revolution.

MUMSIE: Jesus! How long you been up there?

LOMBARD: Forever, my groot bek. [*Jumps from the landing, advances towards MUMSIE.*] Want it again? You want it again?

MUMSIE: [*Aggressively.*] Ja!

PETER: Take it easy, man.

LOMBARD: I am. [*Approaching MUMSIE.*] Where you been voeltjie? Building a nest while all the worms crawl by? What else you been up to? You slipped away . . . leaving me all alone to face the waves. [*Pause.*] Where did you put the other bag? [*To PETER.*] Ag, what a stupid question! Your little voeltjie sang me her song while she was keeping me warm, while she was cruising my high seas.

MUMSIE: Shut up! I never told you nothing.

LOMBARD: She told me everything.

PETER: Then you've got your bag.

LOMBARD: Hey, we don't need to fight. Once we did, but now we can find a way to live together. Can't we, boeta? Did you know one of the bags had four Makarov pistols and two hundred rounds of ammunition? Did you know Lewis was doing that kind of business? Of course, you did. You put him up to it but now you got tired of him.

PETER: Yes, more than tired of the impimpi.

LOMBARD: Lewis, an impimpi?

PETER: I know you put him here.

LOMBARD: And maybe we did.

PETER: You used to take that master-race shit seriously till your bosses ran scared and made you take the rap.

LOMBARD: Tell me something more interesting. Otherwise I'm going to shut you up, my friend – once and for all.

PETER: Ok, let me tell you what happened to Master Lewis's 'postman'. [*Pause.*] Last night you went to the station. You stood in the shadows checking the platform. You saw her go over to him in her whore way, but not too cheap. And you watched him put down his bags, his two, big fat bags. Then you watched her tongue turning in his ear, his skin shivering. But what could you do? She took him by the hand, led him to the toilets. Then you heard the prick coming in the stall. It made you mad – he was having such a good time. [*Pause.*] You didn't expect his scream but you heard her knife fall to the floor. And then, who did you see at the toilet door? Why, it was Elsie! And you watched the two of them pick up the bags and run.

MUMSIE: What's this about Elsie?

LOMBARD: Not bad, my friend, one of your better stories. You haven't left out much. Your little voeltjie, she sings alright. It just depends on how much you paying.

MUMSIE: So I sang . . . and then?

LOMBARD: Then I had you with this. [*Clenches his fist; opens it slowly.*] You want to smell your lover-girl?

MUMSIE: Damn both of you!

PETER: Wait, there's more. . . You watched them, then you got on the same train. But they split up in town. Each one took a bag. So who were you to follow?

LOMBARD: [*Smiling.*] Ok, my friend . . . Very good, but you missed a few things. She started shivering after she steeked him, then she vomited into a basin. She was shaking so much she dropped the blade near the drain. Her hands were full of blood and she tried to wash it off but her sleeves were stained and she had cum on her lips. [*To MUMSIE.*] It was too bad, hey, voeltjie. You could hardly stand. You didn't know what you were doing. It takes professionals to wipe out postmen – not cocksuckers.

MUMSIE: I need more dop. [*Pours herself a glass of wine.*]

LOMBARD: What did Mister Pieter here give you beforehand? A little pep pill? Ja, he gave you a lekker little pep pill. Only thing, the pep got drowned by your nerves.

MUMSIE: What nonsense! You were waiting for me?

LOMBARD: Fucking sure I was! Waiting for my voeltjie to sing her song in my ear.

MUMSIE: I'll scratch your damn eyes out!

LOMBARD: Then I helped her find a taxi.

MUMSIE: Stop already! This is getting boring.

LOMBARD: Ag, she got in the taxi with the bags and fucked off. Voeltjie fucked off before I could get in. I didn't have a chance to even kiss her goodbye. [*To MUM-SIE.*] You didn't even thank oom for the helping hand, jou hoer.

PETER: You've learnt to talk a lot.

LOMBARD: Ja, I've learnt a lot since we last met. [*Slight pause.*] The bag, I want it, voeltjie. And don't lie about madam's fucking wash basket. He may be stupid enough to believe you, but oom knows better. Where is it?

MUMSIE: Up your arse.

LOMBARD: You taking more pep pills so you got the guts to try and make bucks for yourself?

PETER: Now let me see . . . [*Pointing at MUMSIE.*] You followed her . . .

LOMBARD: I don't follow, doos. I track down trash like yourself and this hoer. Then I bring you to God who decides how to deal with you. Ja, I follow the Lord all over the place trying to keep order. I'll do anything to do my duty. Isn't that so? [*To MUMSIE.*] Of course you did what you did to show you're a loyal little somebody.

PETER: You burned so many people you're burnt out, Baas-joker. Go beg for your white pipe somewhere else.

MUMSIE: You fucking junkie. [*Attacks LOMBARD.*]

LOMBARD: Stop your shit. [*Pushes MUMSIE aside and hits PETER.*]

PETER: Enough! Get out! [*Takes the blue screwdriver out of his pocket, points it at LOMBARD.*]

LOMBARD: Throw it away!

PETER: Go!

MUMSIE: Leave him, Peter! He's got a gun!

LOMBARD: She's right, klonkie. [*Takes out the gun.*] I've waited long enough. You both come clean. No more messing. No . . . more . . . messing!

Blackout. Sound of filters.

Scene 2

Sound of waves. MIKE is alone at the promenade railing.

MIKE: I had to get out of there. I couldn't handle him anymore. It became too stuffed up, man. Damn it, I know Sandra loved me. No one could have faked what we had. But then the more she spoke about her disillusionment with him, his hysteria, his bitterness, his drinking – the more sympathetic I became . . . to him. I saw his long, rambling confessions were not a camouflage for us. The man was disturbed. Ja, funny how that got him released. I managed to persuade the others that he wasn't really dangerous, no threat, just big talk. Then Lombard had the idea of placing him where we could watch him. I mean, just in case. So we put him there in the pump room, let Lewis keep an eye on him. [*Slight pause.*] Lewis. You want to know about Lewis? He's a small-time mert who used to buy the mandrax I pulled from the police stores. But after Lombard and I got the chop, we needed him for our own supplies. In any case the new security bosses always want info about the lunatic fringe and will pay quite nicely. So we kept Lewis on the job to watch Comrade Mister Peter. What else can I tell you? [*Pause.*] Lewis was always respectful. He had a way of speaking his mind without being cheeky.

Blackout. Sound of waves.

Scene 3

The pump room. PETER and LOMBARD are still facing each other – PETER holding the screwdriver, Lombard threatening him with the gun; MUMSIE is next to the control panel. A bluish light washes the scene. They all talk past each other.

PETER: Poor little Lewis. He wanted to get out already. He told me what they'd been doing. [*Pause.*] He's too weak to hate.

LOMBARD: Mister Pieter loved his Sandra so much he told us everything to stop us from fiddling with her.

PETER: I fed Lewis what I thought would keep them happy but never enough to move against me. As for the dagga and the mandrax, I made sure he gave them the right cut. And it worked till tonight.

MUMSIE: When George started coming round to Els, I knew there was going to be trouble. I warned her, but she wouldn't listen.

PETER: George did a good job tracking Lewis. He's one of my most reliable people. His security was excellent. [*Slight pause.*] Until he started sleeping with that stupid girl.

LOMBARD: At first when you hit the bastards it sounds bad, but there's also something comforting. It means someone else is crying, someone else is begging – not yourself.

MUMSIE: When Peter first asked me to do the job, I thought he was crazy. Me go and attack a man? But he said he would never forget . . . you know, like he would love me – if I did.

PETER: After Sandra left the country I found out she'd slept with one of her jailers, an elementary tactic that gave her a gap.

MUMSIE: If that fool hadn't moved when I had the knife up against his throat I would never have cut him. I didn't kill him. I'm sure I didn't. I just gave him a fright so he dropped the bags.

LOMBARD: As for Mr. Pieter, when he got out, we knew about his organizing almost immediately. He's the most useless messiah. Now he's trying to join us, become another kind of dealer.

Blackout. Sound of filters.

Scene 4

Sound of the waves. MIKE is still outside at the promenade railing.

MIKE: I'm not sure if extreme situations are the best ones in which to study people's behaviour. In the sense of whether they tell you much about some-one's deepest instincts, if they really cause masks to drop, break patterns of automatic responses. I mean, if someone threatens you with extreme violence, who won't go along with their demands? Who would be foolish enough to risk pain, perhaps death? After all, what principle, what supposed future, is worth the present? [*Laughs.*] Ag, I'm getting fucking serious, hey? [*Takes a bottle out of his jacket.*] Now actors, they know what's up. [*Drinks.*] They know it's all a ques-tion of tone and putting on the right face. They're paid to invent personalities like other people invent excuses to stay away from work. But when it comes to actors who play activists, now that's a more complicated role. They get really creative. And when they're detained, they go to town making up stories, set-ting up decoys, laying false trails, throwing rainbow coloured herrings all over the place. Ja, its quite a challenge to break actors. But I did it. And I got my fuck-ing promotion even if I lost the one woman who could have made me . . .

Blackout. Sound of waves.

Scene 5

LOMBARD has tied PETER'S hands to the sluice-wheel. MUMSIE is on the floor in front of the landing. The screwdriver lies on the floor near her.

LOMBARD: Right. [*Places the gun against PETER'S head.*] Tired? You want to sleep? You want to say a prayer before you join the great Commissar in the sky? One last skyf? [*Hits PETER.*]

MUMSIE: Leave him for God's sake! Leave him!

PETER: You've got me again, Lombard! You've got me. But you haven't finished me. And you won't because I'll kill myself before you manage. Damn you! [*Pause.*] No, I won't ever kill myself. I know what I fought for.

LOMBARD hits PETER again. MUMSIE picks up the screwdriver. She approaches LOMBARD, prepares to attack him but as she raises the screwdriver, he turns.

LOMBARD: Drop it, you silly bitch! Now for the last time – where's the bag?

MUMSIE: Everything's down the toilet, Danie.

LOMBARD: Wait. I know where you've put it.

PETER: Untie me.

LOMBARD: They're up your hot spot, hoer.

MUMSIE: [*To PETER.*] I remember the first time I met you. You were wild that night. You were raving. I couldn't take my eyes off you, you were so powerful. [*To LOMBARD.*] Here. [*Takes two plastic packets out of her bra.*] This was all I could save. I had to stick my fucking arm down the toilet.

LOMBARD: This isn't enough, hoer. I'm not making this trip every night.

MUMSIE: Cut him loose.

LOMBARD: Where's the rest?

MUMSIE: Cut him loose.

LOMBARD: You want this louse loose? Throw whatever else is up against mommy's titty on the floor!

PETER: The day is coming, Lombard. The day is coming.

LOMBARD: I know the day is coming. And this night is crawling towards it just like you're going to crawl for me . . . [*To MUMSIE.*] Dammit, give me more and I'll let him go. You understand?

MUMSIE walks towards the poster. She rips it down; plastic packets filled with pills fall to the floor.

PETER: What! Are you mad?

MUMSIE: [*To LOMBARD.*] They're yours now. Cut him loose.

PETER: When did you bring the bag here? How could you trick me?

MUMSIE: I warned you. You expect me to do what you like but you still kept her up. Well, now she's down here with the rest of us. [*Treads on the poster.*] I've still got the other bag. I'm going to do what I like with it.

She cuts PETER loose with the screwdriver while LOMBARD begins to frantically gather up the packets. The door suddenly swings open and MIKE lurches on to the landing. His clothes are in disarray as is his hair. Behind him strides LEWIS, also looking disheveled and distraught.

PETER: [*To LEWIS.*] Come down! Come down, you impimpi!

MUMSIE: Where's Elsie? Where is she?

LEWIS: [*To PETER.*] You! Shut up! I've had it with your kak. And these Boere. [*Pushes MIKE again.*]

MUMSIE: [*To LEWIS.*] Is she alright? Did you do something to her?

MIKE: She's alive but unconscious. I didn't want to move her.

MUMSIE: What! What did you do to her, you bastard?

MIKE: It wasn't me – it was him.

LEWIS: She's by the rails, by the ice cream shop. [*To PETER.*] Hey, Piet, we got to talk. There's a lot I want to know. But first I'm going to sort them out. [*Pushes MIKE again.*] They won't put me in this mess again.

MUMSIE: I'll kill you! If she's dead, I'll kill you! [*Climbs the ladder, pushes past MIKE and LEWIS. Exits.*]

PETER: [*To LEWIS.*] Did you steek her, Lewis?

LEWIS: No, dammit. Bladdy fog in my head. . .

MIKE: Fucking strangled her . . .

PETER: And where's George? What have you done to him?

LEWIS: Lay off! They both had it coming. And these bastards . . .

LOMBARD: What's with all the threats, mannetjie? Want to blame us for your blow out? We were going to tell you to bugger off tonight. We've got a better connection.

LEWIS: Is that so? Well, I wasn't waiting for you.

PETER: That's right, my friend. He was splitting. He was doing it for Elsie.

LEWIS: Shut up about her! As for George, I never done nothing to George. [*Slight pause.*] I know they were naaing. But he wasn't the first. No he wasn't. She's been doing this for too long.

PETER: What did you do to him?

LEWIS: I let him leave. I'm going to fix him later.

LOMBARD: Ja, let's all get our fixes, hey?

MIKE: There was still a heartbeat.

PETER: Lewis, go get an ambulance.

LEWIS: Ok, but I'll be back for you. You played too many games with me and everyone else. You got to sort your head out, sort it out like the rest of us. [*To LOMBARD.*] Don't come here again. You hear me?

LOMBARD: I don't have to. It's over between us, my friend. [*LEWIS exits. LOMBARD turns to PETER.*] Totsiens con-coon. [*To MIKE.*] You coming? Or you still want the company of this . . . [*Gestures towards PETER.*]

MIKE: What about the stuff?

LOMBARD: Don't worry. I got what we came for. [*Walks up the stairs onto the landing; pats the bag.*] It's all here, Mister Professor.

PETER: Ja, take what you came for. Let's all leave or stay with what we came for.

MIKE: [*Walks down into the pump room and picks up the poster.*] Hey, let me do you a favour and get rid of this. [*Rolls up the poster and puts it under his arm.*] You know, I heard a voice. She said she's tired of this place. She wants some fresh air.

PETER: Just go already. You've left your mark on me, now I need my peace.

MIKE: You're right, Peter – for all us exiles, those who left and those who stayed.

LOMBARD: Ag, come on, man. Stop this kak. Let's go!

MIKE: [*To PETER, holding up the rolled poster.*] Don't you worry – I'll take good care of her. [*LOMBARD and MIKE exit.*]

PETER: Alone again. Nothing new about that. [*Slight pause.*] I've been too clever for my own good, too clever by half. Maybe it was time for her to come down, and for that boy, Lewis, to break their hold on him. As for Mumsie . . . [*Pause.*] But it's time for the pumps. Let them clean out the false words and the hard words, the twisted words and the dead words. Let them wash away the knives and the stones at the bottom of the pools; let them put out the burning tires and the shack fires; let them pump out the stale water with its smells of fear and tiredness; let them bring in the wide ocean with its foam and its jungles of seaweed. Goddammit, let them wash away the trash. [*Pause.*] Now!

PETER begins turning the sluice-wheel. The sound of flowing water becomes audible. He continues turning the wheel. As the flow builds, the lights dim. When the flood reaches a crescendo, the stage is in total darkness.

END

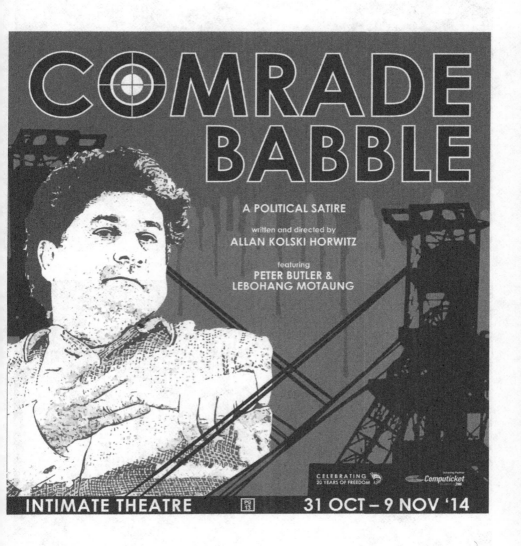

COMRADE BABBLE

A POLITICAL SATIRE

written and directed by
ALLAN KOLSKI HORWITZ

featuring
PETER BUTLER &
LEBOHANG MOTAUNG

CELEBRATING
20 YEARS OF FREEDOM

Ticketing Partner
Computicket

INTIMATE THEATRE   PG 13   31 OCT – 9 NOV '14

BABBLE and PROF (Johannesburg production)

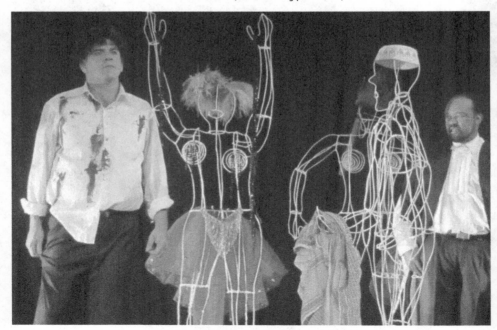

BABBLE and BHUNGA (Johannesburg production)

BUTCH (Cape Town production)

BABBLE and WILHELMINA (Cape Town production)

Program notes

The phenomenon of Brett Kebble, who perpetrated the biggest corporate fraud in South Africa's history and was then mysteriously killed in 2005 (in what appears to have been an 'assisted suicide') is a microcosm of the major fault lines in the New South Africa as well as being an exploration of key universal archetypes. His life and its final moments provide the basis for the play.

Kebble, an articulate, charismatic but paranoid figure, styled himself as an entrepreneur who would overhaul ownership in the stagnant White-controlled mining industry. He promised to do so by bringing in Black partners, expanding existing mines as well giving marginal ones a new life. Together with his father, an experienced mine manager, he took control of Johannesburg Consolidated Investments (JCI), Barney Barnato's old company, as well as Rand Gold, and proceeded over ten years to create and direct over seventy other companies in the mining sector. However, to achieve his objectives he practiced political patronage on a grand scale, buying influence by subsidizing the appetites of numerous Black political figures, including revered ex-Robben Islanders and a new crop of Youth League leaders. At the same time he cultivated a life of extreme affluence, owning corporate jets, five mansions, a fleet of luxury cars and collections of highly valuable watches and art works. However, Kebble's downfall, when the Revenue Service and the Justice department finally unraveled his fraud, was swift and merciless. And when he refused to negotiate a "deal" (as it would have entailed spending some time in jail), it seems he orchestrated his own death.

The play opens with Kebble/Babble's return from the dead in order to present the 'truth of his life' in the face of numerous books and articles which have painted him as a "profiteer and manipulative pirate". It examines him from different perspectives as reflected in his dealings with a group of five other characters – free-ranging portraits of people (or composites of people) who were actually involved with Kebble. As a form of morality tableau with strong satiric influences, it unfolds through a parade of the various forms of corruption which marked Kebble/Babble's rise to eminence; an advance enabled by his skill in influencing (and corrupting) key individuals and interest groups.

By way of an over-arching conclusion (embodying a moral), his empire's collapse and his final humiliation do ostensibly offer an indication that even the most powerful will eventually be brought to account.

The first performance of COMRADE BABBLE took place at the Catalina Theatre, Durban on 13 January 2012 with the following cast:

BABBLE/BUTCH DERATTI/UMSHINI DE BOOM   David James

BHUNGA/PROFESSOR/WILHELMINA   Lebohang Motaung

A second production took place later that year with the same cast directed by Albie Michaels.

A third production, like the first, was directed by Allan Kolski Horwitz in 2013 with the following cast:

BABBLE/BUTCH DERATTI/UMSHINI DE BOOM   Peter Butler

BHUNGA/PROFESSOR/WILHELMINA   Lebohang Motaung

CHARACTERS

Mephistopheles Medici Babble – a white man dressed in a white shirt and black pants (bankrupt tycoon)

Buti Bhunga – a black man dressed in a judicial robe (public prosecutor)

Professor Ndlovu – a black man wearing a hip hop flat cap, a Bafana Bafana top, white track suit pants and sneakers (Youth League leader)

Butch Deratti – a white man dressed as a Mafia spiv (gangster)

Wilhelmina Randridge – a black man dressed (flamboyantly) as a woman; he/she carries a boom box (artiste)

Umshini de Boom – a white man dressed in a sleeveless top and military fatigues (assassin)

SETTING

A double car-seat is placed to one side. Several human size figures (made of wire or of plastic) are placed in different places on stage. One of the figures, dressed in a red-stained white shirt and black pants, is placed on the car seat. Perched on each of the other figures is a different item of headgear: a safari helmet, a woman's straw hat, a jester's hat, a Zionist Church (ZCC) peaked hat, a kaffiyeh and a skull cap. There are also brightly-colored bits of 'jewelry' hanging from the pegs and a long Pinnochio style nose.

The characters make use of the figures to illustrate points, treating them (where appropriate) as people with whom they interact and as lifeless mannequins.

Scene 1

Blackout. Seven gun shots ring out.

VOICE: This is your leading news breaker, Station Overload. Late last night the billionaire mining tycoon Mephistopheles Medici Babble was found gunned down on a suburban road off the M1 near Birdhaven. Mr Babble was found in his favourite Mercedes sedan. He had sustained several bullet wounds to the upper body. Business and political leaders have expressed their shock though over the past few months it was reported that Mr Babble was under financial pressure and the subject of scrutiny for alleged irregularities. At this stage no suspects have been identified. The deceased leaves behind a wife and four children. And now to international news …

A gong sounds three times. Lights slowly up. Babble rises up zombie-like from behind the car seat.

BABBLE: [*Mumbling to himself.*] Easy does it… I'll be right as rain… nothing to it… I'll show 'em… [*Becomes aware of the audience, his speech is still disjointed but becomes progressively more audible, understandable; at different points he lapses back into zombie-like speech and mannerisms; he is alternately arrogant and ingratiating.*] Ah, you've arrived! Wonderful! So pleased you could make it. We're all such busy people, all of us chasing, chasing… now you've come to hear about something profound, something that will make a real difference to your life. [*Slight pause.}* Money. I mean, real money. How do you make it? You borrow. You never use your own, right? You get some suckers to put in. Then you buy cheap with the borrowed money. And then you buy out the bastards who lent you the money. Of course, you sell at the right time. You must always know when to buy and when to sell… at the right time. Leveraging, we call it leveraging. [*Claps his hands.*] Ha, ha! Pioneer, patriot, wealth creator… that's what you called me. Philanthropist, art patron, political facilitator – year after year, article after article! [*Lurches again.*] Easy, easy… I'll be right as rain… no one going to keep me down… no one! Indeed, ladies and gentlemen, you are assembled here tonight because you need to finally know the truth about the phenomenon that was me, Mephistopheles Medici Babble. Yes, finally… [*Talks very excitedly.*] Of course you know who prints the 'Newspaper of Record', who writes the history books, who fills in the Book of Life. Why, it's the one who signs the cheques, the one who can phone the Chief in the middle of the night. That's right, it's the smartest. But I have been robbed of my rightful place in history. The jealous have spread lies about my colossal achievements, invented vile names. No doubt the skeptics among you will ask who can apply objectivity, yes, ob-jec-ti-vity, to his own life? Who can reach high enough to have a bird's eye view? And they are correct – most cannot. But I… I have soared. I have been up there where everything is absolutely clear. [*Pause.*] Now let's not pretend. You know a lot about me already. Bloody press was more than interested in my goings on. And at first they got it right. But, you make the slightest slip, you start to tip, and they give you the treatment, those dark forces and their pale emperors. [*Pause. Sits down on the car seat next to the mannequin.*] Mud. You ever handled mud? Scooped it up, let it ooze through your fingers. Ever done that with your eyes closed, sun on your face, not a thought in your head but the feel of that slow ooze, that slimy, warm squelch? That kind of mud is a treasure for the one they all laughed off as a boy, a fat boy.

BHUNGA: [*Seated in the audience.*] That's right – fat boy with a bully for a brother. Fat boy who preferred books to rugby…

BABBLE: [*In shock.*] Bhunga!

BHUNGA: Fat boy who had a father who mined gold and called him a ninny…

BABBLE: Now, now, sir…

BHUNGA: Night after night while bully brother was snoring, Fat Boy emptied the cookie jar with a thudding heart and the soft hands of a pianist.

BABBLE: Pianist, yes, but…

BHUNGA: [*Stands. Addresses the audience.*] He learnt to play not just the piano but some very tricky games with some very questionable instruments.

BABBLE: Now wait a minute! Don't go too far,

BHUNGA: [*Mounting the stage.*] The day you could order anyone about is over. As for your story, you think you can tell it all by yourself? [*To the audience.*] Please, don't think I'm denying you the right to hear both sides. What I will not allow is his monopolizing the stage to sell you a pack of lies.

BABBLE: Lies? [*To the audience.*] Did I invite you for lies? [*To BHUNGA.*] Please, let's have no unpleasantness. Can I ask my learned friend to kindly return to his seat?

BHUNGA: The seat of justice? Exactly.

BABBLE: Mr. Bhunga, these good people have come here precisely because they know you've been feeding them a diet of falsehoods.

BHUNGA: For ten years I watched you in action. [*To the audience.*] His death wasn't enough – the stench of what he did still lingers. Yes, I've been standing guard…

BABBLE: You and your type hounded me out of my companies and destroyed the mother of all Empowerment deals. And now you want to besmirch my memory and strip my family of the little that's left. [*To the audience.*] That hurts the most.

BHUNGA: Your family… yes, the poor family you've made a fool of. As for the 'little' that's left, I hope that's the case. But I seem to recall that you took out a rather substantial insurance policy just weeks before your unfortunate 'accident'.

BABBLE: What do you mean?

BHUNGA: And how much did you stash off shore? Are there more paintings from your private collection hidden away? A missing corporate jet? Another little palace somewhere, apart from the five we know of? And the watches? Talk, Comrade! What else have we missed? [*Slight pause.*] Dammit, you owe millions but you've stashed away millions. And it's my job to find them.

BABBLE: That is a travesty of the truth! I tried to build this country. I believed in investment, in creating jobs, in everything that Madiba and the Movement stand for. And once I've shared the truth with these kind folk, they'll realize how I've been maligned – and support me against piranha like yourself.

BHUNGA: Piranha are South *American* fishies, amigo. Get your continents right. Of course, we're sharp-toothed. We have to be. We can't let rot like you keep infecting the public.

BABBLE: You'll do anything to keep me down – even countenance murder.

BHUNGA: Murder!

BABBLE: Yes!

BHUNGA: So that's what it was? [*To the audience.*] Do you know what I had to contend with? The conspiracies, the double-dealing. The… but I don't want to talk about that now. Not yet. First I want to . . .

BABBLE: Don't 'first' me! I… I… asked you to leave the stage.

BHUNGA: Leave? Alright! [*Turns as if to leave, then abruptly faces BABBLE again.*] Why did you bring Madiba into this? You want trouble? He may have made some mistakes but he's still a hero.

BABBLE: I helped him where I could.

BHUNGA: [*Smiles.*] Yes, that mansion… I mean, *house*, in Houghton, it wasn't one of your companies that first bought it for him, hey? Back in… But no, I won't go down that road.

BABBLE: Yes, go down that road.[*Gestures to the theatre exit/aisle. To the audience.*] My apologies for this intrusion! [*Slight pause.*] I stood up to the old farts who have run mining in this country for a hundred years. I told them it was right and proper and historically necessary for us to help develop a class of black tycoons but all they would say is "You want to mess with such fellows, well, my boy, you'll get an assegai up the arse!"

BHUNGA: [*To the audience.*] He might have enjoyed that.

BABBLE: To think what I endured to promote change! [*Slight pause.To BHUNGA.*] Now where are your *other* heroes today? After having learnt an awful lot breaking rocks on the Island with an ancient ghostly rabble of exiled chiefs, sheikhs and other imperial lepers, what are they up to?

BHUNGA: That was no holiday camp. On the Island they gave up everything for the People.

BABBLE: Of course they did! [*Whispers to the audience.*] But when I danced in with Lil' Miss Opportunity, they were only too happy to take her arm, and waltz away with a packet of sweeties.

BHUNGA: I heard that. [*Slight pause.*] So you admit to the *sweeties?*

BABBLE: Sir, tolerant as I am my patience is being exceeded. Kindly return to your seat!

BHUNGA: [*Slight pause*]. Alright, I'll sit, for a while, but where I choose, and then I'll let you hang yourself. Go on, Babble – babble! [*Walks back on stage. Sits on the car-seat. To the audience.*] Let's hear him. It may be almost as entertaining as the drama of his last few hours.

BABBLE: [*To the audience.*] You all knew about my proposal to reopen old mines. And my exploration of West Africa. That's right, me, a White African [*BHUNGA pushes the sun helmet along the floor to land at BABBLE's feet.*], no longer a colonial, now developing the continent with patriotic Black African entrepreneurs. Of course I took risks, but considered ones. Growth, as we know, only comes with individual effort. And that effort deserves to be rewarded. [*Pause.*] Is there anyone here who believes otherwise? Of course not! We all know that those who take the trouble to invest their time, their energy and their money, deserve a healthy return.

BHUNGA: *Return* what you stole! Your achievement was to sucker a few investment *specialists*, not to mention accountants of no account.

BABBLE: Ah, being called to account… When I was a child I loved to take communion with my grandmother. We would get up early and walk to church.

BHUNGA: Did you hear me?

BABBLE: It was very relaxing to be with my grandma.

BHUNGA: Babble, did you hear what I said?

BABBLE: She was the only one who listened to my piano playing. She saw that I was gifted and that music truly lifted my soul.

BHUNGA: Enough already! [*Stands.*] I think I'll read out the charge sheet so our friends here can get more of the specifics. Let me see… You controlled some eighty odd companies but almost all of them were shells. You sold shares you knew were worthless. You had a fetish for luxury watches. [*Takes out a watch with a very long chain from his pocket. Dangles it before BABBLE.*]

BABBLE: Of course I loved watches! [*Grabs the watch while BHUNGA holds the chain. A tussle ensues between them for control; each tugs at the chain.*] Who doesn't tremble at the thought of conquering time. Those Rolexus, those Breitlins – they define time, knock it into micro-time, nano-time. Then you can fit more into your day, more into each moment, because on your arm is the precise heartbeat of the universe. [*Pause.*] Envy, brother! Don't let it consume you! Just because you weren't on the receiving end of my generosity doesn't mean you have the right to condemn it. I saved so many of your heroes from hardship… in the nick of time.

BHUNGA: You wormed your way into the belly of the Movement and laid your maggots.

BABBLE: I met many, but selected just those I could see had the guts and the vision to really go places…

BHUNGA: Places you wanted them to go, places that suited your schemes.

BABBLE: I lifted them out of the trauma of financial hardship and gave them hope.

BHUNGA: Hope for a quick buck – provided they could deliver on your needs.

BABBLE: I asked nothing of them but good sense, loyalty and friendship.

BHUNGA: [*Pulls the chain out of BABBLE's hands.*] What *did* you give the Youth League leaders?

BABBLE: The whole world knows what I gave them! [*To the audience.*] And why? Because I believe in the youth of this country, in their right to a bright future.

BHUNGA: You gave them sports cars, rooms in your mansion for whoring, an endless supply of booze…

BABBLE: 'Booze'? You never have a drink? Not even a little tipple with your buddies on Saturdays when the soccer's on? [*Shakes his head.*] Don't lie, Bhunga. Ours is a country that appreciates its liquor. We're not namby pamby teetotalers.

BHUNGA: No, we're not namby-pambies. We're connoisseurs who spend thousands on the best of wines. Especially you, Comrade.

BABBLE: Why you such a self-hating Black? Why do you try to drag down men and women of colour who succeed?

BHUNGA: Don't try and make a fool of me like you did with the others.

BABBLE: Fools... mockery... [*To the audience.*] Have you ever felt that fire, that crazy feeling when you're about to clinch a deal? That tightening in the guts when the bastard sitting opposite you is about to sign and you know you've run rings round him. [*To BHUNGA.*] At least some of your leaders realized that to be part of the future you have to pass on the past. [*Replaces the sun helmet.*] Yes, I admire them for their courage, Mister Buti Bhunga-Bhunga, Bhunga-Bhunga ...

BHUNGA: Don't take liberties with my name – you know it's just Bhunga.

BABBLE: Come now, what's an extra 'Bhunga' between friends? Always buzzing around... isn't that what your name means? [*Slight pause.*] Ah, the thrill of the deal... why, it's almost as *stimulating* as having a...

BHUNGA: I don't want to know, you pervert.

BABBLE: Perversion, my learned friend, is an art that someone as unsophisticated as you will never master. [*To the audience.*] The main thing about money isn't how you make it, but what you do with it.

BHUNGA: And what *did* you do with it?

BABBLE: I reached so high.

BHUNGA: [*To the audience.*] Yes, but then over a period of three months he was booted off his throne and cut off from the slush funds that made him irresistible to so many. No matter what his spin doctors said they couldn't put up a big enough smoke screen.

BABBLE: [*To the audience.*] Things did get a little stuck but there has been no ending, not a proper and just one, that is. Why do you think I've come back? You can't imagine what it's like down there. It's... it's unbearable!

BHUNGA: [*To the audience.*] He and so many like him. Instead of serving the common good, they turn their 'good fortune' into vast *private* fortunes.

BABBLE: Ha, 'The Wheel of Fortune'! How very poetic, Your Excellency! You wax lyrical for a servant of the Law.

BHUNGA: Yes, I am a *servant* of the Law, and a proud one at that. Strange to think you were once a practitioner. You did your articles under the direction of some smart arse, didn't you? Every morning the two of you would sit on the slopes of Devil's Peak and plot.

BABBLE: Really! Has 'planning' now become 'plotting'?

BHUNGA: Your fraud has left tens of thousands without jobs.

BABBLE: I kept mines going even when they weren't economically viable, I paid wages to thousands of men when it made no financial sense. I don't come from wealth. When I was a kid we moved around all the time. My dad was chasing jobs all over the country.

BHUNGA: A simple mine captain…

BABBLE: Yes!

BHUNGA: But with your help he became a director of more companies than he could count.

BABBLE: Yes!

BHUNGA: What an achievement! Pity he had to wait in line to see you at your office – you were so happy to keep his company. Yes, you kept him waiting for hours. [*Pause.*] Pity he thought you a sissy.

BABBLE: Who told you that? My damn brother?

BHUNGA: That one never did spare you. [*To the audience.*] Come on, show a little sympathy for Comrade Sissy Mephistopheles. Give him a clap for standing the sight of his insufferable brother. [*Slight pause. To BABBLE.*] In celebration of your undoubted triumphs why don't you try this on? [*Points to the Pinnochio nose.*]

BABBLE: And why not? School plays forever. [*Puts on the Pinnochio nose; dances in marionette fashion.*]

BHUNGA: Speaking of 'play acting', what was the name of that rent boy? The one you always selected at a certain 'establishment'.

BABBLE: How dare you?

BHUNGA: You liked to treat him. A new shirt, a Ferrari…

BABBLE: Shut up!

BHUNGA: It was quite a joke among your mafiosi.

BABBLE: I thought you had a little more class.

BHUNGA: Tell us how you found the time for all these diversions. I mean you were running from boardroom to bordello, and back again.

BABBLE: I had to spend a good deal of time on the road, I was always so busy. But God knows my dear wife was understanding. And the children.

BHUNGA: Yes, the loving family that supported your odyssey from rat hole to princely mansion – and back to rat hole.

BABBLE: [*Removes Pinnochio nose.To the audience.*] I miss them so much. Especially the little one. You know she was burnt all over, she fell into a bath of boiling water. Poor thing, she's been through a terrible time. [*To BHUNGA.*] Be careful, just be careful!

BHUNGA: Yes, they *were* pretty amazing – to have stomached your lies, your disappearances, your tantrums, your infidelities.

BABBLE: What do you know of the instincts and needs of an exceptional man? Do you know how much energy I had? How much energy I needed? How much effort it took to control dozens of busybodies and make sure they turned a blind eye to certain… [*Whispers to the audience.*] You have to make the right people feel very important. Let them lick the dull stone and taste the salt before you gild it and top it with honey.

BHUNGA: [*To the audience.*] I know most of you thought he was a wonder, a new breed of tycoon. You even gave him the trappings of a state funeral, flew the flag at half mast, wrapped him in the national colours. [*Pause.*] It was only when you found yourselves swindled that you questioned his flair.

BABBLE: Stop insulting my guests! Show respect! That's the mark of civilization. [*Puts on the kaffiyeh.*] Out in the desert, survival is dependent on hospitality and honour. [*Playing with the kaffiyah.*] Ooh, I like this… Babble of Arabia…

BHUNGA: Stop play acting, you…

BABBLE: Yes, I can act. To do what I did, I had to. I could keep more balls in the air than two teams of rugger buggers.

BHUNGA: A deadly web, Comrade Spiderham. [*Slight pause.*] This time I am going. Quite apart from you, I can see I'll make no progress with this lot… [*Pointing at the audience.*]… they're holding tight to their illusions. [*Leaves the stage and starts walking down the aisle towards the exit.*] You're allowing this country to go down the drain because you all want to be in on the action, and the action is rotten. [*Exits.*]

Scene 2

BABBLE: There goes the epitome of Black piety. Thank God, there aren't too many of him around though lately there are a few that stand out in the public service. [*Picks out a person in the audience, addresses him/her directly.*] I mean I tried my damndest to find solid Black partners who were serious about uplifting the masses. Doesn't my track record speak for itself? Doesn't it? [*Stops as he notices the ZCC hat. Takes off the kaffiyah and puts on the ZCC hat.*] Now this certainly takes me back… when we lived in Brakpan we had a garden boy who was in the Zionist Church. I think Philemon was his name. He used to stick up for me when my brother was pushing me around, 'making a man out of me'. Ja, that Philemon saved my skin more than once. Wonder what he'd say if he saw me now? [*PROF enters at the back of the theatre singing "My mother was a kitchen girl…"*]

PROF: [*Advancing down the aisle. Speaks with an American accent.*] Yo, your hero was a ZCC gardener!

BABBLE: What? Who's that?

PROF: That's a safe bet. You prefer your darkies simple and superstitious.

BABBLE: Professor! What are you doing here? Who told you about this gathering?

PROF: [*Mounts the stage.*] That's a secret. [*Slight pause.*] Sorry if I'm late.

BABBLE: No, don't apologize. It's actually perfect timing. I was just about to start the show when that thug Bhunga pitched up and cut me short. I'd hardly got going when he jumped up and started heckling me, making out that I was this scumbag. I mean who the hell does he think I am? For that matter who does he think he is?

PROF: You said it, bro! But don't worry yourself. He's history.

BABBLE: What do you mean?

PROF: Man, he got the chop, he's past tense.

BABBLE: Right now? Where did it happen? He was here just a… wait… you… you organized it?

PROF: Whaddaya you think? You think we gonna stand around and let a nigga like that give you the heat? No, we don't stand for shit like that – not me and the brothers.

BABBLE: I hope you didn't kill him! I just wanted him roughed up enough to back off.

PROF: I can read your thoughts, bro. And you whisper real loud. [*Laughing.*] Comrade Prosecutor Bhunga just got a visit from Police Intelligence. I asked them to take him away for a little questioning while you're here addressing these very important opinion makers. You see, we finally got through to the Vice Prez – he's also got beef with Bhunga. Dere's elements want him out. Dey say he bin too open with his dependencies. You dig? And now dey wanna nail him. Shit, Comrade Bhunga in de wrong camp, man – I mean, we got proof he was a CIA spy, a System man, a motherfuckin' tool of the Boers.

BABBLE: I wish you would stop this fake American accent, Prof. [*Takes off the ZCC hat and puts on the peaked hip hop cap.*] It's almost as fake as me wearing this.

PROF: Come on, what's with you, bro? Me and my Yankee cousins are like this. [*Holds up two fingers pressed together.*] Yo, dem Yankee bitches are hot for me, and I'm like hot for dem. [*Takes the cap off BABBLE, puts it on his head.*] Now, don't dis look right? Where's de Chivas? I'm thirsty.

BABBLE: You're always too damn thirsty. And cut the 'bitches' talk. [*Takes the hip hop off BHUNGA and puts it on his head.*]

PROF: Why? You never used to be like this. Hell, man, you wuz so generous in understanding a man's needs. But then we done you plenty good turns, me and de brothers. [*Takes the cap back.*]

BABBLE: Good turns, yes. Except for the ones when you went behind my back and brought in other investors.

PROF: Bullshit!

BABBLE: Like that deal in Congo. You went to the bloody minister of Land Development and offered him the jet I'd given you in return for a bigger slice for yourselves. [*Takes the cap back.*]

PROF: Non-sense! Who told you this shit, man?

BABBLE: What does it matter? [*Pause.*] It was Butch.

PROF: Yo! You believe dat cheap ass gangster? Dat man's got no politics.

BABBLE: [*Smiles.*] Why, he's got plenty of politics. [*Slight pause.*] But let's rather talk about Elephant, the most… the biggest… the mother of all Empowerment Deals! Why didn't you hang in there? Everything would have come right.

PROF: Man, you got it wrong. We gave you de Black Face but de bankerman turned it gray. [*Takes the cap back.*]

BABBLE: [*To the audience.*] Ag, how rude of me! I should have introduced my good friend here at the start. Professor Ndlovu is a comrade of note. A rising star of the Youth League, a real rough diamond… [*Clearing his throat.*] Always at the service of the youth of this country. Always aware of his fiduciary duty, you know, always accountable for every cent. Always reporting back and then getting a mandate for the next step. And needless to say, we have always gotten on.

PROF: Definitely! Who's the man?

BABBLE: You de Man! I did some things well, and you did other things *better*.

PROF: [*In a Rasta accent.*] Yeah, mon. Dey call dat 'division of de labour'. You see me bin reading dem books you gave me. I bin burying me poor little curly head in dem white man's books.

BABBLE: Oh, my God – he's now doing Jamaican.

PROF: An me tell you, since den I and I bin doing bizness like nobody's bizness. Come rain or shine, lil' ole Professor bin doing bizness just like Selassie On High said: O ye Chillen of Afrika, hit dem streets and buy out Babylon. Me was de star, man. Me was king.

BABBLE: What's wrong with just being Shangaan?

PROF: [*Returns to American accent.*] Nothing, man. Pity you told Lungi I was a has-been. You said I had my dick in my eyes and couldn't see straight.

BABBLE: Well… that was…

PROF: You acted bad, man – after all I done for you.

BABBLE: You got the car you wanted, and cases of…

PROF: Bling, dat's all bling, man.

BABBLE: Bl…ing!

PROF: Yeah, I need cash for my old age. You think you the only one with family to look after?

BABBLE: I took care of my children alright. You've never paid a penny in maintenance all your life. How many garnishing orders were served on you at my place?

PROF: Dose weren't my kids. De bitches was just looking for easy airtime. Dey knew I was workin' hard and savin' and dey wanted a piece of de pie.

BABBLE: [*Turns away.*] Stupid dickhead… [*Slight pause.*] Anyway, you didn't come here to insult me, did you?

PROF: Fact is – I didn't know you wuz around. I was just passin' by but someone sent me in.

BABBLE: Someone? Who?

PROF: Guess. We wuz just talking about him. [*Smiling.*] Mr Butch Deratti.

BABBLE: Are you telling me Butch is outside?

PROF: Dat man is a liar. And a thief. But he wants to see you.

BABBLE: [*Grimly.*] Well, Butch… Why doesn't he come in? He knows I'm here.

PROF: He wants to… clarify…

BABBLE: Yes, he'd better. The two timing bastard.

PROF: … a few things regarding the last operation.

BABBLE: Right! I'll step out for a few minutes and sort him out. [*Claps his hands.*] In the meanwhile you stay here. Tell them a few stories, you know, reminisce… [*Exits.*]

PROF: Move your butt, chief. [*Sings "My father was a garden boy…" Laughs. Switches to a working-class Black South African accent.*] Did I really sound like an American? Took me ages to learn the lingo, man. I used to sing along, you know, in front of the mirror. And my homeboy, Izwelethu, he and I used to get the DVD's, man, one after the other and check the style. Now Babble always used to hum a tune to himself when a deal was buzzing. Meant he had something up his sleeve. Not that he didn't teach us how to play. It was 'willing teacher, willing learner'. You got something useful to teach us, something that will bring in the bucks, we gonna listen, we gonna sit on your lap and lap it up. But I never really sat on Babble's lap! Not me! Ha, ha! You think we don't know about *interest* – bank interest, self interest – and what side the bread is buttered? Maqabane, we know how to make interest so interesting the sweetest bantwana start popping up at your elbow. And you better believe we know exactly how to use a Mephistopheles Medici Babble. [*Slight pause.*] Ha! He coughed up plenty. Why sell out cheap to the umlungu? Anyway, I was on the road to nowhere when this majita who lives next door says there's plenty opportunity in the League. League? What league? The soccer league or the cricket league? No, no, he says, it's the real top league if you want to help yourself – and if you want to help abasebenzi. Help? In what way can I help anybody? He grabs my arm. No, man, don't be like that, baba! Open your mind to opportunity like the Prez says. Step out. Go to a meeting or two and take the wax out your ears. Amagents are serious. They know time is not on our side. The umlungus are cashing in and amaChina and amaKhulu are robbing us blind. [*BUTCH enters behind PROF.*] I mean, you heard the Prez say we need to nationalize. Amandla! We need to take back the land and the mines. We must stop being patient. [*Slight pause.*] I mean, who's supposed to be driving the fancy cars? [*Sings "My mother was a kitchen girl…"*]

Scene 3

BUTCH steps forward, grinning madly. When speaking to Prof he uses a fake Italian accent.

PROF: That was quick!

BUTCH: Well done, me boy. [*Hands PROF an envelope.*] I finished with Mephistoph-eles. [*To the AUDIENCE.*] I'm here to share with you a few secrets that are maybe not so secret. [*Laughs. Slight pause.*] He's having a little chat with Happy.

PROF: Happy?

BUTCH: Si, si. Happy Happy.

PROF: You serious? I thought he was under guard in hospital.

BUTCH: His kidneys are finito but he'll live.

PROF: Well, done! Well, done! The press made such a fuss when Naidoo got parole I thought it would be real trouble to get Happy out of jail.

BUTCH: My boy, there's nothing we can't get done. And you? I hear only good things. You going for deputy minister?

PROF: True, me and the homeboys are chowing very, very nice. But hey, you also doing well. You won in the end. It was tricky but you pulled it off.

BUTCH: Cross my lines – you end up with an *assisted suicide*.

PROF: Hey, that was top shit, man. And then you destroyed Happy, and got away with that too.

BUTCH: Sh…

PROF: And now to show you're absolutely, totally, in every fucking respect, uncon-ditionally de Boss, you get him out of jail.

BUTCH: Quiet now!

PROF: Haai Baba, we got to give it up for you! [*To the audience.*] Let's all give it up for Butch Deratti Ngwenya, King of the Swamp! Ngwenya… the croc, man. That's your clan name, bro. You one of the family – sharp, sharp… [*Opens his mouth and taps his teeth.*] Chicken, steak, prawns, anything else you put on the plate… Shake on it, Baba! [*Tries to do a hi-5 with BUTCH.*] Don't you know how to shake with a brother?

BUTCH: Hey, shut the fuck up! I'm not a bambino.

PROF: Kid? No, *youth*, man. *Youth*.

BUTCH: And what is the maximum age these days to be a *youth*? I hear you changing your constitution so at forty you can still become… whaddaya-call-it…

PROF: An office bearer? That's bullshit, man. Thirty-five's the limit, thirty-five and
not a day more.

BUTCH: Really? Your Mister Mashaba's a rather mature looking thirty-five. And that
signorina, er… Nomsa, the one with the big arse, she's definitely…

PROF: Hey, bro – there's five Nomsa's with big arses. You gotta grade them…small,
medium, large . . .

BUTCH: I'll leave that to you.

PROF: Whaddaya mean? There's plenty umlungus that likes mpundus. You people
got plenty women on the *extra* large.

BUTCH: [*Looking at his watch.*] Shit, Happy taking his time.

PROF: No, it's Meph what got plenty to say to him. I mean, you were the *connection* but you kept him from meeting Sidney while you played your game.
Makes sense, bro. After all, that's how you made your…

BUTCH: [*Laughs.*] How do you know about that?

PROF: Meph complained to me. He said he was pissed off that Bhunga's investiga-
tion wasn't being squashed by Happy – considering the bucks he moved your
way to make it happen.

BUTCH: Basta! We all had a cosy dinner. Man, dey talked about de Struggle days.
You know how Mephistopheles fancied himself as de messiah of you lot. Now
I'm not in de business of making and breaking chiefs of police. I keep every-
body smiling – especially Happy.

PROF: Yo, you testified against the dude in open court! You turned state's evidence
to save your fucking skin. How low can you get!

BUTCH: I can go lower.

PROF: Yeah, the lower you go, the more skirts you can look up.

BUTCH: Happy hang himself. He got de shakes from all dose single malts. [*To the
audience.*] We discuss every fucking detail before hand, but in de box he start
talking kak.

PROF: [*To the audience.*] You should have been at court. Butch turned up every day
with a fresh shave and a smile while Happy looked like a hobo.

BUTCH: He gotta sloppy with de paper work. Why de hell bring the wife, the old one, into the story? [*Phone rings.*] The way he was drinking ... [*To the audience.*] Scu-si... momento... [*Takes the phone out of his jacket pocket.*] Buena Serra. [*Pause.*] Ah, you finished. Go alright? [*In a whisper to PROF.*] It's Happy. [*Pause. To the caller.*] Mephistopheles wants to see me again. No way. [*Pause.*] Tell him to go to hell. [*Pause.*] He's already there. Good. Let him stay put. [*Pause.*] I'm coming to fetch you. You must be back in an hour. We pay de nurses just enough to get you out tonight. [*Pause.*] See you in the car park. [*To PROF.*] I gotta go now. Nice to see you, my boy. [*Slight pause.*] Dat Happy! What a nerve saying it was me, Butch Deratti, took him down! [*Raises an imaginary glass.*] Here's to the next fucking police chief! And the next... and the next... and the next. [*Exits.*]

PROF: Good riddance to that baboon! I've heard the stuff his outfit is dealing is cut with so much shit it's worse than the nyoape on Rockey St. Why Meph pulled him in beats me. What a dirty mouth to go with that big, big smile! But he's got connections. Bouncers, guys who do collections. [*Slight pause.*] Ag, I also better be going. Got a date with you-know-who. Anyway Meph will be back in a moment. For sure he's going to deny any involvement with Happy and tell you he never *bribed* no cop, never mind politician. And he's got a point. When in Mzansi, do as the Romans. [*Slips back into a hip hop accent.*] So let's get one thing straight - I don't wanna knock de man when he's down. I already told you how much he done for us in de early days. Pity it had to end so bad for him. [*In his 'normal' accent.*] Be sure to run into you guys sometime – the whiskey boys are sponsoring so many of our meetings and I can see we're all on the same guest list. [*Exits, whistling "My mother was a kitchen girl..."*]

Scene 4

BUTCH steps forward; addresses the audience.

BUTCH: I thought he'd never leave! Can you believe it, Happy and Medici still jab-ber, jabber... [*Slight pause. Switches to a "normal" white South African accent.*] You know, Mephistopheles and me, we went to the same school. Chubby little bastard, not much good at sport, but full of himself... and very smarmy, paid the bigger boys to protect him from de bullies. [*Laughs.*] And that brings me to the affidavit they say I signed, the one about a meeting to discuss... eh... Mephistopheles's future. Sure that meeting took place but Mephistopheles was there. He was the one to come up with the idea! Everything crashing down, what's he to do? And that old frog behind him, that Aussie, you know, his fucking guru, that Colonel Suction, he got no answers. That one no fuckin' mining expert, just an old wanker... a British spy. Now you get it? Mephistopheles begged me to rub him out! So I help the man. I get in touch with Glint. Now Glint's a real gentleman. He's got the boys. But what a bunch! First time, the car stalls. Second time, the fucking gun jams. [*Pause.*] I know you hear shit about me, that I only gave the affidavit 'cause I did a deal with Mister Buti Bhunga about *recreational medication*. That business not my show. [*Reverts to the fake Italian accent.*] De Greeks ordered de goods. Me, I just help with warehousing and sales, ok? [*In a "normal" accent.*] As for how the cops come to know, I got my suspicions. [*Slight pause. Laughs. Steps off stage, walks down the aisle; stops mid-theatre.*] Doos clowns of Glint's, it's one thing to do a job properly, but why did they have to fill him with so many holes?

Wilhelmina Randridge dances down the aisle towards the stage holding a boom box.

WILHELMINA: They sure did, honey.

BUTCH: [*Reverts to his fake Italian accent.*] You!

WILHELMINA: So many holes the man didn't know which way the wind was blowing.

BUTCH: You! I thought you gotta some scholarship to Britain after dat… dat competition.

WILHELMINA: Which I won, darling. The inaugural Babble Art Award for Mzansian Genius. I won it by a mile. [*Breaks into song.*] "She shall have music wherever she goes." [*Slight pause.*] You can also sing, hey?

BUTCH: Me… sing?

WILHELMINA: We all admired your performance in the dock.

BUTCH: [*Slight pause.*] What you doing here?

WILHELMINA: I want to see Meph. [*Mounts the stage. Puts the boom box down.*] I heard he's giving a show tonight. Come back to tell it like it is before more books come out and trash him.

BUTCH: You will have to wait. Medici, he's outside with Happy. Come tomorrow night.

WILHELMINA: Ag, no. Tonight's the night.

BUTCH: Why? Is there something I don't know?

WILHELMINA: There's a lot you don't know, Mr Bimbo.

BUTCH: Don't 'bimbo' me, babe. You not too loaded upstairs from what Mephistopheles tells me.

WILHELMINA: Then how did I win the prize?

BUTCH: I know how your art world works.

WILHELMINA: Ag, even on Pluto you have to know the right people. That prize brought a sensational new artiste into the public eye and got me a little something to live off while I created the next show-stopping installation. [*Slight pause.*] Just five minutes with my grand patron, my Medici, that's all! Just a fiver to cheer him up and let him know some of us still appreciate him.

BUTCH: Don't make me into a stupido. I seen dose lousy paintings of yours all over his houses, but most down in the cellar.

WILHELMINA: The dealers would tell us he'd just say, "this one", and "that one", and "this one"…

BUTCH: [*Laughs.*] There was nothing he couldn't have. And that idiot Colonel Suction used to blab to me about it. [*To the audience in a 'normal' accent.*] Come to think of it, he only talk to me about things he want me to tell others.

WILHELMINA: [*Dramatically.*] "Behind every Puppet Master is a Puppet Master." Picture this: a hellava storm, great bolts of lightning flashing over the city, and these bolts are coming from the finger tips of a great 'puller of strings'. [*Slight pause.*] Speaking of God, I heard that when the shit started and he couldn't find enough bucks to pay people, Meph went and had himself baptized, there in his swimming pool at the house. [*To the audience.*] He worked out how to sell himself – and how to buy others. It all came so easy, but then, poor darling, he went cuckoo.

BUTCH: What you complaining about? You play de game as cool as anyone else.

WILHELMINA: What do you expect me to do? Roll over and die because I'm *disadvantaged*?

BUTCH: Ok, ok – don't get too excited. I gotta go. People waiting.

WILHELMINA: Off you go. Ciao, ciao, capitano.

BUTCH: [*Venomously.*] Ciao, ciao, bambino! [*Exits.*]

Scene 5

WILHELMINA: Slimeball deluxe! [*To the audience.*] Anyway the good news is that now I can do my special dance. You're in for a treat. [*Pause.*] God, the people you meet when you're hustling for patrons! We, artistes, are really a tough bunch. I mean the whole crew I ran into trying to win Meph over are 'colourful' enough to make you cry tears of inspiration. Ag, but now for that special dance. I call it 'Devil's Delight'. [*Puts on the ladies straw hat. Switches on the boom box. A disco song blasts out. Dances wildly for a short while.*] Whew, that was fun! Agree? You loved your Scarlet O'Hara come from Ikasi? Well he did. At first Comrade Mephistopheles Medici Babble charmed me like he did everyone else. He could talk, the fucker. And I thought he actually did value art. In no time he put me on the map. But now…

BABBLE: Wilhelmina!

WILHELMINA: My Medici!

BABBLE: I thought I recognized the dulcet tones. [*Embraces her.*] Of all my unexpected 'visitors' you're the only one who is unreservedly welcome. And in such fetching gear!

WILHELMINA: It is lovely, isn't it? [*Takes off the straw hat. Points at the headgear on the different mannequins.*] This your collection?

BABBLE: As a matter of fact, no. Must be the management's idea of a joke. Leftovers from the last performance.

WILHELMINA: Come, come! There's extreme method here. And who would have the taste and the imagination to put it together? Think hard, Comrade. [*Pause.*] Why, *this* is my latest installation.

BABBLE: Oh! What's it called?

WILHELMINA: "So Many Caps to Wear… [*Bows to BABBLE.*] … but Only One Head" by Wilhelmina Randridge.

BABBLE: How very clever! You've always got something to say and you know how to say it.

WILHELMINA: And you've always had a way of making me feel worthwhile. Glad that hasn't stopped.

BABBLE: [*Sits on the car seat next to the mannequin.*] Until the scale starts to tip, tip to the wrong side, you can't believe it – you refuse to believe it. You wait for it to swing back. But when it doesn't, and you feel it dropping faster and faster, then no matter how calm and in control you've been and how many risks you've faced, you start to go down, down with it. And then you see that the higher you've climbed, the faster the downhill is going to be.

WILHELMINA: My poor Medici! Don't feel depressed! Your exploits will always be remembered!

BABBLE: Will they? [*Pause.*] You're right! My dear, you've inspired me. Give me that jester's hat!

WILHELMINA: That's the spirit! Don't let the bums get you down! [*Passes BABBLE the jester's hat.*]

BABBLE: [*Puts on the jester's hat.*] Bums! Yes, Bhunga, and the other gatecrashers, the grudge brigade.

WILHELMINA: [*Gestures to the audience.*] But not these good people! They've come to applaud you – just as I have. You took the temperature of our time and said, "I'll show Mzansi how to play in the Big League. They won't call me the new Barney Barnato for nothing. I can see exactly what to do".

BABBLE: Yes, let's show them! Let's show them the Babble empire!

WILHELMINA: And there she was, still covered with birth blood, the babe kicking and screaming and ready to face the global onslaught. Ja, she was ready for them, all 'resource heavy', busting out with gold in her hair…

BABBLE: [*Begins dressing WILHELMINA with the baubles and chains decorating the mannequins.*]… and iron ore up her arse…

WILHELMINA: … and titanium along her crotch…

BABBLE: … and platinum tickling her armpits…

WILHELMINA: … and bauxite beefing up her six pack…

BABBLE: … and a little diamond flashing in her eyes. [*Places the last 'jewel'.*]

WILHELMINA: She was a heavy duty queen of the mineral world, and the suitors were queuing up to strip her, but why let foreigners take it all?

BABBLE: That's exactly how I saw it! Go on, go on… [*Jumps up onto a chair.*]

WILHELMINA: You said, "They may have made my life a fucking misery as a kid but now *I'll* be the boss, the Force of Nature whose unleashing tsunamis in the mining business, the boss who'll show good old daddy and rugger-bugger boet and those old tarts in the Rand Club where the future lies."

BABBLE: Say it again!

WILHELMINA: I will, I will, Your Excellency, Il Duce Medici.

BABBLE: [*Steps off the chair.*] It was going so well till Suction started pushing me. There were a few deals I thought were too crazy but he kept on saying it was psychologically necessary to close them.

WILHELMINA: I can't see you keeping quiet and hoping the butler would call him to order.

BABBLE: Gosh, I'm feeling a bit faint. [*Pause.*] It's pretty taxing to have to deal with the old stuff. Those last few weeks were awful, absolutely awful. And the worst was worrying about my kids.

WILHELMINA: [*Puts an arm round him.*] Poor baby, you go and take a power nap.

BABBLE: Really?

WILHELMINA: I'll wake you in half an hour so you can finish your story.

BABBLE: How sweet of you! [*To the audience.*] And you? You don't mind me having a quick nap? [*To WILHELMINA.*] But I'm keeping this. [*Points to the jester's hat on his head.*]

WILHELMINA: You do that, darling. Now off you go. Have a good rest. I'll set the alarm. [*BABBLE smiles, waves to the audience. Exits.*] Do you know how much weight he's lost? And his colouring! Nothing should amaze me, but Comrade Meph, a True Son of the Soil, risen from the grave? [*With great vehemence.*] Must say, it's a miracle. Seven bullets. That's what the papers said. Ja, fat boy copped it real good. And who planned the deed? Now, that's a juicy one. Some say it was that dried out Suction – he wanted Meph dead before he could spill the beans. But others say it was a certain Mr X. Meph needed five bar real bad for immediate expenses. Everyone had turned him down but then this Mr X offered him a fat bag of sparklers. Sadly something went vrot and hey presto Meph had to more than bite the bullet. As for *assisted suicide*…! Hell, no! He could have just fiddled with his brakes and driven that Merc he loved so dearly off a cliff. I don't believe he would've had the guts to face a gunman, eyeball to eyeball, knowing he was about to be snuffed.

Scene 6

UMSHINI: [*Advancing down the aisle with a crash helmet over his head.*] Wait a second! You better believe it, ou pal! I was there, on the spot so don't talk shit! First he asked Glint for a pill, something to stop the old ticker that no autopsy gonna pick up. But we ain't got nothing like it in this part of the woods. So we got no choice, we gotta make it look like a… fucking hijacking, you know something *criminal*.

WILHELMINA: Hello, hello! Who are you?

UMSHINI: [*Takes off the crash helmet.*] You don't recognize me? You don't read no papers, you don't check the tv?

WILHELMINA: Why would I do that when I got my own private circus to star in?

UMSHINI: Ja, you look like a right proper queen of the Mardi Gras. But let me bring you up to speed. Sit down… [*WILHELMINA sits down on the car-seat.*] I reckon these arseholes here… [*Points at the audience.*]… will also be interested. [*To the audience.*] Glint was Babble's security boss, earning good but nothing special. But, hey, when Babble tells him what he needs done, then Glint knows he can really burn the bastard. So Glint says, "Who you gonna get? A bunch of moegoes who work for the taxi bosses… bunch of clowns. No, you want class, you want guys who got the skills, man, and the hardware, and the fucking temperament. Guys who got gees, who won't blink when it comes to the big day. Quick in, quick out. 500 G's each and we need at least three on the job and then there's me. I need my slice of the pie for sewing it all up." [*Pause.*] Ha, what a meal Glint makes of it! And Babble tunes, sweet. And we get the whole fucking thing rolling… me, Gerrie and Nappy, all of us long in the game and tight, man. Then Babble tunes we gotta do it when it's quiet, no cars or any mense around, and he can meet us near his pozzie, and the boys can just blow him away. Then the big night comes and, man, Babble was a star… I mean the gat didn't wanna go off and the fucking jam made me nearly drop the fucking thing. And there he was just checking me out and not saying a word. But his fucking eyes, man, his eyes were saying, "Please, please, just fucking kill me, I've had enough, they're crucifying me, the whole world thinks I'm a fraud". Ja, the man was proud and he had no more tom to pay the pin stripes. He just looked at me and fucking prayed the gat would kick in. And when it did, shit, I went fucking bedonnerd and pumped him I don't know how many times. I mean, I just kept on to make sure I'd fuckin' wiped him for real. [*Slight pause.*] And I did. [*Pause.*] Hey, I can see most of youse is lahnies. Admit it, you think I'm a low-life. But let me tell you I got a woman and kids that shows respect. And not just because I was on TV. [*Pause.*] No one gonna tell Umshini De Boom what to do.

WILHELMINA: [*Clapping.*] Dead right! I'm sure your chick is here tonight to support her Man.

UMSHINI: Knock it off.

WILHELMINA: And if I don't?

UMSHINI: Don't push me.

WILHELMINA: Me? How could I push you, brother?

UMSHINI: You working on my nerves, fairy. Go play games with your bum-chums.

WILHELMINA: What? You and I aren't chommies?

UMSHINI: Don't chaff me! You know who I am. And you know I got principles.

WILHELMINA: Like pulling the trigger on a hero of the masses.

UMSHINI: He was no fucking hero and me, I just did the job he paid us to do.

WILHELMINA: Just a buddy doing another buddy a favour.

UMSHINI: Business, boet, business. Business with heart.

WILHELMINA: [*To the audience.*] You buy this crap?

UMSHINI: Zip it, sonny. I'll show you what happens to laaities who rag Umshini de Boom. [*Grabbing WILHELMINA by the throat.*] This tight enough?

WILHELMINA: Hey, let go! You fucking strangling me!

UMSHINI: Had enough, bitch? Enough?

WILHELMINA: Ja, ja! Let me go!

UMSHINI: Say sorry, cunt.

WILHELMINA: Sorry, cunt!

UMSHINI: Louder.

WILHELMINA: Sorry! I'm fucking sorry!

UMSHINI: That's better. Now shut the fuck up. [*Releasing him.*]

WILHELMINA: Peace, brother! [*Makes a peace sign. To the audience.*] No more lip for the brother – you hear that. No, no. The brother's a fighter, a contender!

UMSHINI: Hey, watch it. One more poep out of you and I'll really bite your tits off…

WILHELMINA: Ok, Ok. [*To the audience.*] There's nothing new about a beautiful girl hogging the limelight.

UMSHINI: Bugger off, already!

WILHELMINA: I am. Just collecting my shit. [*Gathers up all the baubles draped on the wire figures. To the audience.*] Maybe I'll come back when Meph's ready. But who knows, he might have second thoughts about hanging around, might have got word that you're all getting restless and want to gooi him with tomatoes. [*Waves and blows a kiss. Points at UMSHINI. Exits.*]

Scene 7

UMSHINI: [*Puts on the crash helmet. To the audience.*] You want to throw me with tomatoes? Go on throw! Throw! You think I'm the one you should be aiming at? Go for the real fuckers! [*Pause.*] Shit, I don't wanna go on about this, but I can see you scheme I'll do anything for a buck. And sometimes I think so myself. But that's only when I'm so goofed I can't fucking piss straight . . . or when I'm so pissed I can't goof straight . . Shit, you know what I mean. Lucky that's past tense, hey? I mean, can a ou's life get so screwed up you just want to fucking die? I been down that road, believe me I had my days, but to get so low? No, that will never happen. And you know why? Coz inside me is a fucking survivor. I stopped the booze and the pills and the screwing. I went back to my wife and kids. You don't believe me? I'll phone Gerrie and Nappy right now. [*Takes out a cell phone.*] You can mos cross-question them the whole bladdy night. They'll tell you it's true. Anyway, we didn't know nothing of the shit behind old Babble's story. All we knows is he wants out. [*Slight pause.*] But come to think about it, who can blame him? Tjoekie's plenty rough for a white ou at his age and God, the life he was leading. Be fucking locked up with scom when you had all he had – the *whole* bladdy world in your pocket. No, man, tjoekie ain't no fucking joke.

BHUNGA enters.

BHUNGA: No, it isn't a joke, absolutely not. But your story is too much of a joke.

UMSHINI: Buti Bhunga! You following me? [*Stands.*] I thought they took you off the case. I mean, shipped you out. Jissus, you the one who needs this. [*Throws the helmet to BHUNGA.*]

BHUNGA: To think that a bunch of killer-clowns like yourselves walked free because we had to use you to nail more serious threats. [*Throws the helmet back to UMSHINI.*]

UMSHINI: That's right, Mister Babble was no longer a threat to *society*. Now that's a big word, Mister Lawman. Not sure what it means. Sure, you had to bust Happy. But it's not very pretty, all this plea bargaining shit. [*UMSHINI throws the helmet back at him.*]

BHUNGA: [*To the audience.*] Decisions, priorities … sometimes I wasn't sure if I was making the right ones, if I myself wasn't being expedient.

UMSHINI: Blah, blah, blah! Man, you gotta learn to build up your… what do they call it? … fucking immunity system, so that when you in the shit and suck your fingers they still taste of roses.

BHUNGA: Roses… you almost killed that investment banker In Cape Town.

UMSHINI: Man, he had it coming. Fucker was asking too many questions. Anyway, he survived. He's still a fat cat. Not like you, hey?

BHUNGA: [*Slight pause.*] Yes, it is over for me – in a way. [*To the audience.*] You are all no doubt aware that despite the positive ruling of the commission into my competency, the President over-ruled its recommendation that I remain in my position. And the special unit responsible for investigating cases like Babble's has been disbanded and a watered down version installed.

UMSHINI: Stop moaning, man! Get on with your life!

BHUNGA: [*To the audience.*] The whole trade off made me puke. [*Throws the helmet back to UMSHINI.*]

UMSHINI: Then why did you do it?

BHUNGA: Happy can appeal as much as he likes but the mood in the country is changing. He doesn't have too many friends to bail him out.

UMSHINI: Just like Babble.

BHUNGA: Yes, just like Babble.

UMSHINI: So his lekker big funeral in Cape Town in that cathedral with all the big bosses and the fucking government people – what was that? Never mind his name, what about mine?

BHUNGA: The game must go on, Mr de Boom. And these good folks in front of us also don't give a damn. {*To the audience.*] You just want to be titillated, alternately gobsmacked by the brazenness of power junkies. [*To UMSHINI.*] In any case, Babble's the one who organized this event. If he wants to stir the pot some more, that doesn't mean you have to join the party.

UMSHINI: Quiet! [*Pause.*] Did you hear that? Thought I fucking heard his voice.

BHUNGA: How opportune. Now you can renew your acquaintance. Maybe set your sights on those eyes again…

UMSHINI: Fuck off!

BHUNGA: Do a rerun of that last *operation* and show us your expertise.

UMSHINI: [*To the audience.*] Shit, I can't take this anymore. I'm off to the gym.

BHUNGA: Exercise restraint, my friend.

UMSHINI: Spare me the sarky, sparky, or I'll bang a few heads before I get there. And just remember… Butch, he's the scum bag. Gone an ratted on Happy and the others to save his fucking skin after the cops got onto his bladdy warehouse dik with dagga and kif. They're all like fucking swollen pythons – swallowed the bucks, now it's time to lie in the sun. I never done evil. You hear that? I just pulled a job. [*Moves to stage rear. Stops, walks back to one of the wire figures and picks up the scull cap.*] Better put this on. You're a preacher, man. Suits you. [*Holds it out to BHUNGA who ignores him.*] OK, be like that. But you don't fool nobody. They fucked you over good and proper, mate. Man, you look real washed out. Pity. A darkie like you can make a fortune these days. [*Drops the skull cap on the floor. Exits.*]

Scene 8

BHUNGA picks up the skull cap; puts it on.

BHUNGA: [*To the audience.*] It's true – I am tired. [*Sits down on the car-seat.*] But I can't afford to be. So what's my next step? To help you understand your historical responsibility? Or is it to just let off steam? [*Slight pause.*] Between the White Trash and the White Overlords, we've now got this layer of Black Scum. I mean it's just too much! [*Stands.*] Survive? Is this how we want to survive? [*Pause.*] I'm sorry. I let my emotions take over. But you have no idea how much tension builds up in me. Can't sleep, snap at people, my wife is thoroughly upset, says I ignore her. [*Pause.*] A lead from a leak, a routine tax inquiry that throws up a funny, a disgruntled employee who wants to get even, thieves fall out . . . and so it starts, the whole damn process – the collecting, the cross checking, the double checking, trying to hold on to the thread that will guide you through the labyrinth. [*Pause.*] Yes, mountains of documents . . . months, sometimes years building a case, then the bargaining, the horse-trading . . . most unnerving, unsettling . . .

BABBLE: [*Enters. To the audience.*] I can't tell you how much I resent seeing these killers walk off scot free. Insurance scam! Do you think they would've paid my family if there was the slightest suggestion of fraud?

BHUNGA: The jury's still out on that one.

BABBLE: The minute my murder was reported they were all over the place. The media, a few bungling cops, my own security people...

BHUNGA: Everyone came looking for something – and what did they find?

BABBLE: They found me filled with these... [*He opens his shirt to reveal the bloody holes in his chest.*]

BHUNGA: Yes, and you still haven't been cleaned up. Those undertakers were a sloppy bunch.

BABBLE: That baptism in my pool wasn't just for the cameras. I made a vow, a sacred vow, with the Lord. His other Son also prophesied his death. The Great

Father ordained that both of us should die. Otherwise how could we set an example?

BHUNGA: An example of what?

BABBLE: Redemption.

BHUNGA: How can you ever redeem your crooked life?

BABBLE: I had to create that empire and be crucified for my boldness. And I did this to bear the cross of White Guilt.

BHUNGA: [*To the audience.*] The cross of *White Guilt*…

BABBLE: The Lord was building me up so that by the time I had to fall, to please Him, I was untouchable to all but Him.

BHUNGA: And now you've come back to save a few souls and check that your beloved family is quietly living off the loot so they don't mind your absence too much.

BABBLE: I told you not to mock them!

BHUNGA: You're back to lure hardened devils away from Lucifer's army. After all, you're the perfect missionary.

BABBLE: And your role was also ordained.

BHUNGA: Indeed! We *are* making progress!

BABBLE: What are you going to do now? Do you appreciate the harm your lies have done to my children?

BHUNGA: The sins of the fathers invariably blemish the fruits of their loins.

BABBLE: No!

BHUNGA: I thought you would have been told that when you were baptized. [*Gestures to BABBLE'S shirt.*] Couldn't you at least have gotten rid of the blood stains? No, wait! I get it. Your *drama coach* said it would make an impression, drum up some sympathy.

BABBLE: And it did. [*Gestures towards the audience.*] Look at their faces! You saw their response.

BHUNGA: How can they not applaud a man who's sincere? Especially someone who bankrolled school feeding schemes and never turned a beggar from his door – especially a black one.

BABBLE: I would have thought your battle with your own kind would have been enough without your always having to attack Whites.

BHUNGA: [*In a preacher's voice. To the audience.*] Amen, brother. And listen further to what the Lord has to say. "Black Man you're on your own. Do not take the helping hand proffered by the white folk. For it is a crooked hand, a hand smelling of perfumed dung."

BABBLE: Look, I've been patient, but I've come to the end of my tether! Shut up and leave!

BHUNGA: Just try and touch me.

BABBLE: I just want to … go home to my kids. I just want to go home.

BHUNGA: Home?

BABBLE: I'm lonely.

BHUNGA: Get a grip on yourself, man! This is most unbecoming. After all, the Lord put you where you are. You were just following His orders.

BABBLE: That doesn't mean others don't have to show me mercy. [*Pause.*] And love.

BHUNGA: So now its mercy *and love* you want.

BABBLE: Of course, I do. Isn't that what everyone wants?

BHUNGA: Mr Babble, right now I don't want to hear about mercy and love – I want justice.

BABBLE: That's outrageous. No one is allowed to favour justice over love.

BHUNGA: The show is over.

BABBLE: I've come to repent.

BHUNGA: No, you just want to check on your kids to see how they're handling their shame.

BABBLE: They aren't ashamed.

BHUNGA: Really? Do you listen in when they're talking among themselves?

BABBLE: I said I'm sorry! [*To the audience.*] Do you want me to leave? Have you heard enough?

BHUNGA: They've heard enough. You're only repeating yourself.

BABBLE: [*To the audience.*] But I haven't really told you about Elephant, the biggest empowerment consortium anyone has ever put together... Elephant was going to change everything!

BHUNGA: A final throw of a loaded dice to raise cash. Thank God it didn't get off the ground.

BABBLE: Don't blaspheme! [*To the audience.*] Tell him to stop! [*Runs down the aisle. Addresses individual members of the audience.*] Dammit, tell him to stop crucifying me! I'm just like you! I only want forgiveness! Please... [*Starts sobbing again.*]

BHUNGA: [*Leaving the stage and running to BABBLE.*] Stop making an exhibition of yourself! Have some dignity!

BABBLE: With these all over me? [*Touches the bullet holes.*]

BHUNGA: [*To a man in the audience.*] Sir, will you help me? It's time to take action and show we won't be held captive by his stratagems.

BABBLE: Do you know what I've been through?

BHUNGA: Sir, are you with me? [*To the audience at large.*] Are you with me?

BABBLE: How can they be with you? You're a megalomaniac!

BHUNGA: That's *your* diagnosis. [*To a man in the audience.*] Are you going to help me, sir?

BABBLE: [*Sobbing.*] I want to see my family. [*On his knees.*] I want to see my kids...

BHUNGA: No more tricks! No – more – tricks!

BABBLE: I just want to see my kids...

BHUNGA: [*Pause.*] Is that really all you want?

BABBLE: Yes, yes! If only you could take me! Say you will! Please! [*Sobs more hysterically.*]

BHUNGA: [*To the audience.*] You know I'm a man of my word. [*To BABBLE.*] If I was to say I will take you, then I will.

BABBLE: I won't do anything bad! I just want to be with them!

BHUNGA: Not another word? No more whining? [*Pause as BABBLE nods in agreement. To the man in the audience.*] What do you say? Should I take him?

BABBLE: Please, please, I beg you! Let me see them just this once! I did no wrong!

I did what every one of you would have done given the circumstances. [*Goes down into the audience.*] Friends, thank you! Thank you so much for coming. You can't still think what you did when you first walked in this evening. And those books you've read, you've seen through them, haven't you? Thank you, thank you again! [*Grabs the hand of a woman in the audience and kisses it.*] God bless, God bless! [*Sound of a gong.*] Time!

BHUNGA: Who's waiting for you, Comrade? Who's laid down your curfew?

BABBLE: Don't pretend you don't know.

BHUNGA: [*To the audience.*] Wasn't this an experience? You did get your *show* after all. [*To BABBLE.*] Come here! [*Walks towards the car seat; BABBLE follows, reaches the seat and sits.*] Comrade Mephistopheles Medici Babble, at least you had the guts to expose yourself to popular judgement. Now finally the good folk here sense your agony. They appreciate your return to the bowels of Hell, they know you'll never stop living those last minutes alone in your Mercedes in that dark avenue off the highway… waiting… Yes, it is too late to go to your children. It is too late.

Seven gun shots ring out. Blackout.

END

**Downstairs Theatre
Wits. Jorrisen St,
Braamfontein**

Performances:
29, 30, 31 July (7.30pm);
1 August (7.30pm);
2 August (2pm)

Tickets: R60
Students: R30
Groups: R20

Featuring Robert Hobbs & Khutjo Green
Written & directed by Allan Kolski Horwitz

Boykie and Girlie have been together for several years; they live in a comfortable but unfashionable flat somewhere in Johannesburg. They are no longer in the first flush of their lives, experience has roughened their edges. On this particular evening, Girlie returns home & once again finds Boykie in a foul mood. The past and the present collide and what ensues exposes their many different faces: values, ambitions, sexual needs & ability to love.

THE POLITICS OF A PARTNERSHIP

BOYKIE & GIRLIE

The Politics of a Partnership

PERFORMED BY
KHUTJO GREEN &
CRAIG MORRIS

WRITTEN & DIRECTED BY
ALLAN KOLSKI HORWITZ

...One evening when the past and present collide...

All photographs from
BOYKIE and GIRLIE first
production

Program notes

Boykie and Girlie have been together for several years; they live in a comfortable but unfashionable flat somewhere in Johannesburg. They are no longer in the first flush of their lives, experience has roughened their edges. On this particular evening, Girlie returns home and once again finds Boykie in a foul mood. The past and the present collide and what ensues exposes their shared history and reflects on their values, ambitions, sexual needs and imperfect love.

Set in their kitchen and in the toilet Boykie habitually escapes to, the play seesaws from mood to mood, subject to subject, while Girlie prepares the supper Boykie refuses to eat. It has moments of pathos, of profound emotion, of madness and clarity as the couple spar and cajole, testing each other's resolve and intentions. In language that is both poetic and coarse, they alternately celebrate and denigrate their relationship dominated by Boykie's dead end. In a telling exchange, the 'blocked' writer and activist calls out to Girlie, "It's not you that I can't live with. I'm not strong enough. It's all so absurd, so trivial, so demeaning . . ." To which she replies, "Hey, you're vomiting over a pretty full plate."

Boykie and Girlie are thus both agents and victims, switching from one to the other as the evening unwinds. His 'hunger strike', his sexual experimentation, his punctured ego and subsequent sense of self-loathing – all place an enormous strain on Girlie as she has to bear not only the responsibilities of her demanding and important work as a lawyer but the pressure of living with a partner who, despite experiencing exuberant, almost ecstatic epiphanies, is mired in depression.

However, by the end of the play, after having discussed or revealed almost all the facets of their lives, they reach a point where it is mutually agreed to 'give ourselves a rest'. And so we see them prepare to exit from the sites of battle (the kitchen and toilet) and 'retire to their bedroom' rather than throw themselves into the abyss of separation. In this way there is no apocalyptic denouement, no neat conclusion – their lives will continue, probably in much the same way, even as their final matter-of-fact discussion about 'Tony and Brenda', two mutual friends they plan to visit after their 'rest', degenerates into rhetorical side-stepping.

~~

The first performance of BOYKIE AND GIRLIE took place at the Wits Theatre, Johannesburg on 29 July 2014 with the following cast:

BOYKIE	Robert Hobbs
GIRLIE	Khutjo Green

A second production was staged in 2015 with the following cast:

BOYKIE	Craig Morris
GIRLIE	Khutjo Green

Both productions were directed by Allan Kolski Horwitz.

SETTING

An old block of flats; a kitchen and toilet in one of the flats. The space is furnished with a kitchen table; two chairs; a stove; a side unit with storage space which stands next to the stove; a rubbish bin; a clothes horse; a pot plant; a few pots and pans; tins of food; bottles of alcohol (both full and empty; a toilet with a door.

BOYKIE brays off stage; strolls in with a book of Samuel Beckett's plays and begins to read aloud from Krapp's Last Tape.

B: "Box 3, spool 5." [*Brays. Pause.*] "Slight improvement in bowel condition." [*Brays. Pause.*] "Memorable equinox." Now, that's a really peculiar line. [*Brays. Shakes his head. Laughs. Takes a pot out of the side table. Places it on the stove.*] "Hard to believe I was ever that young whelp. The voice! Jesus! And the aspirations! And the resolutions! To drink less, in particular." [*Stops. Brays. Opens one side of the side unit, looks at the array of bottles of alcohol inside. Shakes his head. Close sit .*] Drink less . . . [*Brays. Enters the toilet. Sits.*] "Good to be back in my old den in my old rags. Have just eaten I regret to say three bananas and only with difficulty restrained a fourth." [*Brays. Laughs.*] If only . . . [*Brays. Concentrates on shitting. Gives up. Continues reading.*] "Spiritually a year of profound gloom and indulgence until that memorable night in March at the end of the jetty in the howling wind never to be forgotten, when suddenly I saw the whole thing!" [*Brays. Stops.*] The whole thing . . . fuck it. [*Brays. Tries again to shit. Gives up. Resumes reading.*] "How do you manage it, she said, at your age. I told her I'd been saving up for her all my life." [*Brays. Stands, pulls up his pants.*] Mister Krapp! What utter kak!

G: [*Enters carrying shopping bags. Sets them down, takes off her 'smart' shoes, arranges the delicacies. Lifts the cover of the pot on the stove. Looks around.*] Boykie! How did it go today? [*Pause.*] Get anything done? [*Boykie emerges from the toilet.* Anything from your agent?

B: [*Brays. Points at the shopping bags on the table.*] Don't you think you've overdone it?

G: Why?

B: There's food here for a month.

G: Nonsense, there's barely enough for a week, my darling.

B: No, really Girlie, it's a waste – of food *and* of money.

G: Let me be the judge of that. [*Places bags on a side-board.*] After another day of thankless struggle in the human jungle . . . yes, that case didn't go to well today, they had a long line of very dodgy witnesses but did that make His Worship a little disbelieving? Oh no, the good man lent his ear to their nonsense. Yes, that was my day. But still she spent her *hard* earned time and cash on rare delights, exotic pastries and pies to please her *hard*-to-please mate. [*Spins round with two small boxes.*] Look what I've brought for you!

B: Don't try and sweet-talk me. [*Slight pause.*] You've gone overboard.

G: Eat now or later?

B: Nothing for me.

G: Pity, I'm ready for more than just a bite. And I'm sure you didn't cook for yourself. So you must be hungry.

B: Are you deaf? I just said I'm not hungry. [*Pause.*] You know full well why I don't have an appetite.

G: I do?

B: [*Mockingly.*] I'm starving for my art.

G: [*Points to some groceries.*] Please put this stuff in the cupboard.

B: No.

G: [*Slight pause.*] You're really not hungry?

B: No.

G: But I can't leave you every morning knowing you're on a *hunger* strike.

B: Strike one, strike all.

G: Never mind my *wasting* good money on food for the two of us, you'll *waste* away. Ag, don't turn our little love nest into a *wasteland* . . . ha, ha. [*Slight pause.*] You know, you look terrible. This has got to stop. You must start eating normally again. [*She begins arranging vegetables on the kitchen unit next to the stove and places a cutting board on the table. She then lights the stove and places a large pot on one of the plates and takes a large kitchen knife and starts to chop them up. Throughout the play she will busy herself preparing a meal.*]

B: What's the fucking point?

G: [*Puts her arms round him.*] Come on, I'll make something special. Something light.

B: Something so light I won't even *feel* it.

G: It will flutter about in your guts . . .

B: [*In a fake accent.*] Without making you feel that you've consumed the slightest morsel of life-giving substance. [*Brays.*] You're a bloody marvel.

G: I *am* a marvel. The restorer of lost desires.

B: Ja, the filler of holes. But some holes can't be filled. Not even Girlie the Marvel can fill certain holes. [*Getting up from the table, claps his hands.*] I'm off. [*Slight pause.*] I'm going.

G: [*Dryly.*] To the cemetery? I mean, that's what you call your study these days.

B: Study? What is there to study?

G: Nothing, of course. But I won't be nasty. And why not? Because a graveyard is a cheerful place to make a relaxing meal of yourself. [*Pause.*] Boykie, have a snack. Humour me.

B: Alright. [*Slight pause.*] Just . . . one dry biscuit.

G: No, five crackers with a little something on top. [*Slight pause.*] Eat all of them and I won't stop you having another midnight snack with my sister-witches on top of a mouldy marble slab in memory of Lady Macbeth.

B: No doubt you'll join me in that fitting tribute to all ambitious wives. [*Slight pause.*] Where's the spade?

G: What do you need a spade for?

B: Don't play dumb. You've pointed the way. [*Slight pause.*] I need a *spade* to dig a *grave*.

G: My Boykie, a grave digger? Ag, shame– such hard work on an empty stomach. [*Slight pause.*] For chrissake, go and lie down. Have a nap. I'll call you when the food's ready.

B: I'm going to finish off what I started.

G: Yes, always finish off what you've started. [*Slight pause.*] Fact is, you've only managed to dig about *half way* down to the necessary depth. You know . . . [*SHE mimes digging a grave, using a broom.*]

B: No, deeper, much, much deeper.

G: Come to think of it, you were deep enough only minutes after you were thrust out of your *mother's* unloving womb.

B: [*Takes the broom from her and pretends to dig.*] I dig and dig but there's still not enough room for my carcass. The soil flies out, but then, for some damn unfathomable reason, it keeps falling back in. [*Acts out the scene.*] Ah, the soil. . . *Mother* Earth's dank and shitty soil . . . [*Pretends to dig up soil and sniff it.*]

G: Ah, so it's the *shit* in the soil that's saving you. [*In a preacher's voice.*] "Oh brother, who can tell from whence salvation will come." Now get out of the kitchen and have a little sleep. Maybe you'll wake up in a better mood.

B: My mood is . . .

G: Sombre, mournful, funereal . . . and has been for how long now?

B: Back off. My mood is irrelevant. It never interferes with my commitment to the task at hand. And if I perform it diligently, it will save you hiring someone to finish the job. Then that saving can be used for something more . . .

G: Life-affirming? [*Caresses his cheek.*] I promise that after a good rest and a snack you can go and meet Dr Death and his bunch of 'last resting place' inspectors. They will check if you've reached the required depth of . . . shall we say . . . *depression*. [*Punches him affectionately.*] Get going already!

B: Don't talk to me about *depression*.

G: No, I won't. [*Affectionately mocking.*] Let's rather talk about love – mine for you, you for me, you for you, me for me. And finally – our love for our love.

B: No, Girlie, please! Spare me this . . . this little . . .

G: Why, what are you risking? Aren't you a regular junkie?

B: Aren't we both. But I pass on this domestic drama. Besides, I risk letting you down even more than I have.

G: So what? You've walked the tightrope more or less successfully for long enough.

B: No, I haven't.

G: Yes, you have. We forgave each other when lines were crossed so long as we didn't deny responsibility. And we're both still here. Even though you, my fine friend, are seriously guilty of ignoring a chance to plant a very sweet-smelling flower on top of your half-empty, half-filled . . .

B. But Girlie, it's not you. It's not you that I can't live with. *I'm* not strong enough to deal with . . . [*Embraces her. Breaks off.*] It's all . . . it's all so absurd, so trivial, so demeaning . . .

G: Hey, you're vomiting over a pretty full plate.

B: [*Sneering.*] Ja, despite the ongoing wave of capitalist *accumulation* there are still millions of children starving in South Sudan. [*Slight pause.*] I'm not being self-indulgent. I resent your saying that. [*Moving away from G.*] Ok, I *am* whining. But it's the truth. I've got nothing ...

G: Going for you right now?

B. [*Sitting down again.*] I'm bored. I'm ...

G: [*Sharply.*] Come on, stop this. I'll make something light.

B: I've done nothing today. Nothing. I need something, dammit ... something ...

G: Challenging? And am I supposed to confess that you're *my* challenge? [*Laughs.*] Alright. How about washing the floor? There's the mop. Get cracking. Wash the floor down. Give it a good shine, Boykie. No doubt about it, it *is* your turn. [*Sings.*] 'Turn, turn, turn – for every season, there is a turn, turn, turn ...'

B: [*Pretending to whine like a child.*] No, no. Anything but the floor. I'll do the next lot of dishes. Leave me the *next* full sink.

G: Yes, go full sink ahead.

B: I swear I'll do it.

G: Don't. I know all about your vows. Their shorti-ti-vity.

B: Wait a minute ... I cooked the last few meals. And the one who cooks doesn't also wash up – a very *fair* division of labour.

G: Rubbish. There are hardly any dishes – for obvious reasons. And most of the time you get takeaways.

B: That's not being lazy. That's being smart.

G: Yes, you are *smart,* though lacking in .... more basic intelligence. But I must say, when there's absolutely no way out, you do cook rather well, my darling. And always have.

B: Ah! Recognition of my magic concoctions.

G: Especially those laced with rhino horn.

B: A rhino horn or two, thrown into the stew... [*Starts to strut around thrusting his pelvis. Stops.*] Me. I'm not a chef – I'm just a stirrer, a simple stirrer ... just chuck it all in and ... stir the pot.

G: A sir of a stir! Yes, what a stirrer! You're such a stirrer it's no mystery why you got kicked out of every bloody organization you ever joined.

B: What do you expect me to do? Stand by and watch power games run riot. And then have to kow-tow to petty egos once they're entrenched.

G: Exactly! Why bow down to petty egos? They've none of the grandeur of your little specimen.

B: Mine is a rare species of ego. Sometimes a little swollen but never to the point where it overwhelms others.

G: No, no, never one to seek the limelight.

B: You think I'm looking for fame? [*Brays.*] Come on, Girlie. That reminds me of a great insight, made decades ago, mind you, by old whatshisname . . . Andy Warhol. And what did he say? He said not to panic. The new technology will ensure that we'll all be famous for fiifteen minutes, every one of us known by the world, held in utmost esteem, for a full fifteen minutes. [*Slight pause.*] But these days it's gone down to fifteen fucking seconds.

G: Well, that's more than *zero* seconds.

B: It doesn't matter how much attention you get. Today, after your latest acquisition/hit record/starring role/top award/knighthood/first prize/gold medal/inauguration into the Hall of Fame, what do you have to show for it? Barely fifteen seconds of adoration or notoriety. Just fifteen fucking seconds when you've had countless wet dreams of an eternity where your work is on everyone's lips, your face on every billboard, and every network is buzzing with your latest tweet. Forever and ever, the centre . . .

G: Of the fucking universe.

B: Yes! A lootah continua!

G: So play it! Show me *you* as the centre of the fucking universe! Go on, let's see you do it! Play it! Carry the world on your broad back! [*B stands, smiles but does not move.*] Go on, do something! Show you're worthy! Carry the world on your broad shoulders! [*B. picks up a pot plant from the kitchen unit and begins to dance with it as if he is carrying the world. He whirls round and round as G. encourages him.*] Yes, that's it! Now you've got the hang of it – keep going! Very good, Mister Superman! You can return to earth. You've done your stint up there in the clouds. What joy to breathe in the perfumes of power and ignore the stench of envy!

B: An envy-fumigant is a useful item for us, super-stars. It's not easy dealing with our rivals. Scenting the sweetness, they want more sugar in their coffee. While those who know they haven't a chance of scaling our heights keep applauding us for want of anything better to do, the ones coming up, the ones really sniffing success . . . why, they're a motherfucking bunch of . . .

G: Just as well you fell off those exalted heights long ago so there's nothing to lose.

B: [*Smiles.*] Yes, it has been a while, quite a while. A sudden coup. Forced retirement from the mafias that run this demented backwater. [*Brays. Slight pause.*] Damn . . . I'm feeling . . . a bit nauseous. [*Stops. Walks over to the toilet. Opens the door. Tries to vomit into the bowl. Then drops his pants, stands for a few moments.*]

G: [*Goes to check on him.*] Are you alright? [*Slight pause.*] Close the door. [*B ignores her.*] I said 'close the door'.

B: [*Mimicking her.*] Close the door. [*Sits.*]

G: I don't want the smell in my kitchen.

B: It's not 'your' kitchen.

G: Yes, it is. I happen to have purchased just about everything in this room that qualifies it as a *kitchen*.

B: Including the drama. [*Brays.*] Don't be so . . . crude about your financial prowess, my darling. In any case, how can an empty stomach give off a smell? Any sort of smell.

G: Gas, there's a buildup of gas in your guts. You know, sulpher, carbon monoxide . . .

B: Bio-fuel, dammit, I'm creating bio-fuel!

G: Then take a container to trap it.

B: Ok, pass me one.

G: One of your old vodka bottles?

B: Why not?

G: Coming up. [*Turns her back and searches for a bottle. Picks one up from under the table.*] And this one's still got a shot left.

B: Bring it! I'll drain the last precious drop before attaching the aperture of the vessel to my rectum. Get it here fast, Girlie, or I'll crawl out and get it myself. [*Slight pause.*] And add some orange juice!

G: With ice?

B: Yeah, why not.

G: Wait . . . you usually want tomato juice.

B: I said *orange*.

G: There's hardly any orange.

B: Quit stalling!

G: But we've got three cans of tomato.

B: Damn, can't a man change his habits? Pour 'em down the drain and stop this crap.

G: You're the one who's got to stop the crap. And close the fucking door.

B: I can't believe it! Why the sudden fuss? I've taken plenty of shits with the door open.

G: Indeed, you have, my precious. But God's the one who decides and she's decided no more foul odours wafting into the kitchen from this moment and this moment on.

B: Fuck that. I'm blocked.

G: Argh! The day we move to a bigger flat so you can get some action away from my sharp nose will be a mighty blessed day. But till then – vodka and orange juice with ice coming up! [*Walks over to Boykie and hands him a bottle.*]

B: Thanks, babe. I knew you'd have mercy. [*Takes a swig.*]

G: A poisoned chalice from your 'One and Only'. [*Mimes closing the door.*]

B: [*Stopping her before it's completely closed.*] Hey, there's no bloody vodka in here! I don't want juice! Where's the vodka?

G: First close the door.

B: No! First put the bloody vodka in . . .

G: I can't trust you.

B: Then I'll close the door.

G: Close it.

B: Vodka first.

G: No. [*Laughs.*]

B: You'll have to trust me.

G: No, I don't have to.

B: Then the door stays open.

G: No, no, no, Boyo! No more vodka. In fact, better the stench of your bowels then the stench of your alcoholic breath.

B: Lay off, Girlie!

G: You're hitting the bottle a little too much of late.

B: The search for meaning needs to be lubricated.

G: How would I know the truth of that? I'm just one of those worker bees who keep on buzzing without knowing or wondering why.

B: Ah, a moment of humility!

G: But there is one thing I do most certainly know: I can't stand the reek of alcohol coming out of your body every night.

B: Then bring me an empty container so I can at least continue with my ecologically sound recycling of gasses.

G: If I do, you promise to eat my little light something?

B: Promise.

G: So help you God.

B: Hey, leave the bitch out of this. [*Covers his face with his hands.*] At last! [*Closes the door.*] Only joking. Now bring me my vodka!

G: Don't be disgusting! You promise to eat when you're out?

B: What's the point of shitting and then eating? Or eating and then shitting, or shitting while you're eating . . .

G: There doesn't have to be a point. You have to live before you can die. So . . . you have to eat before you can shit. Point of fact, you spend half your life in that little room. And why? Because . . . once upon a time, you were a compulsive eater. And, most of that time, of trash.

B: Then you should be happy that I'm now cutting back on non-essentials.

G: Like what? Moaning and groaning about how lousy and useless you feel.

B: [*Opens the door.*] Like potatoes and rice and pasta and bread and . . .

G: Shut the door – you've no idea how offensive this is.

B: Ok, relax! [*Shuts the door.*] I'll eat, goddamit! Just make it simple, and not too much garlic.

G: But you like garlic.

B: I do like garlic.

G: Then what's your problem?

B: Light hand, Girlie. Apply with a light hand.

G: What have *hands* to do with garlic? It pours itself out of a container without my help.

B: [*Opens the door.*] Where's my bloody vodka?

G: Just wait with decorum for what's coming.

B: Does that include a dose of your *loving kindness*? [*Slight pause.*] As soon as I'm done here, I'm going.

G: Hey, we had an agreement.

B: What? For me to sample another one of your unmentionable . . . ?

G: Try *unnameable.*

B: Just don't take liberties with my recipes.

G: How could I? I'm the mother of precision.

B: And of derision.

G: No, no. I'm far too soft when it comes to sorting you out.

B: [*Rises from the toilet. Brays.*] Soft. *Soft* as the gentle rain touching the faces of the casualties of civil and uncivil war. [*Hitches up his pants.*] *Soft* as the flight of radioactive particles from tsunamied nuclear power stations. [*Brays. Pause.*] Have you added the garlic? [*Sits down at the table.*]

G: I decided on chili.

B: No, you're even more heavy-handed with chili! I'll have to drink so much water that sometime between three and five in the morning, pissing in our beautiful, lumpy bed will become an inevitability.

G: Thanks for the warning. I'll sleep on the sofa.

B: No, sleep here. [*Motions to the kitchen table.*]

G: But then the mattress comes with me. You can soften those broken bed springs with towels.

B: Not a chance. I'll take your forty-four fur coats.

G: Forty-three, my darling.

B: Dammit, Girlie, you know how sensitive my palate is.

G: No, I don't. I only know how sensitive your stomach is – not to mention your soul. In fact, I know only to well how sensitive every bloody part of you is except the right side of your brain. That's a dead zone where fruit bats fly.

B: Funny you should mention fruit bats. I was just reading about them. They're massive, really big flying rats. You find them all over India. In the late afternoon they come down in these gigantic flocks over lakes, darkening the whole bloody countryside.

G: Where did you get that from?

B: Some damn book . . . the autobiography of . . . some bloody actor. He went holidaying there with his boyfriend. They were on a pilgrimage, you know, seeking the *spiritual* in nature. [*Brays.*] And there, by that Indian lakeside, as the fruit bats came pouring in, they experienced nirvana: an invisible God saturating the sky with their velvety wings. And afterwards they would go out in the jungle on elephants, watch the predators do their thing, then stroll off and *wash* the damn things in a river.

G: Wash who?

B: Why, the elephants.

G: Come on! Serious? [*B. nods.*] And how much did they pay for this *supreme* ecological wank?

B: I imagine quite a packet. But if you've got money to burn, why not? Scrubbing an elephant must *definitely* be an experience. Especially cleaning their ears, then polishing their tusks. Then . . .

G: No! These guys must have concentrated on the *bulls* and had a pretty nice time soaping their . . . . Hey, maybe you can write a porno script with that as the climax? "There by the banks of the Ganges, only metres away from an ashram, two bronzed hulks slowly lather a young bull's monstrously large member."

B: [*Comes up behind her.*] And while one of them's soaping away, the elephant gets so excited he falls on the . . . bugger! [*Pushes her down onto the table and pulls up her dress.*]

G: [*Pushing him away.*] Hey, watch that word 'bugger'! Not allowed anymore.

B: The word or the activity?

G: Certainly not the word. And the activity has to be performed gently and with appropriate protective equipment.

B: Of course, *we* know all about that.

G: Well, you're not trying it on me again.

B: [*Slight pause. Smiles.*] Why not? I thought you enjoyed it.

G: No, I didn't. I was too self-conscious and it was painful.

B: But you told me you'd done it before and it was ok. With that guy, that American you went with to Vic Falls . . .

G: I didn't enjoy it then and I didn't enjoy it with you.

B: But you made all the right sounds.

G: The *right* sounds?

B: The haunting sounds of extreme pleasure.

G: Oh, really?

B: Don't pretend! It was only during the very last *occasion* that you complained.

G: I was always doing you a . . . a *favour*.

B: Didn't I use enough vaseline?

G: No, you didn't.

B: Sorry, my darling. I'll make up for it next time.

G: There won't be a next time.

B: Was just a thought.

G: Is *that* what you call it?

B: This reminds me of a mate I had at school. He moved to London and met up with this Irish girl who liked water sports.

G: What?

B: Water sports. Ja. Fuck, hey, this girl was really into it. He didn't know how to take it. He was out of his depth. He'd never come across this type of stuff before.

G: What's the big deal? Breaststroke, backstroke, thighstroke . . .

B: Come on, Girlie – I'm talking about people pissing on each other and stuff like that . . . hardcore, crazy stuff.

G: [*Ignores him. Pauses.*] Stop this nonsense. Go and have a lie down. I'll finish supper in the meantime.

B: [*Holds out his hand.*] Alright . . . but don't wake me too soon. Give me enough time for a wild fantasy.

G: My dear boy, we've already noted your deficiency in that department.

B: [*Throws up his hands.*] So I'm over it, am I? A neutered stallion, a castrated gladiator . . .

G: Go and lie down.

B: Lie down with the toothless attack dogs . . .

G: Go and lie down before I boil the kettle and throw it over you.

B: [*Runs round the table singing.*] 'Boil, boil, boil . . . who the hell needs cooking oil?'

G: Get out of here!

B: [*Still running round the table.*] 'Boil, boil, boil . . . who the hell needs cooking oil?'

G: [*Starts following him round the table.*] 'Out, out, before I shout! Out, out, before I turn you inside out!'[*B. picks up the kitchen knife from the table, grabs her and holds it to her throat. They look nervously at each other without speaking then after a few seconds start laughing.*] Sweetie pie, lie down and close your eyes. Then feel your body, your whole maggot-ridden body, slowly decay further till you're a mass of worms. [*B. kisses her.*] A last kiss before the final rot.

B: I just hope what's in that pot is a little tastier, a little more exciting, than the usual . . .

G: Slop and vleis. And this time it's horse meat. [*Whinnies. BOYKIE brays in return.*] Go already. I need to carry on chopping.

B: Oh, you do that my single-minded beauty. Let me have a little shut-eye.

G: [*Pushes him towards an exit.*] 'Get thee hence, thy foul visitation.'

B: 'Leave off, thou pestilential hag.' [*Exits.*]

G: A man for all seasons and master of none. A man who oozes compassion but only for failed messiahs; a man who gives charity to the poor so long as the small change comes from my pocket; a man who uncovers the secrets of the universe by injecting himself with rat poison; a man who knows himself to be a colossus in waiting, in the making, the unfinished masterpiece his mother always dreamt he would be.

While she is finishing her 'speech', B. re-enters.

G: What *is* wrong with you today?

B: I just had the weirdest flashback.

G: I'll bet. And how long did it last? As long as it takes me to run round this table again?

B: Don't try and be funny. Remember that Ethiopian woman I was involved with, the one who was selling coffee machines.

G: Of course I do.

B: I just suddenly thought of her.

G: A waking dream of this *Sheba* you laid while exploring the upper reaches of the Nile.

B: You know, the time we spent together was very sweet and tender.

G: [*Half-smiling.*] In marked contrast to the hell you and I are living in.

B: My darling, let's face it. These days we go through the motions of respecting each other, of helping, supporting, providing. We're only *shadows* of emotion.

G: [*Sarcastically.*] Motions of blocked emotion . . . and of course, its' my fault. [*Slight pause.*] Do I really need to hear this?

B: She had big breasts and a slightly thick waist but her bum was perfect, not too big, not too small, but well rounded, you know, just rounded enough so it sits in your hand perfectly while the other hand is moving up her back slowly massaging her so she starts to squirm with pleasure and then your lips are on her ear lobe and she begins to push against you and you feel yourself harden till you are so fucking hard with the pleasure you want to kiss her on the lips, and you fucking kiss her on the lips and she pushes against you with such sweetness, the fucking sweetness of holding her and kissing her as she moves up and down against your groin is over-fucking-whelming.

G: [*With utmost scorn.*] Pity the poetry stays locked up in the mind, trapped on the tongue.

B: You've also inspired me, my darling. [*Comes up behind her.*] I've been besotted with you. You know that. You know how good it was. Once all that mattered was to hold each other and slowly kiss and lick each other's eyelids and nuzzle each other's necks. [*Pause. Caresses her.*] You remember the times in that place, that flat on Klein St? We once stayed put in the flat for four days. All we did was . . . yes, all we did was . . . make love. We were blessed. [*Silence. B slowly exits.*]

G: [*Sings.*] '*Midnight on the long road, I've read your book to the end, I cannot accept the load, you lay upon your friends. But I will be true to you, like the sunshine and the dew, I'll be true. Midnight in the tree-flying park, I've read your palm and all its lines, I cannot explain the dark messages its contours define. But I will be true to you, like the rainbow's red and blue, I'll be true. Midnight . . .*

B: [*Reappears. Sheepishly.*] I can't sleep. [*Slight pause.*] Food ready?

G: [*In a 'mad' voice.*] Vot a question? Foodie-foodie . . .

B: God, I'm hungry now.

G: And vot for is my Boykie hungry?

B: For . . .

G: Foodie-foodie . . . Boykie hungry.

B: Boykie hungry for . . .

G: Peace? A piece of pie, a slice of action?

B: Funny you should say *peace.* [*Sits at the table.*]

G: [*Laughing.*] Knocked zis vey, knocked dat vey, oy vey, Boykie wants respite. [*Pause. In a serious tone.*] No money for rent, no money for food, no money for medicine, no money for movies, no money for books . . .

B: Hey, hey, can I eat now?

G: *Now* he wants it . . . snaps his fingers . . . Well, it's almost ready, almost but not quite. [*Slight pause.*] Speaking of money, *honey,* when you getting that payment?

B: What payment?

G: For that last job.

B: What you talking about?

G: That last job. For that old woman. When you getting paid? It's been months now . . .

B: Oh, *that* book. Ja, it has been a while.

G: *Much* more than a while. Give them a ring.

B: Yes, I should.

G: Give amagents a ring. Give them a little buzz in the ear. Bzzz, bzzzz bzzzz . . .

B: Shit, that was a funny project.

G: But it kept you on your toes. It's been a long time since you were on your toes.

B: Crazy old bitch. But I did a good job. [*Slight pause.*] What a ridiculous life story. The way she inflated her importance.

G: But it was a good rate for a *ghost* writer.

B: Ja, come to think of it, it *was* a good rate.

G: Just a pity the ghost doesn't get paid.

B: I'm surprised they haven't given me more work. [*Slight pause.*] The more I think about it . . . funny how I forgot about payment.

G: You forgot? How could you forget?

B: I'm joking. Do you think I'd forget? I just . . .

G: Never got round to pushing it.

B: Shit, I have been slack. I'll ring them tomorrow.

G: You do that. They must get off the roundabout and settle with you.

B: But I'm not going to work for that agency again.

G: Buddy, it's better to have someone try to take advantage of you than to leave you altogether high and mighty and penniless.

B: I'll sort it out.

G: But when?

B: I said tomorrow.

G: You know something . . . I'm pretty tired of your . . .

B: Stop this, Girlie! Stop harping on my . . . Let's not go backwards!

G: No, of course not! Let's go sideways, crossways – anywhere but *that* ways.

B: I know I'm not perfect.

G: [*Pause.*] Phone them. Phone them now. Tell them, if they don't pay within forty-eight hours you're going to . . .

B: Sue them? Yes, I'll sue them. [*Laughs.*] What have you made? I'm not joking, I'm really hungry now.

G: Tell them you're going to hire bouncers. [*Slight pause.*] Wait, you're scared to confront them.

B: Me, scared? Don't fucking insult me. [*Sarcastically.*] Ok, ok, keep it up, keep up the pressure. I mean, you took on the job of *managing* me. And if I recall, no one forced you.

G: Only my sense of compassion for the helpless.

B: I wasn't a charity case.

G: True, not entirely. Not then.

B: Not then and not ever, but certainly not then because you wouldn't have come to live with me if I'd been broke. Let's go back awhile.

G: How far back?

B: Back to when we met and *you* were the one who was short of cash. Remember? Who supported you while you were finishing your articles? Let's face it, Girlie, you have, like *most* women, at one time or another traded your *favours* for a little help with the rent.

G: Oh! Of course, we're all whores. Ultimately, we're all *whores*. [*Slight pause.*] Emotionally you were a charity case.

B: Sometimes the only *access* I could get depended on a whole fucking truckload of groceries.

G: You were flaky then and you're flaky now.

B: [*Sarcastically.*] Just because my alcoholic father hit my alcoholic mother and abused my little sister who started cutting herself doesn't mean I'm emotionally retarded . . .

G: Stop trying to belittle what I'm saying.

B: I suppose I always have. But maybe it hasn't done you any good. [*Idly picks up an egg beater on the side table.*]

G: Oh, no, of course not! It's the rod I want. Here on my bare bum. Where's a nice, flashy cane to whip up a little excitement on my masochistic cheeks? [*Pulls up her dress.*] Come on, lay in, Boykie! Weigh in with a will! Come on!

B: [*Looks bemused then, as she taunts him, starts beating her with the egg beater.*] This enough? This enough for you?

G: Go on, harder! Is this the best you can do? Harder! Much harder! [*He continues to beat her. They suddenly both stop.*]

B: We're fucking crazy.

G: Yes, we *are* crazy.

B: About each other.

G: But we come out the other side . . .

B: Smiling at each other.

G: And the whole . . .

B: Wide fucking world.

G: So that's what the world thinks.

B: That we're crazy and that we're crazy about each other.

G: Let's keep the world thinking that.

B: Ok. Let them think we're ok.

G: But secretly we're not so . . .

B: Ok. [*Slight pause.*] Secretly, we're taking strain.

G: Secretly, we're in trouble.

B: Secretly, we're in deep water.

G: [*Accentuating the bantering tone.*] Treading water. For years now.

B: You and I treading in deep, cold water.

G: Our knees are freezing.

B: My whole bloody left leg is cramped.

G: And the middle one.

B: What does my limp prick have to do with your frozen cunt?

G: Beastie-beastie-beastie. . . . [*Slight pause.*] Go and sleep. I'll wake you when the food's ready.

B: But when *will* it be ready? I mean, what have you been doing the whole evening? *Meditating* on what immaculate dish to serve? [*Tries to embrace her; she slips away.*]

G: It won't be long. It's something *very* special. [*Suggestively.*] Actually, it's a new recipe. I've got everything set out but now I need to decide *how* to cook them.

B: Whether to bake or fry or boil or poach or . . .

G: Exactly.

B: And what energy source to use? The hot plate, the gas stove, the micro-wave, the solar powered geezer . . .

G: Hey, let's braai! We haven't braaied for ages.

B: That's an idea. We could put a braai stand on the toilet.

G: No. Let's put it on the bed.

B: Yes, we'll keep the fire going with those romances under your pillow.

G: A good choice of fuel.

B: Ja, I'll light away.

G: You do that, my precious. God, I *must* get going with this meal.

B: Ja, please do! I could have already redug the bloody Big Hole never mind a *ridiculously* modest grave.

G: Fortunately it's never too late to stop being ridiculous.

B: And what else do the sages say?

G: Ridicule should be my best friend. But instead it's . . .

B: Procrastination.

G: No, bro, that's your forte. Besides, you're always too late to catch it from my lips.

B: It's something else I want from your lips. [*He sits on the back kitchen unit.*]

G: My . . . sweet . . . lips? [*Pause. She leaves the table and goes down on her knees in front of him, slowly pulls down his pants as if she is about to perform oral sex and then abruptly pulls away.*] Tell that to your Sheba.

B: [*Runs up to her.*] No, I'll spare you more. After all, you have to bear the brunt of my longing. [*Pause.*] Yes, that woman kissed like nobody's business . . . ah, the most lingering and twirly of kisses.

G: Twirly?

B: Ja, they'd go up and down, and in and out and just tie me up . . . kiss after bloody kiss. Often, we'd just lie down and . . .

G: And, and . . .

B: We would just kiss.

G: [*Sharply.*] How old was she?

B: Now that's a question.

G: How old?

B: I don't know . . . maybe . . . ten? [*Laughs.*] At any rate, old enough to give a *special* kiss. [*Stands.*] My darling, as flavoursome as yours. Come, a quickie, my love! Just a little nip of the lip before I hit the sack. Come to Boykie!

G: [*Pause.*] What if I was fat? Like really fat [*Walks about as if she is very fat.*] I mean, really, really fat. A big fat mama. Would you still want me?

B: Silly question.

G: Why's it silly?

B: Because you aren't.

G: But if I was.

B: But you're not.

G: Answer me.

B: Alright, let me apply what's left of my oxygen deficient brain. This question is as relevant as me asking . . . [*In a high pitched childish voice.*] "Would you still love me if I had a hunchback or one arm or no nose or a beer belly as big as a . . ."

G: It wouldn't be a make or break a thing for me.

B: No, of course not.

G: Am I too thin?

B: [*Poking her all over.*] What's going on with you? You're my perfect girl, Girlie. My perfect woman.

G: Don't lie. You've never gotten over her.

B: She wasn't massively fat.

G: I know.

B: And that's why you're insecure.

G: How often do you think about her?

B: At least twenty times a day.

G: Especially when we're fucking.

B: Yes, for the last ten years it's been her fucking ghost under my *thrusting* pelvis.

G: No doubt.

B: Give me a break.

G: I will – once I get the truth from you.

B: Don't be so fucking obsessive! Go and cook. All this *performing* has really made me hungry.

G: You still feel she's your ultimate . . .

B: There's no bloody ultimate. [*Pause.*] We did have a . . . we had a . . . but it was way before I met you, Girlie. I don't hold your past against you, I'm not jealous of things that had nothing to do with me.

G: But maybe you should. Maybe you shouldn't be so relaxed. Maybe you don't know as much about me as you imagine. I might have lied to you. I might have left out all sorts of very important things and people and other stuff that is critical to understand me but for some reason I've never told you about them.

B: Why? Why wouldn't you tell me? Am I untrustworthy? Have I ever shut you up when you're telling me about your old boy-friends? No. I listen, and I listen with interest.

G: When you aren't snoring.

B: I just grunt. [*Slight pause.*] Why don't you go and sit on the toilet while you're telling me about all your past *beaus*.

G: It's not just about old boy-friends. That may be the least of it.

B: Ok. So girl-friends.

G: Don't be one-track minded. My *significant* relationships don't have to have been sexual.

B: No, they don't. But they usually are. [*Slight pause.*] Alright, these were *intellectual* and *spiritual* relationships, ones you selflessly *nurtured* over the years.

G: I want to tell you about an amazing man. [*BOYKIE brays.*] Don't try and shut me up.

B: How could I? I'm a coward.

G: It was just when I started studying. But I was also working. I had a night job, a very ordinary job.

B: My darling, you've never been or done anything *ordinary*.

G: I was on my own and I had my mother to support. I was working as a cleaner. You know, in office blocks. And one day while I was working, I met a man on one of the floors. He was a security guard. We got talking, and after a while he invited me to go down to his office and have a cup of coffee. I went down and though the coffee was bad, we ended up talking till day-break. Or should I say, he talked. He told me about his life in prison. He had been sentenced to fifteen years for running phony investment schemes. He had defrauded thousands of people, lived the high life and then lost everything.

B: Ok, so you fell in love with a chastened fucking crook. What was special about that?

G: I didn't fall in love with him. But I learnt from him.

B: You learnt, I'm sure, like . . . how to smile at a new punter even when he's a ninety-nine year old pensioner.

G: I learnt to concentrate on the essential. And the essential, Boychik, is to be able to . . .

B: Laugh at yourself. Ha, ha, ha.

G: There's truth to that, but there is also the small matter of what you do to other people *while* you're laughing at yourself. Because most people, while they're laughing at themselves, are also laughing at other people. And that's . . .

B: A problem because this causes them to treat everyone and everything as a joke and fit subject for fraud.

G: Just listen! In jail he couldn't bribe the guards and make life easier for himself because he really had no money. He had to accept just what the ordinary prisoner had to accept. And that was tough. But even more life changing was that he began to feel ashamed of what he had done. He had cheated so many people. They had put their trust in him. And this began to gnaw at him.

B: But why? He didn't have to feel guilty. They were greedy idiots who deserved to be conned. That's what enables every trickster to become and continue to be a trickster.

G: Hear me out! [*Pause.*] Maybe now *is* a good time to run away to the toilet.

B: It's not my fault you're so pissed off with me that you feel obliged to talk more than your quota of . . .

G: [*Sits on the toilet.*] The point about this man is that he was writing a novel based on his life and he wanted me to help him edit it.

B: Oh, editing! But that's where *I* should have come in! But, no, you edged me out and gave him first class advice free of charge so that he could go on to sell the sentimental shit first to Nollywood and then to Bollywood and finally to Hollywood, and soon every fucking film company on the planet was making movies about the repentant crusades of armies of shysters – subsequent, of course, to their making teensy weensy little fortunes.

G: He was black-listed once he got out of jail so he couldn't get a job for almost three years.

B: And the security gig was the first thing that came up.

G: Do you have any idea how difficult it is for someone with a criminal record to get a job?

B: I like that – ex-fraudster gets a *security* job. I like it. Keep going. Don't let this story fall apart.

G: He asked me to edit it after I told him I was a student.

B: Someone literate, someone with *grammar* and *spelling* and . . .

G: So I edited his book and he was so grateful he started sending me money every month.

B: Every month like clockwork the ex-con pyramid scheme trickster sent you enough for you to give up the night cleaning job and concentrate on your studies and pass with distinction and be employed after just one five second interview by the top legal firm in the country.

G: Yes, that's right.

B: And that's why your shit smells of the eau-de-cologne only bonuses can buy.

G: Exactly. A little reward for exposing government cover-ups not to mention the *very* private sector. [*Flushes the toilet.*]

B: We're quite a pair. [*Slight pause.*] Is that your story? Is that what you've been hiding from me? That you were a secretary to a crook?

G: [*G. leaves the toilet.*] Boykie, you had so much going for you.

B: Did I? Going, going, gone.

G: It didn't have to be like that.

B: No, it had to be. It's called karma.

G: You can get back into it. You used to know so many people.

B: And spend every day running around poking my big fat nose into other people's business – their greed, their deviousness, their vanity. No, Girlie, that's your job.

G: Don't be so cynical.

B: Why not? [*Slight pause.*] Look what you're doing? You just serve these fuckers.

G: No, I don't.

B: Yes, you do. You draft their contracts. Their *con-tracts*.

G: There will always have to be contracts of one kind or another . . . our species needs to be regulated.

B: Bullshit! Bring on the black flag! [*Slight pause.*] Have *we* signed a contract?

G: No, we haven't. But what if one day we . . .

B: Separate? [*Slight pause.*] Ok, let's separate.

G: Don't be crass.

B: What's the big deal? It wouldn't be the last time.

G: But we . . .

B: We don't need a bloody contract to keep us together. In any case, what do we own? From the start I refused to buy a house. I thought you agreed.

G: This flat is worth quite a bit and the cars.

B: What are you talking about? My car's a wreck. [*Slight pause.*] Alright, so when we going to separate?

G: Right now if you won't admit you don't know everything there is to know about me.

B: But what secrets can we still have from one another? [*Pause.*] Ok . . . ok . . . we all have certain . . . let's say *private* thoughts. Things you don't want anyone to know about. That's only natural.

G: You let it all out. You tell me everything that's in your head except when it comes to the Ethiopian you can't tell me the whole truth.

B: Christ, it happened so long ago, Girlie!

G: But if she still matters to you – it must matter to me.

B: [*Pause.*] It shouldn't matter to you. [*Kisses her.*] Do you really want my mind to always be an open book? A running conversation with you no matter what's flowing under and over the bridge.

G: [*Embracing him.*] Yes. I want to know everything about you.

B: But you do, Girl. I need you.

G: Sometimes I don't know that and it frightens me.

B: There's nothing to be frightened off.

G: Then why have you been a monster over these past few months?

B: I've told you it doesn't mean I'm unhappy with *you*. I'm unhappy with *myself*.

G: Boykie, you've achieved. You've been *long-listed* for so many prizes.

B: Stop making a fool of me.

G: But you have.

B: I never made it to the short lists – never mind won anything.

G: So what? Prizes aren't everything.

B: Don't change direction now! I write what I have to, dammit!

G: [*Smiles.*] And so did Shakespeare.

B: The only fucking difference is that he still packs out houses. You know, they still fucking run in, stampeding, to see a bunch of kings and queens and clowns and misers and murderers and . . . why have I had such miserable luck?

G: Darling, you're a Taurus and ungovernable. You kick too many people in the industry around.

B: It's not an *industry*.

G: Yes, it *is* an industry. And yours is the *entertainment* industry.

B: Well, I can't fucking entertain myself never mind anyone else.

G: You're abrasive, you're unsubtle. And there's no *entertainment* in political . . . what do they call them? . . . meringues. [*Laughs.*] You only entertain me.

B: I only entertain dark thoughts.

G: [*Pause.*] Ok, let's say you've written a new play and its been given a slow reception in Joburg. That doesn't mean it's not going to be accepted in Durban.

B: Durban! And stage it in on the beach or in the middle of a bloody sugar cane field?

G: Rework it. You just have to make it more dramatic. Throw in more *physical* theatre, less talkie-talkie.

B: But you know my style!

G: Yes, I do! All those monologues.

B: Alright. What if I start it like this. . .

G: Don't tell me! There's a man shitting on stage. [*Runs to the toilet. Sits down.*] He's shitting there when the audience comes in. And he never gets up. He just shits there and talks for an hour about weight loss.

B: Beckett. Too damn Beckett.

G: What's wrong with paying homage? He was a great playwright.

B: Yes. That's why *he's* recognized. But *I* won't be recognized by trying to be Beckett. I'd rather try and be . . .

G: Boykie! Of course, be Boykie. But maybe there's too much Boykie. My darling, every one of your characters is actually you and you and you.

B: Good God, Girlie. All art is a reflection of the artist.

G: Ja, fifty takes of the same cracked mug.

B: This one will be a *profile* – of my noble lineage.

G: Your lineage – that's rich! Your blood-lines are so mixed up they can't flow straight.

B: You mean *talk* straight.

G: Exactly, my love. You're recognized as one of our foremost social commentators disguised as a. . .

B: Dead art in a dead time practiced by a dead giveaway for a dead playwright. Dead. Dead. Dead. [*Pause.*] No, wait a moment. Let me try something. The curtain opens. In the background you'll hear a donkey braying. A man comes out of a 'long drop'. This will be his opening speech. [*Brays.*]

G: A donkey! Why a donkey?

B: It's a rural piece about dispossessed peasants and a little mbongolo whose sound city people won't even recognize but will know is part of the barnyard symphony of those who chew the cud . . . So this man comes out of a long drop and says, 'Friends, I know this is a cliché and a fucking feeble device, but I've been a little stuck lately for brilliant ideas so this is all I can deliver on this stage at this stage. Kindly pardon me and come back in an hour. Perhaps by then I'll have hit the funny bone.'

G: Oh, my God.

B: [*This section done with mimed gestures for each action.*] Then the curtain will come down and people will be given little pieces of paper . . .

G: Yes, yes. Keep it interactive.

B: So they get the papers which say 'Come back when the bell rings. Meanwhile, go to the foyer and watch TV'. And once they get to the foyer the TV will be playing a movie. The movie will be of the man on the toilet telling them to wait for an hour and in the meanwhile they're to go outside to a nearby restaurant and watch TV. And at the restaurant they'll have to . . .

G: Eat shit. My God, what an old style *happening*.

B: In this dump of a city, in the absence of anything else *happening*, why not? Or am I labouring the point?

G: Like the poor donkey.

B: No, *she* can go on forever but she doesn't want to. She's seen through her master's tricks. She wants a new life.

G: Like her inventor.

B: She's examining the alternatives but then she's struck dumb and can't bray for her pipe and her fiddlers three.

G: Just make her determined to take over the field and cultivate it herself.

B: Like ride the tractor and sow the seeds.

G: Ja. She becomes her own boss and no damn farmer tells her what to do.

B: A revolution.

G: Right on.

B: No, right *off*! People are sick and tired of *your* feminist agitprop masquerading as art. [*Pause.*] On the other hand – why not? I like this little donkey. [*Brays.*] I like her more and more. [*Brays.*] She can be magical. [*Brays.*] I can make her fly. [*Brays. Flaps his hands.*] I can turn her into a human. A little baby don-key with chubby cheeks. [*Brays.*] "I have had a most rare vision. I have had a dream past the wit of man to say what dream it was. Man is but an ass if he go about t'expound this dream. Methought I was—there is no man can tell what. Methought I was, and methought I had—but man is but a patched fool if he will offer to say what methought I had. The eye of man hath not heard, the ear of man hath not seen, man's hand is not able to taste, his tongue to conceive, nor his heart to report what my dream was."

G: [*Her thumb pointing down.*] Nice try, darling. In the end you may get it right.

B: Ah, it's not the truth that hurts – its little Ms Girlie who hurts. [*Pause.*] Fuck off!

G: And if I do, where will that leave you? [*Pause.*] What did I say earlier about you finally getting that payment?

B: Don't dig that up again! I told you I'll follow up. [*Sits at the table.*] I thought you were ok about my not being able to contribute to expenses for a while.

G: Yes, for a while. But how long is *for a while*? A month? Six months? A year?

B: My darling, why this vulgarity? Is it . . .

G: Don't say it's my period. Please, please!

B: Bravo! [*Starts to exit.*]

G: Where you going?

B: Where do you think?

G: You can't run away when the conversation's getting *relevant*.

B: To who?

G: [*Pause.*] Listening to all your whining it makes me edgy.

B: You mean 'scratchy'.

G: [*Scratches her head violently.*] Ok, my flea, go and have a lie down. [*Stirs the pot.*] I'll put the finishing touches to what's here.

B: After we've eaten I think I'll pop out and see Tony.

G: Tony! You saw him last night.

B: So what? He's got the germ of some new idea. We need to discuss it further.

G: As always. [*Slight pause.*] Admit it! You're off to your Ethiopian.

B: No! This time it's a Tunisian.

G: Surely, boyo, surely! Now get out of here before I throw . . .

B: Up?

G: Before I throw this knife at you.

B: Come on, throw! [*Parades in front of her.*]

G: Feel how sharp it is. [*Holds up the cutting knife.*] Come on, feel it!

B: I've already been snipped.

G: I'll snip your head off.

B: First let me . . . [*Runs back into the kitchen past her to the toilet. Closes the door.*]

G: I said out of here! Now!

B: [*Holds the door closed.*] You try and get me out.

G: Get out, you stupid . . .

B: I'm not leaving. You can't make me leave.

G: [*Standing at the door.*] Alright, then I'll leave. You can cook yourself something. I'm going.

B: Where you going?

G: To lie down.

B: With me?

G: And then I'm going out.

B: We'll leave together. [*Pause.*] You going to Brenda?

G: No.

B: Where you going?

G: To Tony.

B: Stop kidding. You're not going to Tony.

G: Why not?

B: Because *I'm* going there.

G: So what.

B: Go to Brenda.

G: I don't want to go to Brenda.

B: Alright, go to Tony. But then I won't.

G: Why not?

B: Because I haven't seen Brenda for some time and this is a good opportunity to check her out while you're visiting Tony.

G: What if I bring Tony over to Brenda?

B: Why would you do that?

G: So he can see Brenda. He also hasn't seen Brenda for a long time.

B: I don't think Tony *wants* to see Brenda.

G: Why not?

B: Because he wants to see *me*.

G: But maybe Brenda wants to see Tony.

B: That's too bad.

G: Bad for who?

B: Bad for you and for Brenda.

G: What about Tony?

B: I'll handle that.

G: Ok, you handle that and I'll go and see Brenda.

B: [[*Stands, pulls up his pants. Opens the toilet door.*] You see, it wasn't difficult for us to talk this through.

G: My darling, there's *nothing* we can't talk through.

B: There's nothing we can't talk through if we make an effort.

G: Effort – yes, an effort is necessary.

B: But we're lucky. Our efforts are effortless.

G: So to speak.

B: We can make an effort look anything other than an effort.

G: [*Picking up the knife on the table.*] Did you think I would use it?

B: No, my love. I knew you wouldn't. I knew you *couldn't*.

G: Why not?

B: Because you're short-sighted and wouldn't have known where to stab me.

G: Apart from that I'm too superstitious to stick a knife into a 'living dead'.

B: Gosh, these vegetables look a bit tired.

G: What! I just bought them.

B: Supermarket stuff – it's never fresh, my love.

G: [*Holding up a vegetable.*] Yes, it does look a bit tired.

B: Maybe open a tin.

G: No, no. That would be making a mockery of making an effort.

B: Better let them rest.

G: [*Holds different vegetables up to the light.*] Yes, maybe you're right. [*Begins putting the vegetables into a bag.*] Let's give them a rest before making an effort.

B: Come, we've done our best.

G: We've done our best.

B: Nothing fallen down? [*Looks under the table. Checks the toilet.*] Nope. Everything accounted for. Let's go. [*Stands at the toilet door.*]

G: Yes, let's go and rest. [*Stirring the pot. She lifts the lid as if to close it.*]

B: [*About to exit from the toilet.*] A rest, yes. Let's give ourselves a rest.

They freeze. Blackout.

END

Biography of
NAMATSHEGO KHUTSOANE

Tshego is a Performer, Director, Applied Theatre Practitioner and Theatre-maker with an MA from Wits University. Having majored in Directing, Acting, Contemporary Performance and Applied Theatre during her time of study at Rhodes University, she is highly committed to her performance craft and to the Social, Educational and Developmental aspects of the arts. Tshego has experience performing in and directing for stage, site and varieties of community based theatre. Facilitating applied drama and theatre processes with schools, target groups and communities as well as collaborative-educating and creating in the areas of performance, improvisation, voice and applied drama and theatre techniques. Her areas of research and interest include drama in education; site-specific performance; community narratives and collaborative theatre-making; inter-cultural and inter-disciplinary performance; gender studies with a particular focus on role, expectation, identity and behavior; contemporary performance in the specific fields of movement; gesture and embodiment; performance-art practice; voice exploration, aesthetics, devising and improvisation.

Biography of
JÒVAN MUTHRAY

Jòvan Muthray is a South African actor, writer and director who received his training at the University Of Witwatersrand. From an early age, Jòvan has had dreams of becoming an actor. He became fascinated with the idea of entertaining those around him and has devoted all his time to engaging and entertaining audiences. His formal training gave him exposure to some of South Africa's greatest artistic minds in the industry whereby he developed a strong and powerful ability as a character actor. Jòvan has done a great many theatrical productions. Still fresh in the industry, Jòvan landed roles in short films for various film festivals as well as featuring in both local and international series.

CITY PROPERTY
Pioneering the Future

Ticketing Partner
Computicket

STATE THEATRE

an agency of the
Department of Arts and Culture

THE SOUTH AFRICAN STATE THEATRE IN ASSOCIATION WITH ALLAN KOLSKI HORWITZ PRESENTS

JERICO

WRITTEN AND DIRECTED BY
ALLAN KOLSKI HORWITZ

STARRING : TSHEGO KHUTSOANE | LEBOHANG MOTAUNG | JONATHAN TAYLOR | KELLY EKSTEEN | JOVAN MUTHRAY

MOMENTUM THEATRE | ALL AGES | 2 - 19 MARCH 2016

SPY 1 and SPY 2

VIZIER, the KING and QUEEN of Jerico

SPY 1, the WHORE and A CANAANITE SOLDIER

The WHORE, SPY 1 and SPY 2

135

Program notes

The mythic story of the conquest of Jerico, a wealthy trading city in the Land of Canaan, by the Israelites, as related in the Hebrew Bible's 'Book of Joshua', is the foundation for this play.

Moses, the spiritual giant has died; Joshua, the warrior, has replaced him. The Israelites, a group of twelve tribes who had escaped slavery in Pharoah's Egypt, have spent forty years traversing the Sinai desert in search of a home. During this time they have suffered all the privations of a hostile terrain including attacks by other nomads, notably the tribe of Amalek. However, they have succeeded in consolidating their new religion and armed with a growing sense of confidence are ready to attempt the invasion of Canaan, the land of 'Milk and Honey', that their God has promised to them if they obey His laws.

The play opens with Joshua's selection, prior to the invasion, of two spies entrusted with scouting out Jerico. We witness their farewells from their families and are given insight into their personalities and past histories. We see them test each other as they carry out their mission; and this contestation of views and personalities continues even as they find shelter with a local whore. At this point the play diverges from the biblical story and shifts to the people of Jerico, and in so doing, explores their responses to the threat of conquest and occupation.

Apart from the Whore, we meet the King and Queen of Jerico and their vizier, and are exposed to their fears and attempts to deal with the looming danger. And so, as the action unfolds, we are presented with varying possibilities: Can the Israelite need for land be accommodated through negotiation and compromise? Can the spies play a role in achieving this outcome? Can the Queen's desire to forestall male aggressiveness trump the king's vacillation and ultimate return to the predictable tactics of deceit and counter violence?

Finally, we confront the historical lesson that those 'who live by the sword, die by the sword'; for when negotiation is abandoned and gives way to war, the inevitable crimes committed by the warring parties return to haunt coming generations. Many tribes and nations have suffered at the hands of those with greater military power. However, should the means they themselves use to defy and survive this suffering not be subjected to moral scrutiny? And as a corollary, should the collective need supersede individual fulfillment and well-being?

The ongoing Israeli-Palestinian conflict, and the global debate about how to find a just solution to competing rights, shows that as a species we are still unable to rationally deal with struggles over land and security; instead of employing intelligence and compassion, we easily fall back on fanaticism and violence.

Ultimately Jerico is a work that examines moral options as well as providing the dramatic elements of a 'thriller'. Do these strands come together in a satisfying way? Does one overshadow the other? Written in a style that is cognizant of the sonorous tones of the King James Bible, it hopefully does not become ponderous. But, more than anything, I hope that the tragic nature of the conflict grips the audience and provides more than a little 'food for thought'.

~~

The first performance of JERICO took place at The State Theatre, Pretoria on 2 March 2016 with the following cast:

SPY 1/THE VIZIER	Lebohang Motaung
SPY 1'S WIFE/QUEEN OF JERICO/ MARKET WOMAN	Tshego Khutsoane
SPY 2/KING OF JERICO	Jonathan Taylor
SPY 2'S DAUGHTER/THE WHORE	Kelly Eksteen
SHEPHERD/ CANAANITE SOLDIER/ISRAELITE LEADER	Jovan Muthray

CHARACTERS

Spy 1
His Wife
Spy 2
His Daughter
A Shepherd
A Market Women
The Whore
The King of Jerico
The Queen of Jerico
Their Vizier
A Canaanite Soldier
The Israelite Leader
An Israelite Soldier

SETTING

ISRAELITE encampment:- two locations: down stage on either side, small areas on which are spread mats; two stools are placed on Spy 1's side, one on Spy 2's.

WHORE's establishment: low table with three stools; two beds are placed on either side of the stage.

The palace of the KING and QUEEN of Jerico: two thrones.

ACT 1

SPY 1 and his WIFE are on one side down stage; SPY 2 and his DAUGHTER are down stage opposite them. These areas are demarcated by circles of sand. SPY 1's WIFE busies herself clearing vessels on the low table; moves about ordering things. Across from her, SPY 2 is lying down, dozing, on a mat. The light on this side is very low. As the action moves from scene to scene, the light fades and rises accordingly.

VOICE: "Now after the death of Moses, the servant of the Lord, it came to pass that the Lord Spoke to Joshua the son of Nun, Moses' minister, saying: Moses, my servant is dead. Now therefore arise, go over this Jordan, you and all the children of Israel, to the land which I do give to you. As I told Moses, every place that the sole of your foot shall tread upon will be yours. From the wilderness to the mountains of Lebanon, and then to the great river, Euphrates, all the land of the Hitites stretching to the great sea where the sun goes down, these will be your boundaries. And there shall not be any man who will be able to stand against you for in the same way that I stood beside Moses, so will I stand with you, and defend and protect you. Be strong and of good courage, and divide up this land between the people. As I have sworn to you, so do."

Scene 1

SPY 1 staggers in.

WIFE: Where were you?

SPY 1: Where do you think?

WIFE: Answer me!

SPY 1: I have.

WIFE: Where were you?

SPY 1: For once I was doing something *important*.

WIFE: And who was she *this time*?

SPY 1: My good wife, you're flogging a dead camel when in front of you is a man with a . . . what shall I say . . .

WIFE: Yes, definitely a *mission*. And one that has led to your getting drunk and hung over and . . .

SPY 1: [*Sarcastically.*] No, no, not this time. [*Slight pause.*] This time . . . agh . . . your head is always filled with . . .

WIFE: Examples of your treachery.

SPY 1: Stop it now! [*Slight pause.*] I was at a council with the Elders and the generals. It's been too long, this wandering.

WIFE: Yes, it has but . . .

SPY 1: Everything is prepared. And they're giving me another chance.

WIFE: To do what?

SPY 1: A task only the bravest can carry out.

WIFE: Yes, the bravest! But we had an agreement!

SPY 1: [*Raises his arms. Sits at the low table.*] Look, I need to eat. I'm tired and I have to leave in the morning.

WIFE: But you swore you wouldn't serve again!

SPY 1: They need me. [*Slight pause.*] Yes, they need *me*. Do you understand?

WIFE: But you swore!

SPY 1: I did but things have changed.

WIFE: Where are you going?

SPY 1: Jerico. [*Slight pause.*] I'm going to Jerico. There is information I must gather before we attack.

WIFE: You're going as a *spy*?

SPY 1: What else does one do before a battle? And in exchange, and you won't believe this, they're offering me . . .

WIFE: A chance to sell your soul.

SPY 1: You really think you know everything! [*Slight pause.*] The Leader is ready. I've never seen such unity.

WIFE: But how can you work for these people after what we've been through?

SPY 1: Don't be so pious! They say only those who prove themselves . . . will benefit. If I do not *oblige*, where will that leave our family? [*Slight pause.*] I'm talking about the division of land.

Both freeze. Fade to half-light.

Scene 2

SPY 2's daughter enters.

DAUGHTER: Greetings, father. You look tired. What did you do today? [*Sits at the low table.*]

SPY 2: I spent some of the morning taking ticks off the sheep then I took a walk.

DAUGHTER: Oh, where did you go?

SPY 2: Just a walk . . .

DAUGHTER: Over the ridge . . . to the widow?

SPY 2: Child, you know full well that since your mother's death I have . . . .

DAUGHTER: Forgive me, father! I know how you mourn, but more and more I wish for you to have companionship.

SPY 2: But I do! I have . . . the Lord! [*Irritatedly.*] Just look at you! Cover yourself, you're half naked! [*DAUGHTER covers herself. Slight pause.*] I went to the mountain.

DAUGHTER: You climbed to the top?

SPY 2: Yes.

DAUGHTER: That's quite a walk!

SPY 2: [*Quietly.*] I was steadying myself. Becoming ready. I was putting aside all . . . all . . .

DAUGHTER: Father, what *are* you talking about? [*Standing up.*] Are you well?

SPY 2: [*Sitting up.*] Child, I have chosen . . . and been chosen. And now I must show that I am worthy.

DAUGHTER: Of the widow?

SPY 2: Oh, stop your prattle!

DAUGHTER: Why? You're worthy of anyone. [*Running to his bed.*] You're the worthiest, wisest man I know.

SPY 2: [*He goes into a dream-like state.*] This is a sacred hour. At last we are ready to make good the Promise. And how rich a land it is, a land of milk and honey! The old scouts said we had not the strength to conquer it. They had no faith. And so we wandered on at the mercy of marauders and bandits. [*Pause. Almost absent mindedly.*] We must determine their strength. They must feel our wrath.

DAUGHTER: I don't understand.

SPY 2: You will. I must play my part in God's plan for our people. I dare not fail.

Both freeze. Fade to half-light.

Scene 3

As the stage light comes up, they begin talking.

WIFE: The division of land?

SPY 1: Yes, after the war. Among the tribes.

WIFE: This is madness! How can we be *dividing* up what isn't ours? [*Brings two bowls of food.*]

SPY 1: [*Begins eating.*] There's already manouvering. But I'll prove myself, and we'll get our fair share. I'll make sure we do. [*Slight pause. Embraces her.*] Please, don't be stubborn. There is no other way for us.

WIFE: Nonsense.

SPY 1: [*Slight pause.*] My darling, you know I don't wish for war any more than you do but the people are growing impatient. [*He holds out his bowl to her. She ignores it*[Besides, I promise there'll be no cruelty, no looting. We will fight with discipline and honour.

WIFE: You will? [*Slight pause*[And they? How will *they* fight to protect what is theirs? What if this war runs on without *victory* for us?

SPY 1: No, it will be quick and decisive. We are battle-hardened. Except for you, the doubters among us are dead. [*Raising his bowl.*] More.

WIFE: [*Witheringly.*] Help yourself.

SPY 1: [*Laughs.*] Just because you're a better cook doesn't mean I have to become my own servant.

WIFE: [*Suddenly rising.*] Don't go! I can't accept this is the best way to survive.

SPY 1: As the priests say, we will make the Land ours according to God's law.

WIFE: God's law! [*Slight pause.*] Who once said, "The Old Man has disappeared up the mountain, good riddance to his Jehovah, let us return to the gods of the Nile, they served us well enough"?

SPY 1: This is unfair!

WIFE: And then pulled me into the sweaty horde he'd worked up, and once he was well and truly drunk, grabbed my earrings and added them to the fire and while they were melting, jumped up in front of the altar and swore allegiance to the Great Bull and his Golden Calf.

SPY 1: Hypocrite! You were right there at my side.

WIFE: My good husband, you were the chief of the *sinners*.

Both freeze. Fade to half-light.

Scene 4

DAUGHTER: Father, rest easy, you have failed neither God nor Man nor ever will.

SPY 2: I pray that is true and that it will always be so. [*He stands, helps himself to water from a jug.*] My child, tomorrow I leave for Jerico. [*Begins to pace about.*]

DAUGHTER: Jerico? Oh, no, father! There are giants there!

SPY 2: Even giants will succumb to those who serve Israel.

DAUGHTER: Are you going alone? Surely not!

SPY 2: I will have a companion, a warrior. You will have seen him. His forehead is scarred.

DAUGHTER: [*Alarmed.*] His forehead?

SPY 2: Yes, scarred. [*Slight pause.*] His family, I believe, have set their camp near us several times. They have a large flock and many children – mostly boys, almost grown. [*Laughing*[His wife is well known as a gossip, a complainer.

DAUGHTER: [*Apprehensively.*] Yes, I have seen them . . . I think. [*She rises from his bed; walks a little away.*] I think I know . . . him. I mean, them.

SPY 2: He is known to be a brave man but also to be changeable.

DAUGHTER: [*Quietly.*] We all change whether we're ready or not.

SPY 2: But I will steady him.

DAUGHTER: Yes, steady him as you do all of us. [*Runs back to him; puts her arm round him.*] This is so unexpected. . . . and so dangerous. [*Slight pause.*] Forgive me father but I must speak to you of another matter . . . something very important.

SPY 2: [*Breaking out of his reverie.*] Important! What can be more important than that of which we are speaking?

DAUGHTER: Of course you're doing God's work but this is important to me and will be for you.

SPY 2: Don't blaspheme, child.

DAUGHTER: How long will you be gone?

SPY 2: I do not know.

DAUGHTER: Father, I . . . I . . .

SPY 2:   Yes, yes . . . get on with it!

DAUGHTER: I must tell you . . . I am . . . pregnant.

SPY 2: You are . . . ?

DAUGHTER: Yes. [*Slight pause.*] Pregnant.

Both freeze. Fade to half-light.

Scene 5

SPY 1: Alright, it was a damn sin. But we were spared thanks to my record.

WIFE: Yes, your *record*. But how many weren't? Three thousand were lost to the sword by way of *cleansing*. Three thousand of our own people! That's what your precious priests and generals are capable of.

SPY 1: I'm just looking after our interests. Dammit, our family!

WIFE: By sneaking back into that very exclusive club, those who drink with the *Leader*. Don't deny it!

SPY 1: They're my brothers. It was painful to be excluded for so long.

WIFE: I'm sure it was.

SPY 1: And right now we have to be careful and not be seen to step out of line.

WIFE: [*Sarcastically.*] No, let us not offend. After all, the Leader is a strong man and a wise one – a model of reason.

SPY 1: Careful! Lower your voice. Do you want someone to hear you?

WIFE: Why should I be scared? How can a feeble-minded woman be responsible for her thoughts, never mind her *utterances*. [*Pause. Holding him.*] Why can't we all just settle where there's unclaimed water and pasture and build a city? We have the skills. How many cities did we build in Egypt?

SPY 1: Oh, yes, we did build their cities. Who can forget the old stories of slavery?

WIFE: Of course we suffered but this is another time. There's a big difference between defence and attack.

SPY 1: Oh, you've noticed! And sometimes that's the difference between dying and staying alive. [*Slight pause.*] You afraid?

WIFE: Don't make me curse the day I married you.

SPY 1: Then let me say again – we have our sons to think of. Like everyone else, we will plant a stake. [*In a very strong and authoritative voice.*] Now pack me a skin with food for three days and a change of robes. I leave at first light. [*Exits.*]

Both freeze. Fade to half-light.

Scene 6

SPY 2: [*Shouting.*] How can this be? Did I not warn you to remain pure till your wedding night? How could the two of you have not waited?

DAUGHTER: Father, do not think me disrespectful but it is not uncommon.

SPY 2: Uncommon? This is *so* common. You are with child and he has not even . . .

DAUGHTER: He will pay the dowry! He will pay every last goat.

SPY 2: What will people think of me? My own daughter a whore!

DAUGHTER: No, father, he is a God-fearing man like you. He loves me.

SPY 2: *Love*! [*Slight pause.*] How long have you known? Are you not imagining things?

DAUGHTER: I have missed several months. . . . I can feel the swelling very strongly now. I can feel a heartbeat and at times a turning. [*Slight pause*[Truly, father, others my age are married already and have two or even three children.

SPY 2: Yes, I suppose so. You are a . . . a woman now. [*Laughs.*] And he is not a bad young man though he could have been more, how shall I say, *patient* and observant of the law. [*Slight pause.*] Very well, we will seal this with honour. I shall meet with his father.

DAUGHTER: Oh, bless you!

SPY 2: After all we've been through, new life should be welcomed. Our family must grow again. [*Embraces her.*] The days ahead will test me.

DAUGHTER: They shall test all of us.

SPY 2: That . . . [*points to her belly*.] . . . will be the first matter I deal with when I return.

DAUGHTER: Only then? But what if . . . in Jerico something . . . happens to you?

SPY 2: [*Smiles*.] He who does God's work is protected.

DAUGHTER: [*Puts her arms around him*.] Oh, be careful! I love you so much! I know the Lord will be by your side at all times but . . . please go now, please, father, go to his family, tell them you still accept him as my husband, that you have forgiven us.

SPY 2: If only your mother was alive.

DAUGHTER: [*Crying*.] Please, father!

SPY 2: Oh, alright. You have always known how to *get* your way. [*Slight pause*.] I will speak to them tonight.

DAUGHTER: I feel such joy! Return to take pride in me and my child.

SPY 2: Blessings upon you, my daughter. I will pray for you both. And *you* pray that I return with the information we need to win the war.

DAUGHTER: May Canaan soon be ours! [*Kissing him on the forehead*.]

SPY 2: Amen! Now come a little way with me. We have a stray sheep with the neighbour. Let us secure it before we forget to bring it home. [*Both exit*.]

Blackout.

ACT 2

Scene 1

Sounds of activity, hustle and bustle of a market. A Shepherd enters, staggering; engages two women, one is selling vegetables, the other is the Whore.

SHEPHERD: Good people, I have just come from the southern hills. My flocks were grazing there by Shittim when I saw a vast congregation spread out across the plain on the west side of the river, their tents as many as the bricks making up our city walls.

MARKET WOMAN: If that be true, not since the Assyrian army marched by us on its way to Babylon has such a host come near our city.

SHEPHERD: And when some of my goats strayed near them, they cursed me and brandished spears. One of their number, who still spoke the language of Egypt, insisted I was a thief even though they did not find any of their stock mixed with mine. He said theft of their herds would provoke war. Then I was taken to their leader and questioned for they also believed me to be a spy.

MARKET WOMAN: You a spy! For what reason?

WHORE: Ridiculous – you are as innocent as us!

SHEPHERD: Exactly what I told them!

WHORE: And were you believed?

SHEPHERD: No, they beat me. [*Pulls off his tunic.*] See here! See the marks of their lashes.

MARKET WOMAN: Poor man! What barbarians!

SHEPHERD: When they poured boiling water over my hand and I pulled back in pain, they said, so too will Jerico surrender.

WHORE: May the holy Mother of Earth keep us safe!

MARKET WOMAN: [*To the SHEPHERD.*] And then?

SHEPHERD: They made me swear to stay far from their tents and from their flocks – and from their war machines.

MARKET WOMAN: And what is this people's name?

SHEPHERD: Did I not say? Why, it is Israel. They are twelve tribes and their god is One. They say his powers will destroy all who stand against their claiming Canaan. It was outrageous how easily they defeated the Amorite kings on the Moab side.

WHORE: They want all of Canaan? Surely not?

SHEPHERD: There is no glimmer of mercy in their eyes.

MARKET WOMAN: Does the king know of this?

WHORE: Why are there no soldiers here in numbers?

SHEPHERD: That, too, is my worry. I will take my news to the palace. I must reach there before these Israelites march. [*Exits.*]

MARKET WOMAN: This swarm of locusts will devour us! Come sister, let us alert our families

WHORE: And sacrifice to the gods for protection! [*Both exit.*]

Blackout.

Scene 2

The two spies enter. Both suddenly stop and look out as if towards an horizon.

SPY 2: Such green! What flocks of fat sheep!

SPY 1: And see those fields and waterways.

SPY 2: Yes, a feast for the eyes after the yellow desert sands.

SPY 1: And see those city walls! What height and breadth! Imagine the treasures they protect?

SPY 2: Indeed, they are immense but praise the Lord, they will soon fall and the king of Jerico, and then after him the kings of all their cities, will hang from their choicest fruit trees and their palaces and temples will burn to the ground.

SPY 1: Burn?

SPY 2: We will spare nothing! That is our covenant with the Lord.

SPY 1: But brother, Jerico is a well-watered jewel! Surely we will divide up the cattle and the women and the gold and not destroy them?

SPY 2: We must entirely cleanse the pestilence and all around they must hear of its fate.

SPY 1: Of course, we must purge wrong-doing, but why wipe out those things that have value? They will fill our lives with ease and plenty.

SPY 2: And so tempt us to stray!

SPY 1: Perhaps some but not those who . . .

SPY 2: Brother, set aside your 'buts'! Let us be on our way. Did our Leader not command us to arrive at sunset? The sentries are tired then and think only of getting away to their homes.

SPY 1: A wise strategy but there is still time enough to savour the sight of this Promised Land.

SPY 2: [*Slight pause.*] You aren't growing faint-hearted, are you?

SPY 1: Me, faint? No one is more equipt for our task than I. The information I gather will guarantee our victory.

SPY 2: [*Slapping Spy 1 on the back.*] I was just checking!

SPY 1: What were you *checking*?

SPY 2: Just checking.

SPY 1: [*Eyeballing him.*] You think I want to go against orders and endanger us?

SPY 2: Of course, not!

SPY 1: I am committed as you are to serve our people.

SPY 2: As it should be! [*They sit, drink water, start eating.*] You know, they say you are a brave man, invincible in all our wars. But many were surprised when you were chosen for this task.

SPY 1: That cannot be.

SPY 2: Come now, don't play innocent.

SPY 1: I'm not playing at anything. You just said I am known to be a brave man.

SPY 2: I did but there is quite a long list of your . . . indiscretions.

SPY 1: I am no better and no worse than any warrior.

SPY 2: And were you not among the first to desert the Lord at Sinai and worship Baal?

SPY 1: Lies! All lies! No one could swear that I was part of that madness. My chief accusers, if you recall, had all been drunk.

SPY 2: Yes, most *were* drunk.

SPY 1: How that orgy pains me! A sin, a grievous sin. [*Slight pause.*] And now you tell me, brother, when Amalek attacked, what part did *you* play in our defence?

SPY 2: Why, my role is to guard our spirit. I ran from side to side encouraging all to bear misfortune with calm and keep up faith . . . [*Grows very troubled.*] It is many years now but my memory of that battle is still too sore, too pained with slaughter.

SPY 1: I must have killed twenty of the dogs.

SPY 2: No, worse than dogs! We just out of Egypt and they set their ambush, murdering driving off our flocks and herds. [*Covers his face. Tries to compose himself.*] They seized my wife. I found her body . . . in a ravine, torn apart, they had interfered with her . . . used her . . . and my two young sons, they took them. I could not count the wounds.

SPY 1: Forgive me, I had no idea.

SPY 2: I live their loss daily.

SPY 1: [*Puts his arm round SPY 2.*] A lesser god would have allowed us all to die.

SPY 2: [*Abruptly straightening up.*] A lesser *God*? No. Even in times of calamity we must accept His wisdom. We had surely sinned and so His wrath came to purge us. But now with Him in our midst, no force can stand against us. [*Scrambling to his feet, pointing forward.*] And there it lies! Come, let us take what is promised! [*Pulls SPY 1 to his feet.*] Much will depend on our firm alliance.

SPY 1: Rest easy, I am your man.

SPY 2: And I am yours.

SPY 1: Let us keep cool heads and be of good courage.

SPY 2: Amen. Jerico's great walls will not keep out Israel. [*They exit.*]

  Blackout.

Scene 3

The WHORE'S house. She is tidying up the table. SPY 1 and 2 enter to one side.

SPY 1: Greetings! Greetings to you, madam! We come to bless and be blessed!

SPY 2: Blessings! Brother, that is no way to address a whore. Besides, I like not the look of this . . . establishment.

SPY 1: Why not? They swore she is hospitable and discreet. [*Calls out again.*] Greetings to you, madam!

WHORE: Coming! Coming!

  She walks towards the entrance. When she reaches it, she stops and listens to their conversation.

SPY 2: No, really, let us leave. This place is a corruption!

SPY 1: But soldiers and merchants come to drink here. We'll soon find out what they know and think of us and how they're preparing their defences.

SPY 2: Perhaps . . .

SPY 1: Trust me, brother. We will have good reason to bless her. [*Banging again on the door. Calls out.*] Come, madam! Open for us, we bring peace and gold to pay for our lodging!

WHORE: Patience, sir! I will be with you in just a moment.

SPY 1: [*Whispers to SPY 2.*] See how eager she is! Let me go forward. I know the type.

WHORE: [*Opening the door.*] Greetings, sir. I have never yet disappointed.

SPY 1: And from your appearance one can see why travellers flock to lay their heads upon your warm bosom.

WHORE: [*Smiling.*] It gives a poor woman joy to provide comfort.

SPY 1: [*Bowing. Kisses her hand.*] Ah, a smooth and lively hand that can soap away the sweat of travel.

SPY 2: [*In a loud whisper.*] Leave off, brother, enough of this levity! [*To the WHORE.*] Madam, let us find ourselves a quiet corner in this house of . . .

WHORE: Refuge? Rest assured, gentlemen, my hospitality has disappointed no one. Come, sit and savour our wines. All celebrate their excellence. [*Leads them in.*]

SPY 1: Yes, not a moment to soon. My thirst is great. [*The spies sit.*]

WHORE: [*While pouring for them.*] We are an open city, a meeting place for many nations. [*They raise their drinking bowls.*] A toast of welcome to our visitors!

SPY 1: [*Bombastically.*] Indeed. [*Shushing SPY 2 as he follows.*] What a privilege to be here! How fortunate that we may share your lives – if only for a few days while we settle our affairs.

WHORE: The goddess has long smiled upon us. Her sweet waters sustain us though all about is drought. But tell me from where you come and what brings you to Jerico?

SPY 1: Now that is a story but one only to be told on a full stomach.

WHORE: Ah, forgive my inattention! I will fetch you a choice leg and other rare parts.

SPY 2: And bring some fruit. Your grapes are well renowned and, of course, your dates.

SPY 1: And pomegranates red as your lips . . . or is this not the season?

WHORE: Good sir, they are always in season. [*She bows and exits.*]

SPY 2: Brother, it does not become us to joke in such a vulgar manner.

SPY 1: Why? This will set her at ease. She will not suspect a thing.

SPY 2: How loud she is – not like our modest women.

SPY 1: Come now! Loud but not loud enough to deafen. As for her bearing, why she carries herself with wholesome pride.

SPY 2: Wholesome? It is the vanity of false gods and luxury. [*Watches as SPY 1 downs another mug.*] Steady, brother!

SPY 1: Why? Let her imagine me a drunkard – will make it easy to interrogate her without giving offence.

SPY 2: I like not this tactic.

WHORE: [*Enters bringing food. Pours more wine.*] To your good health, gentlemen!

SPY1: [*Spy 1 raises his mug.*] To our stay! [*Drinks it all in one gulp.*] To a future bright as your eyes! [*Pours another and does the same.*]

WHORE: You must have journeyed long today.

SPY1: Indeed, we have. And now need to . . . unwind all our wired limbs.

SPY 2: [*To the WHORE.*] Madam, kindly remove the jug. My brother is becoming uncouth.

WHORE: No, let him drink. [*Laughs.*] That is, after all, the way I make my living. But we will put him to bed if his tongue offends. [*Offers SPY 2 a mug.*] And you, sir? Will you not quench your thirst?

SPY 2: Well, it does look . . . alright but no more than one. [*Drinks.*] We have been three days on the road and my throat is thick with dust.

WHORE: You came past Shittim?

SPY 2: Why do you ask?

WHORE: Only today in the market place I heard a shepherd report he saw a great congregation there, tens of thousands a little beyond the river.

SPY 2: Who are they?

WHORE: Israelites. They were once slaves in Egypt who, it is said, escaped through the power of their god whom no man can touch nor see.

SPY 1: I heard that too.

WHORE: And soon they will march on us.

SPY 1: [*Drinking more wine.*] Ha, what proof do you have of this? Why would they threaten a people peaceful as yourselves?

WHORE: Perhaps it is envy.

SPY 2: Have no fear. They follow the ways of justice. Besides, they were victims of other nations. Surely you have heard of Amalek? They attack the weakest in any caravan.

WHORE: Ama-lek! What a violent name.

SPY 2: And an apt one for a primitive and savage people who deserve to be exterminated.

WHORE: Exterminated!

SPY 2: Rapists, murderers! They loot any holy place.

WHORE: All of them? Are they all so evil?

SPY 2: Indeed, they are and there can be no mercy for evil doers. The pity is that those who follow a righteous path still suffer. Yes, madam, in this world those who cannot stand for themselves are trampled underfoot. It could be said that you live here in a bubble of wealth and do not share your bounty.

WHORE: Not so! We give our fair share to the poor. No one can expect us to open the gates to all in need. [*Pours more wine for SPY 1.*]

SPY 2: Come now, your king, like all kings, offers the hungry mere crumbs, if that.

WHORE: Perhaps but we simple people work hard for what we have.

SPY 2: Indeed, you must. These lodgings are well furnished.

WHORE: Sir, it is for the benefit of my guests.

SPY 1: Even the rough like us? But fear not – we have not come to rob you.

WHORE: [*Pouring him more wine.*] Why, thank you for that assurance. [*Laughing.*] To be truthful you have the look of a wolf.

SPY 1: No, more a sheep dog!

WHORE: Do not take offence but it is your scar.

SPY 1: Oh, that. A relic of an ancient battle.

WHORE: With a woman?

SPY 1: Always, always!

WHORE: Come now, you were a soldier.

SPY 2: We are all soldiers – of a kind.

WHORE: Is that a riddle?

SPY 1: No, leave that to the Egyptian sorcerers.

WHORE: [*Sharply.*] You know Egypt? [*In a serious tone.*] Then you must know more about these Israelites.

SPY 2: We are from the territory abutting Amalek and are acquainted with the histories of many peoples.

WHORE: History! It is written by the victor – is it not? If these Israelites attack and conquer, who will record the screams of our people when we die at their hands? The chronicles will simply say that they prevailed and that their god is powerful. [*Slight pause.*] To be sure, we have our flaws. We do wrong to each other as much as any other people but that is no reason for us to fall prey to those who love war.

SPY 2: Madam, Jerico is safe and so are you. [*Taking a last gulp.*] Come, enough chatter –where are the beds you promised? There is much to do in the morning and we must rise early.

WHORE: Sir, you are a man after my own heart, a man of due discipline.

SPY 2: Why, thank you. Your hospitality has blessed our stay.

SPY 1: [*Shouts out.*] Oh, listen to this! Now he's the one to shower you with blessings! Don't get too hospitable with the old bastard!

WHORE: But why not? I discriminate against none. The Moon goddess is my witness! [*She leads them out.*] Would you like a view of the plain to the east and the vineyards that stretch to the mountain? [*All exit.*]

Blackout.

Scene 4

SPY 1 is lying in bed. WHORE enters with a tray with a bowl of water and some food.

WHORE: Good morning! [*Sets the tray down.*] Did the cocks wake you? They crowed much earlier than usual . . . much, much earlier, then fell silent, then crowed again. All told they crowed seven times and strutted round and round as if under a spell. Then at the last, they made such a monstrous racket it was as if a wall was falling.

SPY 1: I heard nothing. Perhaps it was a dream? [*Slight pause.*] Please, sit.

WHORE: [*Sits on a stool beside his bed.*] Do you also believe that the gods speak to us through dreams?

SPY 1: I don't know about that but my dreams also keep me awake. Often, it's as if I am not really where I think I am, like in another time and place. But tell me about your gods. I hope they're quite different to the ones I know.

WHORE: Why? Are you weary of your own?

SPY 1: Most times my God ... my *gods* ... are blind, deaf and dumb, and certainly ... [*Laughs.*] ... they don't step in to stop me from doing something stupid. [*Touches her robe, begins to caress her.*]

WHORE: [*Allows him to continue.*] For my part, the chief among ours is Astarte, goddess of ...

SPY 1: Don't tell me! She's the goddess of fertility and your identical twin.

WHORE: Hey, leave my robe! You'll stretch it. [*Slight pause.*] And then there's El Elyon, the father.

SPY 1: Ah, the big boss with the big ... [*Wiggles his finger.*] ... whom you serve with equal devotion. [*Leans over the bowl of water and washes his face.*] Now tell me, what is the subject of your *current* prayers?

WHORE: [*Rising.*] Please, don't think me a ... but these reports, call them rumours if you will ... these reports about the Israelites have shaken me – they have shaken the whole city. Everywhere people are alarmed but it seems we're just sitting, just sitting and ... and waiting for them to arrive.

SPY 1: What do you hear from your king?

WHORE: Nothing.

SPY 1: And the Elders? Are your Elders not raising the alert?

WHORE: From them, too, there is no word.

SPY 1: So, you're just ...

WHORE: Yes ... and I don't know what to think anymore.

SPY 1: But that can only mean there is no danger otherwise surely you'd see new detachments of soldiers, special fortifications being built.

WHORE: [*Shakes her head. Sits beside him.*] Jerico is just sunning herself. [*Slight pause.*] I'm so fearful for my family.

SPY 1: [*Moves to the stool.*] Last night while we were walking from the gate to your inn, we passed the markets and the temples, all those places where people gather. There was so much *life*. [*Slight pause.*] And I looked around, and I felt a great fear: how quickly all this could change, all this . . . could end. [*Slight pause.*] What if . . . tell your king to go and talk to them, *talk* to them and find a way to meet their needs

WHORE: [*Breaking off.*] Meet with the Israelites? You think they'll listen?

SPY 1: At least . . . *try*. Yes, try.

WHORE: You think they may hold back? I will offer special prayers and incense. I so much want good things to come to pass. [*Slight pause.*] You see, I was born to a family of goat herders. We lived in the mountains. There were fourteen of us and there was never enough to go round. That's why I came here. There's never been anyone to stand up for me. [*Rises.*] Maybe I will take your proposal to the palace. [*Picks up the tray. Starts to exit.*] But first I'd better wake your partner.

SPY 1: Wait. I want to tell you one more thing. [*Slight pause.*] Something *special*.

WHORE: Stop teasing me.

SPY 1: Why?

WHORE: I'm afraid. You come here and now I . . .

SPY 1: Start to fall in love? [*Embracing her.*] Is it so ridiculous? Isn't everything else around us more ridiculous? Maybe we should allow ourselves to just . . . [*Laughs.*]

WHORE: Oh, stop this!

SPY 1: Why? Because this is your . . . *job* and you've heard this so many times before?

WHORE: Yes. I've heard this so many times before.

SPY 1: [*Smiles.*] Forgive me, I meant no offence. [*Bows to her.*] Thank you for these cakes and honey. They were too tasty.

WHORE: [*Slight pause.*] Don't misunderstand me. Under your beard there's a man I might like and want to know better but right now . . . your brother must be hungry. I'd better take him *his* tray. Jerico is welcoming of all those who are generous.

SPY 1: No doubt! But we'll talk later. [*As she exits.*] I'm serious.

Blackout

Scene 5

The QUEEN and the VIZIER enter. The VIZIER is carrying a basket of fruit.

VIZIER: And how is the King today, My Lady?

QUEEN: Sadly, not much better.

VIZIER: It is many weeks now that he suffers this illness.

QUEEN: True, he is very weak, and sometimes does not recognise me nor the servants.

VIZIER: He must be in great pain to so lose his bearings and this latest crisis is not helping. [*Slight pause.*] In fact, and you'll forgive me for saying so, but I suspect it is the cause.

QUEEN: You believe so?

VIZIER: Madam, he is crumbling under the weight of decision! The Israelites are massing just three days march away and from all our sources, it seems an attack is imminent.

QUEEN: Now, now, Vizier. This is certainly not raising our spirits but tell me in all honesty, do they really constitute a *threat*?

VIZIER: My Lady, they have a new leader, a general. Their old prophet has died and now this general has fired them up with the promise of our wealth. And despite our knowledge of their recent victories over the kings of the Amorite, His Majesty continues to speak of them as a mere rabble of runaway slaves.

QUEEN: Exactly! For is that not what they are?

VIZIER: No, Madam, they are not a rabble. Though our walls are justly famous for their height and breadth, this enemy follows his god with pig-headed devotion and is eager for battle.

QUEEN: So what is the wisest course, Vizier? To wait and test their designs? Or to attack them first and so defend ourselves?

VIZIER: My Lady, if only the King would order . . .

KING: [*Off.*] My darling, where are you?

QUEEN: Ah, he's up!

KING: [*Off.*] Where are you? I want to get up and stretch my legs. Come! The girl has disappeared. Where . . . where is my stick?

QUEEN: [*Calls out.*] I will attend to you now, my Lord.

KING: [*Off.*] Where is my damned stick?

QUEEN: [*To the VIZIER.*] Do not leave. I will bring him out.

VIZIER: Yes, bring him out and support my petition. We cannot afford further delay.

KING: [*Off.*] Come along already! You know I can't get up without help!

QUEEN: I will. [*To KING.*] Another minute! Don't excite yourself. [*Exits.*]

KING: [*Off.*] I am not exciting myself. It is you who is exciting me by being so slow.

VIZIER: [*Calling out.*] A good evening to you, my Lord! I have brought some . . . choice fruits for your good health.

KING: [*Off.*] What is that? What have you brought?

VIZIER: Some fruit, my Lord – dates from my son's palms and grapes from my vineyard. [*KING enters; he is bent over, and hobbles along. The QUEEN supports him. The VIZIER goes over to help her.*]

KING: Fruit. What good is that, Vizier? I need something far sweeter to remove the gall on my tongue . . . there's a bitter taste no matter what I eat.

VIZIER: Indeed, my lord, we all require honey to make palatable unpleasant truths. Speaking of which, my Lord, we need to do more about the threat . . .

KING: Oh, be quiet! Is this all you have to talk about? Yes, don't deny it, Vizier. You want to tell me more about these damned Israelites. You are obsessed with these people! But no, they'll not make a fool of Jerico! I'll need *hard* information before I trouble myself. [*He staggers.*]

VIZIER: Easy does it, my Lord.

QUEEN: [*The KING approaches a chair.*] Yes, sit, my Lord. [*They ease him onto the chair. The QUEEN remains at his side.*]

VIZIER: Sir, just yesterday a shepherd reported that . . .

KING: Don't talk to me about shepherds, man. Shepherds are only good for shepherding sheep or goats or . . . wandering *nomads*. 'No man is mad who says he's madder than a nomad.' [*Begins to laugh.*]

QUEEN: [*Irritatedly.*] Husband, our agents say they are gathered on the eastern side of the river.

KING: They are, are they? And what are their numbers?

VIZIER: It is impossible to give a precise number, my Lord.

QUEEN: It seems they are a large host.

KING: What do you know about these matters, woman? I've still got my wits about me. It's not the first time I've been sick.

QUEEN: Indeed, my Lord. But never this sick and never for so long.

KING: Alright. Let me try again. Where *exactly* are they, Vizier? What *exactly* are they doing and what *exactly* are they planning?

VIZIER: Sire, as I indicated, we have very credible information that they plan war.

KING: Very good. They plan war. And when, pray tell, do they plan to *start* this war.

VIZIER: We do not have that precise detail. But that they are planning is without doubt.

KING: Particularize, man! Make it specific. Have our spies not penetrated the Israelite camp?

VIZIER: Not yet, my Lord. Not yet.

KING: And why not . . . yet?

VIZIER: They are about to, my Lord.

KING: *About* face, *about* turn, Vizier. Kick yourself in the . . . *about*. [*Starts to sway as if he is about to faint.*]

QUEEN: My Lord! [*She catches him as he falls. To the VIZIER.*] Fetch water. Quick! There is a jar in the bedroom! [*VIZIER runs off. To the KING.*] Husband, you must return to bed. This exertion will kill you.

KING: How can you say that? I cannot abandon my post. I must lead!

QUEEN: Then give the order to attack.

KING: No, let them attack. [*Confusedly.*] I dream it nightly.

VIZIER: [*Off.*] My Lord, *we* must attack! [*Enters bearing a jar*.] Here is cold water. Drink deep!

QUEEN: Thank you, Vizier.

KING: They are an insolent mob. [*Drinks greedily.*]

VIZIER: But a mob with power, perhaps an irresistible power, if we do nothing.

KING: [*Slight pause.*] Very well, command the priests to sacrifice our choicest oxen, the choicest!

QUEEN: Yes, let us invoke the gods. But at the same time let us call the elders of the city.

KING: No, only the gods can avert this.

VIZIER: [*Quietly.*] And after the ceremonies and the praying, what then? What do we do? Wait?

KING: Yes, let us wait for them to ... [*Agitatedly.*] Let them show their hand!

VIZIER: My Lord, we cannot *wait* to be besieged! No power can defeat us if we act now.

KING: Act against fate?

VIZIER: Already there are signs of panic. Soon our people *will* abandon hope and hand them the city.

KING: No, that can never be! We cannot show such weakness. *I* cannot show ... [*Breaks down.*]

QUEEN: Sire, the Vizier is correct. Give the order!

KING: I will, but first ... [*Again collapses.*]

QUEEN: Goddess have mercy! The fever has returned with full force. More water! [*Splashes his face.*] Help me, man! Help me! [*She and the VIZIER prop him up.*]

KING: My head throbs as if a demon was inside! Oh, how it blows a trumpet and beats drums and stamps its feet! And my eyes! Burning! Burning!

QUEEN: Come, now, Sire. Quieten all the pounding with sleep, and while you revive, the Vizier and I will put out fires of another kind.

KING: [*Limply.*] Have the priests prepare the sacrifice, put up notices in the market. There must be no panic. No one must act without my authority.

VIZIER: Fear not, our gods will taste the finest flesh. The smoke from their temple altars will blot out the sun.

QUEEN: And the people will see that you are truly their father.

KING: That is my dearest wish. [*To the VIZIER.*] Good man, I will reward you well ... when I am well.

QUEEN: [*To VIZIER.*] Indeed, let us surpass this crisis, and we will show gratitude deep as the springs that make Jerico so green. [*ALL exit.*]

Blackout.

Scene 6

Whore walks in to find SPY 2 still sleeping. She places the tray on the low table and surreptitiously begins to go through his travelling pack. While she is doing so, SPY 2 wakes and observes her.

SPY 2: What are you doing?

WHORE: [*Turning quickly to face him.*] Forgive me, I dropped something and was trying to find it.

SPY 2: Liar! You've been searching my things.

WHORE: It's just a . . . a coin, a small coin, really I . . .

SPY 2: What do you take me for? [*Rises, grabs her.*] Open your hands! Open them!

WHORE: I've got nothing of yours, I swear it!

SPY 2: [*Shaking her.*] Yes, you have! Admit it. Take off your robe! Let me see what you've hidden between your breasts. Take it off! [*Tries to remove her robe.*]

WHORE: Please, please, don't do that! Don't!!

SPY 2: Take it off! [*Twists off her robe so that she is exposed. Gesturing to her thighs.*] What have you put down there? Tell me!

WHORE: [*Beginning to cry.*] No, please, I've taken nothing!

SPY 2: Admit you were searching.

WHORE: No, I wasn't! [*He shakes her roughly.*]

SPY 2: Who put you up to this? Who you reporting to?

WHORE: I'm not reporting to anyone.

SPY 2: No, you're just a simple . . . [*Takes a knife out from under his robe.*]

WHORE: Oh, Goddess, protect me! [*Holding up her arms.*] Please! Put that knife away! Please!

SPY 2: [*Advancing on her.*] What were you searching for?

WHORE: I told you. I dropped a coin. [*He reaches her, raises the knife to the level of her eyes. She suddenly becomes very coy. Plays with the knife point.*] Ah, now I understand. You get pleasure from this.

SPY 2: [*He grabs her, places the knife against her neck.*] I do this for the One, True . . .

WHORE: [*Shouting.*] God, yes, your god! You *are* Israelites! The moment I opened the door . . .!

SPY 2: Stop this nonsense! [*Throws her to the floor. Stands over her.*]

WHORE: You've come to spy on us, and then you'll loot Jerico! I heard you, I heard you when you came knocking!

SPY 2: Know one thing. Jerico has no special rights. Your ancestors took it from some other people, and that people took it from another. [*Kicks her.*]

WHORE: [*Sobbing.*] You'll kill all of us!

SPY 2: If we do, it is to carry out God's plan.

WHORE: Plan! What do you want from *me*? [*Slight pause.*] I won't tell anyone. I swear I won't tell anyone you're here!

SPY 2: You won't? I must trust an idol-worshipping whore . . .

WHORE: I swear it! I'll help you. But spare my family, spare us, all of us. My mother, my father, my sons . . .

SPY 2: And if I *do* spare you?

WHORE: I will hide you from the soldiers. You can leave the city unharmed.

SPY 2: We can leave this city whenever we like. Why were you searching? [*In a low voice.*] Who do you report to? [*Kicks her.*] Who?

WHORE: [*Pause.*] I . . . I work for the Vizier. I give information when the sentries send strangers to me.

SPY 2: You do, do you? And what will you tell your Vizier about us?

WHORE: I'll say . . . I don't know where you come from but that you . . . that you aren't Israelites, and that you just know the stories about them like the rest of us.

SPY 2: [*Sarcastically.*] And that we're also afraid of what they might do.

WHORE: I won't fail you! I can feel the power of your god!

SPY 2: You can?

WHORE: Yes! Through your faith he will triumph! [*Excitedly.*] I will tell the vizier you left at dawn and that you were heading east. Meanwhile you can hide until the search is over.

SPY 2: [*Pause.*] Yes, you tell him we went east and . . . [*In a quiet fury.*] . . . if you come back here with soldiers, my people will tear you . . .

WHORE: [*Falling to her knees in front of him.*] I will do as you say! I swear it! [*Pause.*] But you, you swear on your god, the god who brought you out of Egypt, that you will spare my family! Swear on your god!

SPY 2: Very well. I swear by the God of Abraham, of Isaac and Jacob. We will spare you and your family. [*Returns the knife to the inside of his garment.*] Now go and give your *report* and do not give cause for regret.

WHORE: A thousand blessings upon you! Now hide on the roof. You will find bundles of flax. Bury yourselves under them. I will bring provisions for your escape when I return.

SPY 2: Remember, the slightest slip . . .

WHORE: I will not betray you. [*Exits.*]

SPY 2: [*Calls after her.*] Do not think you serve *me*. You serve *His* promise. [*Exits.*]

   Blackout.

Scene 7

WHORE enters; tidies her dress. SPY 1 emerges from the side.

SPY 1: [*Comes up behind her, puts his arms round her waist.*] There's . . . something I want. [*Embraces her but she resists, pulls free.*]

WHORE: To say?

SPY 1: Yes. [*Embraces her again; this time she responds.*] This is as I hoped it would be. [*Kisses her again.*]

WHORE: Is that what you wanted to say?

SPY 1: Isn't that enough?

WHORE: How can there be doubt? But it doesn't answer the question of your being . . . an *Israelite*. [*Slight pause.*] He told me. Your *brother* told me everything. About your mission.

SPY 1: He did? How come? [*Slight pause.*] You didn't . . .

WHORE: No, I did not! Trust me – I will tell you more of what passed between us later. But at this moment you are not safe.

SPY 1: Very well, since there is no time, I will be direct. [*Slight pause.*] Take *me* to your king. There is no need for war. Let him grant us land. I will speak with him as I speak now, with all my heart.

WHORE: As you do now?

SPY 1: As I do now! Then I will ride with him to Shittim. My people will surely embrace rather than destroy Jerico.

WHORE: I would not have thought that a man so war-like in looks could speak so wisely. Now hide upstairs. Wait for me there. Your *brother* already knows where to go.

SPY 1: Whatever comes to pass, I will do my utmost to protect you. [*They kiss again. She runs out; he follows slowly.*]

Blackout.

Scene 8

The QUEEN enters followed by the VIZIER.

QUEEN: You call her a *trusted agent*?

VIZIER: We use her because of her trade, My Lady. She runs an inn, a drinking hole. Moreover she provides services . . . which lead men to be careless. [*Coughs.*] Now let us deal with the matter at hand. We need to construct alliances . . .

QUEEN: But what if she is lying? What if they *are* Israelites and have paid her to conceal their identity and as we speak, encouraged by our King's inaction, they are returning with all haste to their encampment to incite the tribes and cross the river.

VIZIER: Madam, she has never fed us a false report.

QUEEN: Not until now perhaps.

VIZIER: Very well. I will send out search parties.

QUEEN: [*Cries out dramatically; as if possessed by a spirit.*] Wait! By the Goddess, I feel them! Though your whore be a double agent, our Goddess protects us! They are here, Vizier, both are still here within the city walls! And they are spies!

VIZIER: If you say so, Madam. We will search her inn without further delay.

QUEEN: Now pour me wine. Let me celebrate our ancestors' spirits.

VIZIER: [*Rising to bring a jug.*] Indeed, let me join you in that.

QUEEN: Yes, Vizier, detain these men and may your instruments of persuasion be strong and hot as my resolve. [*Slight pause. Drinks.*] And I agree – send emissaries to the kings of Ai and its neighbouring cities. We must unite and present the Israelite rabble with a show of force.

VIZIER: A wise and long overdue course, My Lady.

QUEEN: And instruct the sentries to close the gates. Let no one leave the city while we search. [*Slight pause.*] And when the Israelites are found, hang her, together with her children.

VIZIER: Hang?

QUEEN: Yes, hang!

VIZIER: But . . . surely she . . .

QUEEN: [*Sharply.*] What is your interest in defending this woman?

VIZIER: I have no special interest, Your Highness. If she has committed treason, she will pay.

QUEEN: Precisely! Hang her and her brats. Do you hear me?

VIZIER: Very well, my Queen. All this *will* be done by morning. [*Bows. They both exit.*]

Blackout.

Scene 9

The WHORE enters, she is quite drunk; sits on a stool nursing her bowl of wine.

WHORE: And so it is I use the little *charm* I have to keep my children and we live despite the toll it takes. But how often I wonder if I am the victim of my body's beauty. All the money men will pay to own it cannot be its true reward. [*Slight pause.*] But what of the two hiding on the roof above? [*Rises.*] If they keep their promise, and I, and those I love, survive, we will walk out of the ruins of this, our city, and face a world of shadows, of hollow memories, a world that stings like a naked desert wind. [*Slight pause.*] We will have to build new lives. And how will we do so? They are an alien people who drive the chariot of their Lord over the bones of unbelievers. Will they not say we are unclean and run their knives across our throats? For if I can abandon my own nation, they may think I will one day betray theirs. And would they be wrong? [*Sits again.*] Ah, the king! That poor sick man, so frail beside his icy queen. When I danced, his eyes were lost, swallowing my story as they undressed me. And so, too, that fool, his vizier, my long-time *employer*. How they gaped at my thighs! [*Slight pause. Rises.*] But I must not celebrate. Better hurry to the roof and prepare the Israelites for escape. [*Bitterly.*] And then light my rarest candle, the most fragrant, for the goddess. And pray to her to pray to *their* God to honour the vow they have taken in his name. Surely she will save me! [*Last sip of wine.*] May the love this Israelite proposes be more than words! [*Pause. Exits.*]

Blackout.

Scene 10

The SPIES are concealed under the piles of flax. WHORE enters with a large bag.

WHORE: [*Overturning piles.*] Where are you? Quick, come out!

SPY 1: Careful! Don't up end me! [*Emerging from under a pile of bags.*]

SPY 2: [*Also emerging.*] As for the rats, families of them!

WHORE: Come, you must hurry.

SPY 2: But did you not tell the Vizier we had departed?

WHORE: I did but then, by chance, as I was leaving, I overheard him command a search be made of my tavern. I will fetch your bags. [*Handing him a bag.*] Here is food and water for several days, certainly enough to reach Shittim.

SPY 1: You spoke to him only of our departure?

SPY 2: Of what else could she have spoken?

WHORE: I spoke only of what we had agreed. But leave that now – the soldiers may well be on their way. [*Runs to the side of the stage.*] This wall of my house is part of the great wall itself. Climb out of this window and you will find yourselves beyond the city. Hurry then and hide in the mountains till they believe you disappeared or dead – there are many leopards and other beasts that roam in those quiet places.

SPY 2: [*Hissing.*] No doubt there are! Now pray the soldiers arrive too late. [*To SPY 1.*] Stay here! *I* will go down and fetch our bags. Watch her carefully. See she does not leave this room.

SPY 1: Brother, why speak so harshly? She has come to warn us.

SPY 2: Warn? Turn your back and she'll run. [*Spits.*]

SPY 1: She has done nothing to earn contempt.

SPY 2: Judge that once we've destroyed this nest of idols. [*Exits.*]

SPY 1: Sanctimonious fool! [*Grabbing her.*] What happened? Did you not tell the king of my proposal?

WHORE: I tried but there was not time.

SPY 1: No time?

WHORE: I was alone with them and they were bombarding me with questions and almost throwing me about . . . so . . . [*Crying.*] Forgive me! I was not certain of what you spoke! This is all so very . . .

SPY 1: But we had an agreement! How could you have kept silent?

WHORE: It was not my intention! It's just that the queen was there and she was so . . . so *harsh* and I could not face her.

SPY 1: You could not? Well, soon you will hear the drums, and see the priests step forward with the Holy Ark, and the river part for them and the whole people cross and march forward to make . . . war. [*Slight pause.*] Can you hear them beat out your death?

WHORE: No! We will live! We must live! [*She grabs hold of and kisses him.*]

SPY 2: [*Runs in. Stops in shock.*] Brother, are you possessed by demons?

SPY 1: What demons? [*Breaking away from the WHORE.*] I am ready.

SPY 2: To still sate yourself on this whore?

SPY 1: She has saved us.

SPY 2: Let her first curse her gods before you applaud her redemption.

WHORE: I am prepared to do so!

SPY 2: I will return to burn them before your very eyes. [*Taking out a red rope from his bag.*] Here is rope. We will lower ourselves to the ground. After we have departed, leave it tied fast to your window, for by it, and by it alone, will our men know this is your house and spare all inside. [*Grabs her threateningly.*] And now keep the soldiers away by any means possible. By any means possible . . . do you understand? [*Shakes her roughly.*]

SPY 1: Easy!

SPY 2: If any of your family wanders out, they will be killed.

SPY 1: Don't hurt her!

WHORE: [*Trying to push SPY 2 away.*] I will do everything you say. [*Suggestively.*] Like last night.

SPY 2: How dare you! [*Moves to strike her.*] Stay quiet till we are gone. [*Slight pause.*] Our God is everywhere. He will strike you down if you betray us. [*Throws the rope out the 'window'.*]

WHORE: Why would I go back on my word? You have promised me life.

SPY 2: [*To SPY 1.*] Come! We cannot stay another moment! [*Exits through the window.*]

SPY 1: [*Calls down.*] Pull the rope three times when you are down. I will follow straight on. [*Turns to the WHORE. Holds her.*] Take me to the king. There is still time!

WHORE: [*Crying.*] This is all madness!

SPY 1: Do as I say!

WHORE: They will not believe you! Go! [*Tries to run away. He grabs her robe. As she pulls to escape, it rips.*] I am naked! Oh, the door! I hear them at the door! [*Sounds of banging and voices.*]

> A CANAANITE SOLDIER runs in with a drawn sword.

SOLDIER: Halt! [*SPY 1 draws a knife. The SOLDIER stops.*] Throw down your weapon!

WHORE: Leave him! [*Coming between the two men.*] He is my guest! He has paid . . .

SOLDIER: Of course, he's paid. Move away! [*Advancing towards SPY 1.*]

SPY 1: Who are you?

SOLDIER: We are sent by the king. Where is your fellow?

SPY 1: I am here alone. I am a merchant from . . .

SOLDIER: Nonsense, Israelite! Where is your fellow *spy*?

SPY 1: I am no *spy*.

WHORE: He is a merchant and sold me . . . !

SOLDIER: Quiet, *madam*!

SPY 1: I come to trade skins and celebrate your city.

SOLDIER: Then do so while we *celebrate* your capture. Pick up your bag. We have questions for you.

SPY 1: First guarantee my safety.

SOLDIER: Your safety? I think it the other way round. It is you who threatens us, Israelite.

WHORE: I swear to you this man is innocent of wrongdoing.

SOLDIER: [*Sarcastically.*] As is his companion whom we shall run down soon enough.

SPY 1: I will only go with you if you take me directly to the king.

SOLDIER: Are you mad? *I* will interrogate you first. And there won't be much left of you after that, my friend.

SPY 1: Take me to the king, Soldier. It is in all our interest.

WHORE: [*To SOLDIER.*] He is a man of peace. Listen to him! He will save us!

SOLDIER: Quiet, you . . . shameless . . . [*Pushes her aside. She runs and shelters behind SPY 1. To SPY 1.*] The house is surrounded.

SPY 1: Please! I have a message for him from my leader.

SOLDIER: Ah, one of surrender? That is all I wish to hear. [*Advances on SPY 1.*] My orders are to take you alive but if you frustrate me further I will have no option but to . . .

SPY 1: Kill me? Kill *me*? My people have done enough dying.

SOLDIER: But have you done enough *killing*?

SPY 1: That will also be up to you.

SOLDIER: We are not cowards like the Amorite.

SPY 1: Soldier, I truly do not wish to harm you.

SOLDIER: Then do not. Throw it down!

SPY 1: And then you'll hear me out? [*Soldier nods. Slight pause. SPY 1 lowers the knife.*] I *have* come to trade. [*Slight pause.*] And, yes, I *am* an Israelite.

SOLDIER: A trading Israelite! Very well, Mr *Trader*. Come and *trade* the information we need for your skin.

SPY 1: Return with me to my people's camp. They will confirm that we come in peace. [*Slowly hands over his knife.*] See?

SOLDIER: [*Takes it.*] Why, thank you, sir. I will cut my bread with it. And the lamb I will roast after you have talked. As for your people, they are known only for their hunger . . . for this land that is not their own. But . . . bring your *proposal* to my king. You may speak with him to better effect after I am done with you.

SPY 1: A treaty will save many lives.

SOLDIER: If there be *honour* on all sides. [*Prods him with the sword.*] Walk slowly! Remember – my men are downstairs. [*To the WHORE.*] Follow us. We will need your evidence before we . . . hang this spy.

WHORE: He is no spy! He must be heard for all our sakes.

SPY 1: Remember your promise, soldier. I do not wish to find myself at the end of a long rope because I have stuck my neck out.

SOLDIER: Why now, I thought all your *stiff* necks could survive even that.

WHORE: [*To SPY 1.*] Please. My robe.

SOLDIER: Yes, clothe yourself. Not all of you *pleases* the practiced eye.

SPY 1: [*Handing the whore her robe.*] Warm yourself and support my cause. There must be no more frozen tongues. [*To the SOLDIER.*] Sir, I put my trust in the justice of Jerico.

SOLDIER: You speak of justice? What is yours? Come! My lord the Vizier is waiting! [*ALL exit.*]

Blackout.

ACT 3

Scene 1

SPY 2, walking in the desert.

SPY 2: I waited for him as long as it was prudent. I stood at the foot of the wall under her window and called out to him. I pulled the rope but nothing, nothing from him – nor from her, the heathen bitch. God, how she smiled at him, how she rubbed up against his chest! [*Stops.*] He must be dead by now, tortured, then hanged or stabbed. Or . . . he survives, having turned traitor and divulged our plans. [*Slight pause.*] I must be close to the river. I will soon be at our camp. What will I tell our Leader? The truth of what befell us? No, I will say he left me to buy bread but did not return and I, alone, continued with our task and counted the sentries and took note of their arms and measured the walls. Then I mingled at the gate and in the temples, overheard the common talk and drank wine with the traders and learnt that . . . they fear us and are confused, they with all their wealth and soldiery tremble at the thought of our advance. And so it is their king is sick with fear and foreboding of his defeat. [*Slight pause.*] Indeed, our Leader will be well pleased with my report. I, the one of faith, and faith alone, emerged the stronger. All will understand we triumph over Jerico not because of spears and swords but with the power of the Lord as it swells out, trumpeting from our lungs, and pounding from our feet. [*Slight pause.*] I must hurry to our Leader. [*Exits.*]

Blackout.

Scene 2

Bound hand and foot, SPY 1 is lying face down on the table. He is sweating profusely and has burn marks all over him. A bucket of water stands next to him. A SOLDIER is behind him preparing an instrument of torture.

SPY 1: No more . . . no more!

SOLDIER: No more water, my friend? Not another sip of sweet water from the famous springs of Jerico! Isn't that what you've come for? [*Grabs his arm and begins to twist it. Pushes his face and holds it down in the bucket. Jerks it back up.*] Now when do you plan to march? At full moon so you can see the scorpions? [*Strikes him.*] How many warriors do you have? Talk, fool, talk!

SPY 1: [*Moaning.*] They're all around! Faces . . . so many young ones, so many women . . .

SOLDIER: Stop this drivel!

SPY 1: The smell, the smell of blood! The smell of blood and . . .

SOLDIER: Your unwashed, filthy body!

SPY 1: What do they want? What have I done?

SOLDIER: Oh, I'll tell you. You haven't done anything but talk nonsense. They trained you well, Israelite. Babble, babble, if ever captured. [*Hits him.*] Clever boy but not clever enough. [*Hits him again.*] Any battering rams? Ladders? Talk, you circumsized prick!

SPY 1: Faces . . . bodies without shadows . . . in the market . . .

SOLDIER: Yes, soon you'll *market* Jerico as a lovely place to holiday. So relax. [*Holds a pitcher of water over his head.*] Here's a drop, just a small one, mind you. [*Pushes his head into the bucket again.*]

SPY 1: [*Shouts.*] Water! Water! But not to drown! Not to drown!

SOLDIER: No, you don't want to drown, do you? Anymore than you *want* to turn Canaan into a wasteland. It's just that your blessed god commands it. [*Hits him again.*]

SPY 1: Round and round and round! And on the seventh day there will be a great shout! And the walls will fall!

SOLDIER: [*Spits.*] Dream on, you . . . [*QUEEN suddenly enters as he raises the tongs. He bows.*] Your Majesty!

QUEEN: At ease. I've heard our guest here seems shy to speak so I thought to pay you a visit. But I trust you've not been *shy* with these, lieutenant [*Takes the tongs from him.*] Has he told you how many sheep he has and how many worn out wives? [*Motions the SOLDIER aside.*] Still nothing?

SOLDIER: [*Mumbles.*] Not yet, Your Majesty. But I've only been with him these past three days.

QUEEN: And in all this time you have not loosened his tongue?

SOLDIER: He just jabbers on about *faces* and stamping feet going round and round.

QUEEN: [*Slight pause.*] Where is the Vizier?

SOLDIER: I believe in his chambers. With his . . . eh . . .

QUEEN: Really! I would have thought he would not rest until we had opened this wretch's mouth. [*Slight pause.*] Faces. You say, he sees faces?

SOLDIER: Yes, Madam, he says he sees them all over the room.

QUEEN: Does he call them by name?

SOLDIER: No, Your Highness.

QUEEN: Not even the Whore's? Come now, lieutenant. They must belong to some-one.

SOLDIER: If they do, he does not say.

QUEEN: And does he speak of . . . anything else?

SOLDIER: No, Your Highness except about that which he spoke from the start. [*Laughs.*] He says there should be talks. He proposes *talks* . . . about land, *sharing* land.

QUEEN: Indeed? *Talks* about *land*?

SOLDIER: He raves, Madam! He wishes us to return with him to his camp and meet their Leader.

QUEEN: [*Aside.*] Ah, then the two bulls will trample the field. [*Approaches SPY1, bends over him.*] Come, my warrior. Speak to me. [*SPY 1 does not answer. She smiles.*] Tell me your innermost thoughts. Tell me . . . something surprising. [*She touches his arm.*] Trust me. [*Slight pause.*] Don't you recognise my voice?

SPY 1: [*Twists round violently even though bound.*] Can it be . . .? Is it? Oh, my wife!

SOLDIER: How dare you?

QUEEN: Hush! [*To SPY 1.*] I am everyman's wife, warrior. I will protect you.

SOLDIER: This is the *Queen*, Israelite! Show respect!

SPY 1: The queen of Jerico? [*Bitterly.*] Mock me not, mock me not! The hour will come!

SOLDIER: Quiet!

SPY 1: The hour will come! The hour . . .

SOLDIER: For stringing you up!

QUEEN: Wait, let him speak.

SPY 1: I know everything of the glory of Jerico. How blessed you are! We are but poor and simple herders.

SOLDIER: Yes, herders of *other* people's cows and flocks.

QUEEN: [*Glares at SOLDIER. Quietly to SPY 1.*] What do you want of us?

SPY 1: Come to Shittim. Speak with our Leader.

QUEEN: But he is a brute who listens to no one.

SPY 1: We can devise a treaty.

SOLDIER: [*Whispers fiercely.*] Now, Madam, who is mocking who?

QUEEN: How should we satisfy your misfortunes?

SPY 1: My people will set aside their spears once you grant us land.

QUEEN: Truly?

SPY 1: We will work for what you give us.

QUEEN: But peace makers disband their armies.

SOLDIER: [*To SPY 1.*] Exactly!

QUEEN: Let your Leader come to *us* and bury your spears at the foot of our walls.

SPY 1: [*Shouts.*] On my honour, that is all we want.

SOLDIER: I'll honour you with a hot coal up your . . .

QUEEN: [*To SOLDIER 1.*] Wait! [*To SPY 1.*] And now Israelite, tell us of your battle plan. Tell us, and my king and I will find a solution to your plight. [*To SOLDIER but within hearing of SPY 1.*] Come, Lieutenant. Let us leave our friend, for say, an hour? Let him reflect. Oh, and free his legs.

SOLDIER: [*Whispers angrily.*] But Madam, we have orders to always keep the prisoner shackled.

QUEEN: [*Pulls him aside.*] Whose orders, Soldier?

SOLDIER: The Vizier's, Your Majesty.

QUEEN: The grand Vizier who has not been down to complete his job? Unshackle his feet.

SOLDIER: Very well, Madam. [*To SPY 1.*] You have one hour, Israelite. Take advantage of Her Majesty's kindness.

QUEEN: [*To SPY 1.*] I leave you praying that our Moon goddess with her wisdom prevails. Be brave.

SOLDIER: Yes, be *brave*, you louse.

SPY 1: [*In agony.*] I thank you, madam. Brave . . . let us both be brave. Who does not wish for peace? All nations since the time of Cain become sick with power and the sins of the fathers visit their children.

QUEEN and SOLDIER exit. Blackout. Spotlight on the QUEEN at side stage.

QUEEN: Jerico, how many times have you been destroyed, and then rebuilt? For the springs beneath our feet never run dry though men war and bloody them. And now, I, mistress of your palm groves, your vineyards, all your flocks, your gold and silver, must save us. [*Slight pause.*] Can it be that our future hangs on a coarse Israelite thread? [*Exits.*]

Blackout.

Scene 3

The stage is dark. The WHORE is in her house. The QUEEN approaches; her head and face are covered with a shawl.

QUEEN: [*Calls out.*] Madam!

WHORE: Who is it?

QUEEN: A woman like yourself.

WHORE: At this hour! Alone?

QUEEN: Yes.

WHORE: I've already blown out the lamps. Come back tomorrow.

QUEEN: I cannot. We must speak now.

WHORE: Why? Trouble with your husband? He throw you out?

QUEEN's: No, no!

WHORE: Then why come to me?

QUEEN: I need your advice.

WHORE: Ah, you're pregnant and want to get rid of the child.

QUEEN: No, none of these things.

WHORE: Please, I have enough burdens to carry myself.

QUEEN: As do all us women. [*Slight pause.*] Madam!

WHORE: Go on your way!

QUEEN: All Jerico may benefit from your wisdom.

WHORE: Why flatter me? You sound like a man who wants me cheap. [*Slight pause.*] Alright, but just for a few minutes. [*Showing the QUEEN in.*] Forgive me, I am very tired and with all this talk of Israelites who knows what dangers stalk our streets.

QUEEN: [*Enters. Her face is covered with a shawl.*] Israelites?

WHORE: You've heard the rumours?

QUEEN: More than that.

WHORE: [*Sits and motions to the guest to also take a seat.*] But what can we poor people do when the king is sick and silent? Curse these men! They know well how to waste the life we bring into the world. But how can I lighten your load?

QUEEN: It has to do with a spy.

WHORE: A spy?

QUEEN: One who is a . . . *guest* of the King. There were two of them who only days ago sat at this very table.

WHORE: How do you know this? [*Rising in panic.*] Who are you? [*The QUEEN lifts the shawl from her face.*] Oh, your Majesty, how was I to know!

QUEEN: You could not and are forgiven.

WHORE: I thank you. [*Bows.*] My Lady, is he to be executed?

QUEEN: Why?

WHORE: I pray not. He is a man of peace.

QUEEN: An *Israelite,* come in peace?

WHORE: Yes.

QUEEN: On what authority do you say this?

WHORE: A woman's knowledge.

QUEEN: We must build our defence on a kiss?

WHORE: Much more fell from his lips.

QUEEN: Though you are a whore.

WHORE: [*Rising.*] Though I *am* a whore.

QUEEN: And you trust this enemy? You are not offended by his scar?

WHORE: All of us carry marks of strife.

QUEEN: Sit. [*WHORE sits.*] Let me be blunt. Is his offer of talks to be believed?

WHORE: Madam, I cannot foretell the future but he has shed much blood and now feels remorse.

QUEEN: Would that all men felt the weight of the bodies they have struck down!

WHORE: [*Rising.*] My Lady, I do not wish to pry . . . but has he been hurt? I understand the Vizier uses . . . instruments.

QUEEN: No, he has not been harmed.

WHORE: Praise the Goddess!

QUEEN: But his ears hear voices and his eyes see faces that do not exist for those who stand beside him. He speaks clearly one moment then the next loses himself in a world of fancy.

WHORE: He was not fevered when last I saw him. Truly, he is strong in his conversion!

QUEEN: [*Rising.*] Madam, I thank you for your frankness. I must leave. The king is ill and every hour calls out for me. [*Begins to exit.*]

WHORE: [*Following her.*] Forgive me asking but how is it that you have come alone?

QUEEN: I had no choice. The men who flank me do not hold you in *esteem* nor give your words much credence. But for my part, in these dangerous times, we . . . [*Touches the WHORE'S arm.*] . . . should stand together. [*Slight pause.*] At first light come to the palace. You may see him. I hope the Israelite loves you as much as I love Jerico.

WHORE: Oh, thank you, Madam! May he stay sincere for all our sakes! [*QUEEN exits.*] To think, the Queen is with me! But now I must gather my family. Who knows where we will be tomorrow!

Blackout.

Scene 4

The KING, the QUEEN and the VIZIER enter. The KING sits on his throne flanked by the other two.

VIZIER: Praise the gods for your recovery, my Lord. The priests have done their work most excellently.

KING: Yes, they have restored my vigour. But what news of the second spy? Have our men returned with him?

VIZIER: They have not, my lord. There is no trace.

KING: None at all?

VIZIER: There has been no sighting and by now he is sure to have reached the Israelite encampment. [*Slight pause.*] We must expect the worst.

KING: Come now, Vizier! You still fear this horde of . . .

VIZIER: My Lord, with his report of our inaction, they will prepare to advance. [*Agitatedly.*] Sire, I have contacted the kings of our neighbouring cities. Their armies are ready to join us without delay.

QUEEN: That may well be the case, Vizier, but let me remind you of the prisoner's offer. For as the Oracle advises, we can only quench the desert's thirst with a canal of water and, to this end, must despatch a delegation to negotiate its path. If we do not, the wind will stir up dust and suffocate our crops and orchards. [*Slight pause.*] Let us go with him to Shittim.

KING: But my dear, they are devious and will accept no compromise.

VIZIER: Well said, Sire! And why should we?

QUEEN: Do you prefer the alternative? "Round and round and round and round . . ." until we all come crashing!

KING: What is this nonsense?

VIZIER: The prisoner's ramblng, Sir. He prophesises that our mighty walls will collapse unless we agree to talks.

QUEEN: My Lord, we have territory to spare. And it would not be for all their tribes. Some can share with other cities. A controlled migration – every step marked by mutual agreement.

KING: And in return?

QUEEN: They sign a treaty guaranteeing our safety. A treaty sealed with commerce and all other manner of mutually beneficial exchange.

VIZIER: Really, Madam, you are painting too perfect a picture! This covenant with their *Jehovah* has puffed them up. They say they are a *chosen people*. Chosen for what? To carry his prophecy into the world and so enrich themselves?

QUEEN: [*To the KING.*] Sire, we are all mindful of this danger. But do as I advise and we will triumph.

KING: When I was sick I had visions of a battlefield. And my eyes were filled with the agony of the dying and those who were to mourn them.

QUEEN: [*Embracing him.*] Precisely! That is all war will bring. [*Aside.*] Strange, the Israelites's eyes, too, were filled with horror.

KING: And yet, how humiliating to have to bargain with invaders!

QUEEN: It will be more humiliating to lose everything.

VIZIER: I will say again: we must mobilize to make sure we keep our city.

KING: [*To the QUEEN.*] My dear, should I not trust you? It is against my honour but ... let us try and negotiate.

QUEEN: Oh, my Lord, we are in agreement! [*Kisses his hand.*]

KING: [*Slight pause.*] But still I cannot rid myself of dark foreboding. They are, from all accounts, a stubborn people and will demand the maximum. [*Slight pause.*] Wait! I have it! Give them gold, give them gemstone. That seems to work with most. [*Excitedly.*] Yes, take our good spy to Shittim with carts of treasure. They will surely celebrate his return. And while the mob dazzled, receives us with open arms, our forces, hidden in the hills, will swoop down and destroy them.

VIZIER: [*Clapping.*] Yes, yes! We will use him as our decoy!

KING: [*Shouts.*] Soldier, bring me the whore! Bring her now! Hurry up, man! [*To the QUEEN.*] We will yet outfox these pretenders to our domain.

QUEEN: But, my Lord, we cannot betray his confidence. It will not be just.

SOLDIER: [*Off.*] Yes, my Lord. Coming, my Lord.

KING: And when I am done with her, bring the prisoner.

SOLDIER: [*Off.*] Very good, sir, immediately, sir.

QUEEN: Husband, this is madness!

WHORE: [*Entering.*] You have called for me. [*Goes down on her knees before the KING. Is encouraged when she sees the QUEEN.*] Good day, Madam. I trust all is well.

QUEEN: Good day to you.

KING: [*Sharply.*] Have you two met?

QUEEN: You forget, my King, I was present when this . . . lady, first came to testify regarding the Israelites.

WHORE: That is so, my Queen.

KING: [*To the WHORE.*] Now this Israelite of yours, he has made us a proposal, one that my Queen argues merits consideration.

WHORE: Sir, he did impress me with his love for peace.

KING: Yes, a piece of Jerico. But never mind his love for 'peace', what of his love for you? Does it survive the morning light?

WHORE: My lord, he is very tender towards me and says he wishes to make me his wife.

KING: [*Laughs.*] Does he not have enough wives over there? But tell me, how deep is your knowledge of him in other respects?

WHORE: Beyond his affection for me, he spoke of building trust between our peoples. He even dismissed his companion as a madman. My Lord, he is truly committed to this path.

KING: So committed that he will be prepared to return to his encampment and there . . . become our assassin and rid us of his Leader?

WHORE: What a suggestion, my lord!

KING: Good woman, save our city! Use his passion for you, make him our agent.

WHORE: But not for murder.

KING: Why? It is a path to peace! Cut off the head and the body will collapse!

QUEEN: No, my lord! Such a killing of their general will only provoke revenge. We need no blood vendetta with the Israelites.

SOLDIER: [*Runs in. Salutes.*] My lord! Forgive me, my lord! [*Slight pause.*] The prisoner is gone. We have searched the palace and the adjoining streets but he is nowhere to be found.

KING: [*To the QUEEN.*] You see! You women, always too believing!

VIZIER: [*To the WHORE.*] Or deceiving! [*Grabbing the SOLDIER.*] Damnation, man! Were you not with him at all times?

SOLDIER: I was, sir, but while I went to fetch him food my companion fell asleep and when I returned . . .

KING: He bribed you both!

VIZIER: [*Shouting.*] Call a squad, call five! Search the city! Shut the gates! If he is not found, I will show you no mercy!

SOLDIER: Yes, my lord, without delay. [*Begins to run out.*]

KING: Wait! [*SOLDIER stops. To the WHORE.*] And you! What have you to say for yourself and your *fine* love?

WHORE: I know not what to say, Sir. There is surely some explanation for his absence. It cannot be that he misled me.

KING: But he has, he has. My dear, you have slept with the *enemy*. [*To SOLDIER.*] Take her back to her dwelling, gather her family and lock them in. No one is to enter or leave until we have located this double-dealing bandit. You hear? Have her guarded day and night.

SOLDIER: As you command it. [*Aside. To WHORE.*] I can only imagine what was *your* price. [*Pushes her. They exit.*]

KING: [*To the QUEEN.*] Negotiation? We would have been led into a trap!

QUEEN: I am distraught.

KING: [*To the VIZIER.*] Send for my commanders. [*VIZIER exits.*] I feel my blood run again. This is a time for warriors. Why, I am ready to break bread with Amalek – they know how to deal with Israelites! [*Exits.*]

Blackout.

Scene 5

SPY 1 staggering in the desert.

SPY 1: What did I imagine? Did I see myself approaching Shittim with the king of Jerico and his soldiers at my side, and there, coming out to greet us, elders from all the tribes and our Leader striding forward, waving palm fronds and giving thanks for my wisdom? [*Falls to the ground. Covers his face.*] Could I have truly believed in such a triumph? [*Slight pause. Quietly.*] I see them. The whole camp is gathered and from every mouth comes the cry, "Traitor! He brings the enemy to our tents, betrays the sacred promise!" [*Falls.*] Dogs eating dogs and so will be forever. [*Cries.*] And now? What am I to do? Seek refuge in another city or stay roaming, a hermit cut off, alone with the wind and the crows? [*Pause.*] How weak I am! To have been seduced by a whore! And a foreign whore at that! But she was so . . . so comforting, so different and yet so familiar. So much more a woman than that poor child I took . . . yes . . . months ago, there at the well while the lambs drank. What have I not done for my pleasure? What have I not done and damned myself! [*Stands up. Falls to the ground again.*] I must reach our camp. And make them believe I was held against my will and betrayed no secrets. [*Rises. Exits.*]

Blackout.

Scene 6

The ISRAELITE LEADER and SPY 2 enter.

LEADER: [*Marching in.*] So, Brother, you confirm that Jerico is unprepared and fears war?

SPY 2: General, as I reported, there is no mobilization, no preparation for resistance. As always, they indulge themselves.

LEADER: Yes, wealth and comfort have brought a rot to their lives and only our anointed swords will cut it clean.

SPY 2: Indeed, sir, the Lord's Will . . . will soon be done.

LEADER: My whole life has been a preparation for this campaign and now your mission has cleared our path. [*LEADER sits while SPY 2 remains standing.*] Speaking of which, is your partner still not recovered? A miracle! A few more hours and he would have perished. And what a loss to Israel that would have been!

SPY 2: It was by God's grace we found him in that desolate place.

LEADER: To still live, despite the heat, the lack of water – what strength! How many days was it before he could speak?

SPY 2: Almost four, sir, and only in a broken way.

LEADER: Is he still incoherent?

SPY 2: All he does is rave and spin out . . . [*Contemptuously.*] . . . visions which . . . to be honest, arouse my suspicion.

LEADER: Suspicion? On what grounds?

SPY 2: My lord, I fear these visions are but a sham. [*Slight pause.*] Jerico *turned* him and he has been *returned* to weaken our resolve.

LEADER: No, my brother, you are surely mistaken.

SPY 2: Sir, there are many marks of torture on his body. How could any man withstand such an ordeal? And you, yourself, know full well the cloud which lay across his person. [*Slight pause.*] Once we were in enemy territory, he showed himself unstable, unstable in all respects, and raised doubts regarding our cause.

LEADER: [*Rises.*] No, that cannot be! After all I've done for him!

SPY 2: And there where we lodged, in the evenings he became drunk and was blabbing in such gross fashion so that I was forced to strike him. And then to compound his recklessness, he spent the nights with the whore who owned the inn and when she did us some small favour, agreed to save her and her family once the city is fallen. Sir, he did this without my consent, in fact, it was over my strongest objection.

LEADER: Come now, my brother.

SPY 2: Indeed, he was *that* undisciplined. And then, sir, in an attempt to further sour my faith, he sneered that you are too old for war and Jerico will stand unconquered.

LEADER: [*Rising.*] Do you swear this?

SPY 2: I do, my General. He said this not once but many times. [*Slight pause.*] And in this questioning of authority, his wife is also guilty. Their neighbours tell us she is much given to belittling the priests and your person.

LEADER: This is a most serious charge. Discipline! A thousand times, discipline! [*Slight pause.*] Thank you, my brother, for your frankness. Malcontents must be exposed. As for his promise to that whore ... was it lust alone that made him offer her protection?

SPY 2: [*Looking uncomfortable.*] That was all, sir. That was all it was.

LEADER: You look abashed, brother. What was the small favour that she did?

SPY 2: Yes, well, she did have ... some role to play in my escape ... but it was minimal, sir, and was only in return for substantial payment, she ... eh ...

LEADER: Stop being so vague!

SPY 2: Well, sir, she . . . she hid us from the soldiers for a time . . . and gave us provisions and . . . some advice.

LEADER: Ah, despite herself a righteous gentile! Brother, we have a debt to her and should reward her with her life.

SPY 2: But sir, she was licentious. She came to *me* after . . . lying with him, her breath all thick with wine and the smell of . . . of course I sent her packing.

LEADER: [*Sarcastically.*] Of course you did.

SPY 2: But he did *not*, sir. That is the point.

LEADER: Come, brother, she was going about her business. We will honour your agreement with her but Praise the Lord you have raised your other concerns. [*Grimly.*] If a soldier casts doubt on his commander's judgement, how will he carry out orders in the heat of battle? [*Slight pause.*] Have him charged and constitute a tribunal from among the elders. I will lead the preliminary interrogation.

SPY 2: Yes, sir. Immediately, sir. [*Prepares to leave.*]

LEADER: And brother, as a precautionary measure, watch the wife carefully together with their sons.

SPY 2: Very good, sir. With God's help we will forestall all traitors. [*Exits.*]

LEADER: To think I trusted him, a man of valor, a man to break the slave's fear and face the enemy, a man to take charge. To think I sent such a man on such a mission!

Blackout.

ACT 4

SPY 1 and his WIFE are again on one side of the stage [as in the first scene]; SPY 2 and his daughter are on the other. The DAUGHTER enters on' their' side, occupies herself with domestic work.

Scene 1

SPY 1 enters. He is completely disoriented, lurches about. WIFE follows on.

SPY 1: [*Running about.*] After my water ran out, all dark in the cave. . . Then the voices! The voices! Days, nights, days, nights . . . just the smell of salt on the wind and the jackals, the howling of jackals . . . [*Shouts. Covers his face.*] The faces, so many faces . . . from the marketplace, from around the gates of Jerico. And then faces here, here from our own people . . .

WIFE: Come, lie down. Give yourself a chance to sleep.

SPY 1: No, no! It is worse, it is worse when I sleep. Then they come like stars– white and yellow stars, as many as grains of sand, exploding in my face. [*Shouts.*] Away! Take them away! Always danger, always death – always, always the threat of . . .

WIFE: The threat of you having to accept the truth?

Both freeze. Fade to half-light.

Scene 2

SPY 2 enters.

DAUGHTER: Greetings, father! [*He ignores her.*] Greetings . . . my father! [*He still ignores her.*] Father! What is the matter? [*He continues to ignore her.*] Are you not well? [*Pause.*] Father, why are you ignoring me? [*She rises and goes to him. He pushes her away.*] In God's name what have I done?

SPY 2: [*Suddenly shouting.*] How dare you let the sacred Name cross your lips! Filth. Filth.

DAUGHTER: Father, what are you talking about? How have I offended you?

SPY 2: You do not know? Liar! Impure liar! The whole camp laughs at your hanging belly!

DAUGHTER: No, father, please! I am innocent of any wrong-doing.

SPY 2: Satan's work! It is *his* child you are carrying.

DAUGHTER: Satan? [*Cries.*] What do you speak of? I knew not *Satan*. [*Tries to embrace him.*]

SPY 2: [*Throwing her aside.*] Shameless! My own flesh so shameless!

DAUGHTER: [*Crying.*] Please, father, please!

SPY 2: Your betrothed! He and his brothers came to me with just complaint. He never lay with you!

DAUGHTER: This is madness! Of course he did!

SPY 2: Do not compound your sin with denial. Confess! The priests know. The people know. You have destroyed us!

Both freeze. Fade to half-light.

Scene 3

SPY 1: The Lord, the Lord will guide me. I cannot die! I cannot die now! Not before we have secured the land! But no blood! No blood!

WIFE: Quiet yourself! They will be coming soon.

SPY 1: And now, alone, I am alone . . . alone on the face of this earth.

WIFE: Yes, you are alone but we have your sins for company. Not even the Nile can wash you clean.

SPY 1: Egyptians! They are here, are they not? [*Shouts.*] I don't want to go back! I don't want to go back to that slave house! Save me from their whips!

WIFE: [*Catches hold of him. Takes out a skinbag containing water.*] Here, drink! Be still! Drink! [*SPY 1 drinks while his Wife bathes his face with water, lulls him.*]

SPY 1: [*Suddenly jumps up, checking if anyone is observing them or listening in.*] Anyone else come to visit? Where are you? Where are the visitors? [*Stops suddenly. Whispers.*] Do they believe I've lost my mind?

WIFE: You've lost your mind over and over again. Just look what you've done!

Both freeze. Fade to half-light.

Scene 4

SPY 2: It is decided. You must both be stoned.

DAUGHTER: Stoned! [*Almost fainting.*] For what? I am innocent!

SPY 2: [*Striking her.*] Witch! Did you think our Lord would not reveal your sin?

DAUGHTER: Of what am I accused?

SPY 2: How dare you pretend!

DAUGHTER: I never lay with any man other than my betrothed. I swear it! [*Cries.*]

SPY 2: [*Watches her cry.*] You have brought a most terrible stain upon our family. Of all the men of Israel, you lay with *him*, with my . . . [*Shouts.*] How could you?

Both freeze. Fade to half-light.

Scene 5

SPY 1: [*Whispering.*] Has he come?

WIFE: Who?

SPY 1: He comes every day, doesn't he? He spies on me! On you, on the children!

WIFE: There is no one spying on us. There is nothing left to uncover.

SPY 1: Don't lie! He is here now. I know he is! Why did you let him in?

WIFE: Lie down and be quiet.

SPY 1: He hates me. Of course he hates me. She went to him – the whore went to him after she was with me and he was so happy, she made him grunt like a . . . boar.

WIFE: Enough already! Stop this . . . this dirty talk!

SPY 1: Then he saw it, saw it in the morning, how she looked at me, touched my hand, my hair. . . He hated me. But I knew she loved me. I was going to save her, her and her . . . He wanted her but she was mine . . . that daughter . . . of Astarte . . .

WIFE: Astarte! You had a woman in Jerico?

SPY 1: I was going to make her mine after the battle.

WIFE: You wanted to take a Canaanite whore for a wife?

SPY 1: I know he's here. And you let him in. You want to destroy me. You both want to destroy me.

WIFE: You should have died in that filthy cave where they found you!

SPY 1: But then I couldn't do it. I couldn't stay there, I couldn't. You see . . . my heart, my heart is here . . .

WIFE: Here!

SPY 1: With you and our sons. [*Grabs hold of her.*] Don't let them torture me! Please God, don't let them torture me! Not again! [*Collapses.*]

WIFE: But they will. As you have tortured others. [*Hesitates, lingers over him, covers him with a blanket.*] I pity you but I pity the poor girl you used even more. [*Exits.*]

Both freeze. Fade to half-light.

Scene 6

SPY 2: How could you? [*Spitting it out.*] The *warrior*! My partner in Jerico!

DAUGHTER: [*Crying.*] Oh, father, forgive me, father! He was waiting for me . . . near the well . . . I did nothing to . . . invite him . . . he led me away . . .

SPY 2: Led you? By force?

DAUGHTER: He made me . . . I did nothing . . .

SPY 2: Answer me – was it rape? Did he rape you? Did you scream? Did you . . .?

DAUGHTER: [*Still crying.*] Yes . . . I mean . . . no, he was there with his sons, they were there . . . and he told them to take their flocks a little way off and leave him with me . . . and so . . .

SPY 2: What did you do?

DAUGHTER: He said the man who truly wants me is him . . . not . . . not . . .

SPY 2: He knew to whom you are betrothed?

DAUGHTER: Yes.

SPY 2: And you went with him of your own accord? [*Pause.*] Answer me!

DAUGHTER: Yes. [*Almost in a trance.*] I don't know. I don't know how . . . I went with him. [*Pause.*] We lay in the shade. He opened my robe, he touched . . . my breast, and placed his hand, his hand moved between my thighs, his hand moved very slowly, it was warm. His hand was very warm. [*Pause.*] Then we kissed. [*She collapses.*]

SPY 2: [*Standing over his DAUGHTER. Very slowly, very sadly.*] My child, you kissed your life . . . away.

Both freeze. Fade to half-light.

Scene 7

WIFE: He's been sleeping for hours but his body moves so violently – there are whole armies fighting inside him. [*Pause.*] The Law is the law. They will take him away and stone him. They will stone her. They will stone *them*. [*Pause.*] And when their bodies are lifeless, the people will begin to march. Tribe by tribe, the people will follow the priests, follow the Ark with the Law, will cross into the Land this God they say has given us. Drums, trumpets, banging and shouting, the people will march to take Jerico. [*She moves to his bedside.*] He twists and turns. Does he dream of the slaughter to come? [*Slight pause.*] And the poor girl he used for his pleasure – of what does *she* dream? What dream stirs her soul while she waits for her fate? [*SPY 1 suddenly screams. She addresses him.*] You, what more can I say to you, *my husband*? The shadow of your sword darkens my womb, bruises me when I should be golden with your sons. Our youngest . . . how he suffered to see you break our marriage vows! How he suffered to know you used even . . . our neighbour's child. He did well to go to the priests though their judgement is too cruel for your victim. [*A recording of German Nazis shouting "Judenraus", snatches of Hitler raving, is broadcast. SPY 1 screams again, rolls over, covers his face. The voices continue their rant as his wife runs to his bed.*] What is it? What do you see?

SPY 1: [*The German voices start again. He puts his hands over his ears.*] Quiet! Quiet!

WIFE: Speak it out! Speak it into the light!

SPY 1: [*Sitting up on his knees, swaying as if in a trance, he chants in a staccato, broken rhythm.*] People, so many naked people, pushed, all of them pushed into a room by soldiers, so many soldiers there at the door, shutting the door till the door is shut closed. And the naked people stand, they stand silent, shouting, crying till there is no air, no air to breathe. Then the people hear a noise, a soft noise, a hissing. And the people breathe in, they breathe in the hissing, and what they breathe fills their lungs, fills their bellies. [*Very slowly.*] Till the hissing stops, till the hissing stops and all the people die. All the people die. All the people in the room die. [*Pause.*] Then men, blind men, men without eyes, without hearts, come with small carts. They load the bodies onto the carts. They load them and burn them. They burn the bodies. They take the bodies from the carts and burn them. Blind, broken men burn all the bodies. [*Pause. Addresses his wife. Almost shouting.*] And on that cart was your mother. And on that cart was your sister. And on that cart was your brother. And on that cart were our sons and our daughters. [*Pause. Very, very slowly.*] And one of the men, one of the blind men loading them onto the carts ... one of these ... men ... was ... me. [*Slight pause.*] And the last body on the cart, the last body to be burnt ... was ... [*Points to his WIFE. The WIFE stands rigid. He raises his hands above his head.*] So it is written and so it shall be. The smoke is the smoke of Jerico and all Jericos that were and are still to come.

He lowers his arms and as he does so an Israelite soldier enters.

WIFE: Go with him. Answer for what you have done. I will not march with the priests and the people. I will return to the desert with our children. But how I long for water! For springs of water! How I long for the calming rush of water!

ISRAELITE SOLDIER: [*To SPY 1.*] We must purify the nation, cast out your sin, mark it with a pile of stones. Then we will cross the river and the years of wandering, of helplessness, will become a story of distant sorrows. [*Slight pause.*] Come.

'Normal' stage light comes up on this side of the stage.

SPY 2: [*To his DAUGHTER.*] Come, the priests are waiting. [*They slowly exit.*]

ISRAELITE SOLDIER: [*To SPY 1.*] Be strong and of good courage. Once you are buried ... we will bring on days of milk and honey.

Spy 1 follows him silently. As he moves off, and only his wife is left on stage, a cacophony of drums, trumpets, bells and voices are heard.

The voices speak and sing in Hebrew and English. They call out, "Death to the adulterers, death to the defilers of the Lord's law. Forward to the Promised Land, forward! Shema Yisrael, Adonai Elohainu, Adonai echad".

This is followed by another set of voices shouting in Arabic and English, "This land is our land. Death to the invaders, death to the destroyers of our altars, the rapists of our daughters. We will not be moved. This is our sacred soil!" The shouting/chanting from both sides rises to a crescendo. Sound of bombardment. Silence.

END

BOOK MARKS

A tragi-comedy about friendship, racism and decolonization
(as well as reading ...)
on the wrong side of the rainbow

**They are all on the edge. Each has weaknesses.
There are no innocents.**

These people are **Vish Naidoo** (Luversan Gerard), a divorced, Indian businessman/deal-maker, **Stanton de Villiers** (Craig Morris), a white, gay man of Afrikaner ancestry who is a consultant to the new government and is the host for the evening; **Macedisi Julius Matanzima** (Pule Hlatswayo), a black consciousness activist involved in youth development; and **Cornelia Hendricks** (Campbell Meas), a young Coloured primary school teacher and feminist.

Twenty years have passed since the 1980's Struggle when the three men lived and worked together. Over time they have gone their separate ways and much has changed but on a summer's evening in Melville they come together to launch a book club. In this they are joined by the daughter of a former woman comrade, whose life experience is essentially only that of the post-Apartheid period but who is very aware of the recent and historical past. She brings something from that past with her and as the evening progresses different revelations reveal the fault lines in all their relationships.

Come and spend the evening with them ... join in the discussion!

For more details contact 082 512 8188 or email: botsotso@artslink.co.za

Produced by Botsotso   with support from the NAC:

NATIONAL ARTS COUNCIL
OF SOUTH AFRICA

A tragi-comedy about friendship, racism and decolonization (as well as reading)

BOOK MARKS

with Luversan Gerard
Campbell Meas

Pule Hlatshwayo
Craig Morris

Written and directed by Allan Kolski Horwitz

PERFORMANCES

POPart	Olive Tree Theatre	AFDA	Hillbrow Theatre
286 Fox St. Maboneng	2nd fl. Yarona Mall, Watt Ave, Alexandra	41 Frost Ave. Auckland Park	14 Kapteijn St. Hillbrow
26,27,28 January 8pm	2,3,4 February 7pm	9,10 February 7:30pm	16,17 February 11am
29 January 3:30pm	5 February 3pm		18 February 6pm

A tragi-comedy about friendship,
racism and decolonization
(as well as reading)

BOOK MARKS

with Luversan Gerard
Campbell Meas

Pule Hlatshwayo
Craig Morris

Written and
directed by
Allan Kolski
Horwitz

Soweto Theatre
cnr Bolani Link &
Bolani Rd
Jabulani, Soweto

NATIONAL ARTS COUNCIL
OF SOUTH AFRICA

DATE & TIME
23,24 February
7pm

VISH

MNCEDISI , STANTON and VISH

CORNELIA

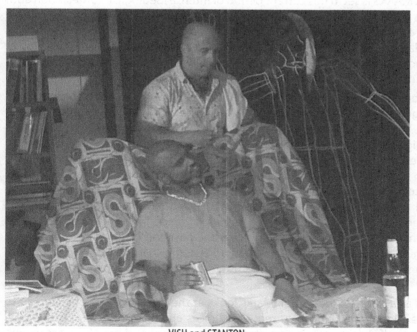

VISH and STANTON

Program notes

The debate on decolonization and racism which started in earnest at several universities in 2015 was initially focused on the University of Cape Town regarding the commanding presence of a statue of Cecil John Rhodes. Rhodes was the arch British imperialist who colonized the country now known as Zimbabwe and set in motion the Anglo-Boer War in order to control the Witwatersrand gold-fields and cement European rule over southern Africa.

The protests provoked wide attention in all sectors of South African society and showed how the surface unity of a 'Rainbow Nation' is cracking under the weight of an ever-widening economic divide between the majority of black people and the white population (despite the emergence of a sizeable black middle class) and how institutions such as universities (but also in the corporate sector) which had formerly been reserved for whites had still not undergone sufficient transformation for black academics (professionals) and students to feel accepted and respected. As such, the movement, inspired by the radical critiques of Frantz Fanon and Stephen Bantu Biko, is an expression of the rage of a new post-apartheid generation that feels cheated of victory despite the handover of political power that took place in 1994. Its desire for an Afro-centric South Africa that defines itself without apology to Europe and the United States is creating shock waves to the assumption that the status quo (of implicit white control) can continue forever.

BOOK MARKS is set in this current period of intense ideological contestation and examines the reactions to it of three comrades from the 1980's 'Struggle'. They come together on a summer evening at the house of one of their number in Melville, a middle class suburb of Johannesburg, to launch a book club and are joined by a young woman whose life experience is essentially only that of the post-Apartheid period but who is very aware of the recent and historical past.

Stanton de Villiers, a white, gay man of Afrikaner ancestry who is a consultant to the new government is the host for the evening. The first to arrive is his old Struggle comrade, Vish Naidoo. They chat while waiting for the others. Vish is agitated because a big business deal is scheduled to be sealed later that evening but he cannot locate the Saudi business man involved. Stanton and Vish talk about many things including the fate and present identity of Mncedisi (aka Julius) Matanzima – the third member of the NGO they had worked in, and resident of the communal house they had shared during the late 1980's in Yeoville, a more working class suburb. Thereafter, Cornelia, the daughter of a female comrade from the Eighties, arrives and begins the process of 'contestation' over the past and its truths. These interactions begin to wear away at appearances and become sharper and more exposing by the time Mncedisi finally makes his entrance and the play moves to its conclusion.

Billed as a tragi-comedy, Book Marks looks at the delusions of erstwhile South African revolutionaries whose current life choices and life styles are shown to be hollow and self-defeating. It is an epitaph for the vibrant and hopeful mass movement that promised so much but which has, over the past two decades, dissolved into the corruption and mismanagement of a black-led neo-colonial regime led on by persistent white racism and economic control. The only hopeful aspect is the clarity of thought and courage of Cornelia, voice of a new generation, who is prepared to take on the burnt-out remnants of the old Struggle and forge a new path.

~~

The first performance of BOOK MARKS was at POPart, Johannesburg on 26 January 2017 with the following cast:

VISH NAIDOO	(middle-aged Indian man)	Luversan Gerard
STANTON DE VILLIERS	(middle-aged White man)	Craig Morris
CORNELIA HENDRICKS	(young Coloured woman)	Campbell Meas
MNCEDISI JULIUS MATANZIMA	(middle-aged Black man)	Pule Hlatswayo

SETTING

Evening. Stanton's house. A garden patio: pot plants; a deckchair, garden chairs, a table, a braai stand. A garden hose, connected to a tap, lies coiled up in a corner of the patio. The general stage lighting is muted on the sides as would be on an outside patio on a summer's evening.

AUDIO COMPONENT

The three songs used as a soundtrack are from the author's albums *No VIPs* and *Look in the Mirror*. These can be accessed online at soundcloud under the name 'All Clear official'.

ACT 1

Play in with STILL NO HOUR OF LIBERATION. STANTON enters mid-way through the song; fusses around, preparing for the book club. He is followed by MNCEDISI who checks out the books in the book case. As the song is playing out, VISH enters.

VISH: The key question isn't whether the working class has the ability to change society so as to do away with violence, inequality and injustice. But whether human beings as a whole, as a species, have the ability to achieve this. We don't want to throw away years of our lives trapped in mindless jobs that may or may not pay well. We don't want to waste hours stuck in traffic jams or crammed in overcrowded trains. We don't want to have to read about endless corruption in government and the big corporations. Or have to tolerate dirty neighbour-hoods and broken sewerage pipes. No, we most definitely want our shit to float as far away from us as possible. But what about what we do want? [*Slight pause.*] After the houses and the cars and the private schools and the luxury trips and the latest smart phones and . . . and . . . and . . . we want romantic as well as comforting relationships. But above all, at a humbling 'number one', we want safe drugs. Ja, drugs. But in this case, I'm talking about mind-expanding, body-enhancing drugs that are cool. In other words, and, boy, this is really uto-pian, drugs that don't fuck us up even when we abuse them. Ja. [*Slight pause.*] Alright, alright . . . stop laughing.

MNCEDISI: I won't start with the usual spiel about where I was born and my very humble origins in the desolate dongas of the Transkei, and how I pulled myself up by my bootstraps and got a varsity education despite the fact that my mom and dad were illiterate. I'll leave that to my official biographer whom I've already appointed. And would you believe it, she's a . . . no, no, not an umlungu princess with peach skin and tits like Charlize but a Korean. Yebo, a real live, genuine North Korean journalist who cut her teeth and her nails as an army correspondent in Matabeleland with Uncle Bob's 5th Brigade when they put down the Nkomo revolt leaving behind just a few casualties. Ja, I've always wanted to do 'stand up'. My heroes were comedians. I won't rattle off all their names but Idi Amin, Big Dada, was number together with the emperor of the Central African Republic, old Jean Bedel Bokassa, right, who built a fucking cathedral to rival Rome in the bush. Ja, 'Your Excellency, the President; Your Honour the Judge. They and their natural-born get on board with the whites and smile for their supper. As long as they're around, we South Africans, and by South Africans I mean real Blacks, will never be allowed to have the power to do what we have to do.

CORNELIA enters. She moves as if she is in another 'zone', is a visitor to the one which the three men inhabit during this scene. She 'glides' around listening, ob-serving them and the environment. When she speaks, she must signify that she is breaking into the audience's space, and then signify her exit in a similar manner.

STANTON: If you've wondered what kind of a name 'Stanton' is, well, that's my English side, from my mother. Came here in the 1860's – diamonds, my great-grandfather was a prospector round Barkly West. Made a bit of money, not that much mind you, and bought a farm in the area near where my dad's family had a place. Of course on his side we've been here a lot longer. As you'll know, de Villiers is a pretty typical Huguenot name, the first one came out to the Cape in the late 1600's. And then, not too long before my folks were born, there was that piece of trouble, the Boer War. In fact, quite a few of my dad's family were in the English concentration camps – something he never forgave nor forgot despite his crossing over and marrying my mother. So here I am, an only child who never took over the family farm – a great betrayal: wat is 'n volk sonder sy land?

VISH: My mom died after my youngest sister was born. My dad was a cop. Ja, you heard right. And for my sins I grew up in Verulam. You know where that is? Just north of Durban, or should I say, Ethekwini. And who lived in this little sugar town? Indians, man. Indians and more Indians and more Indians and quite a few Zulus and a handful of bloody umlungus. Now my Old Man had a low rank all his life because that was as high as a coolie could go. At school half the class hated me because I came from the family of a sell out and the other half thought my dad was smart because any job is a good job and six kids ain't easy to feed. Shit, he told me to also become a cop but after my two elder brothers, who were arseholes, went and joined up, I said, fuck this, who the hell do they think they are? I'm not going to wipe any white man's arse for a miserable pay packet. So I left home, went to Durbs, got a job in a clothes shop. The owner, old Moosa Ebrahim, was a UDF type. I got roped in. Ja, I learnt a lot from old Moosa. Then his cousin said he needed someone to run a shop in Joburg, and I said what the hell, and I took the job and went to Joburg. And I carried on with the Struggle stuff and soon I was one of the leaders in the branch. And after six months I met Stannie and Julius at a meeting. Didn't take long and they asked me to join this NGO they started. [Slight pause.] And that's where I wrote those bloody useless poems.

MNCEDISI: Izwe lethu! Our brothers in Zanzibar – they kicked out the Arabs. In Uganda they kicked out the Asians. In Kenya and Algeria and Mocambique and Zimbabwe, they kicked out the Whites. The time has come for Azania to turn inwards, to draw a line so that in our minds we can go back to where we were before slavery, before colonization, before the missionaries and the mines and the factories – before they took what we had. We have to go back to that time before we believed them when they said we were a dark continent. [Slight pause.] Ag, don't worry. I won't eat you. I've got a little bit of Rasta in me. I'm a vegetarian.

CORNELIA: Once I arrive I'll have to live up to what Stanton wants. I'll have to play a certain role. [Laughs.] Not that it's a particularly negative one but, all the same, it's annoying. I mean he hardly knows me but he's going to project all sorts of stuff about my supposed intelligence and spunkiness and my representing the 'born frees' and all that jazz. He'll demand that whoever is there likes me and at the same time, because he's a sly bastard – or so I've heard from my mom – he'll dare them to challenge whatever I say. And why is he doing this? Does his being gay make a difference? For so long he had to hide who he really is. He knows what it's like to be on the outside and have a massive chunk of your life seen as a sickness. Who knows, maybe that's why he wanted to join the Struggle. As for straight Afrikaners, they're scared of us, bruinmense. They think we're the bruised fruit of their loins, the living shame of their randiness. Just look at our names. I mean, mine is Hendricks!

STANTON: I was about fourteen and like most farm boys I went to boarding school, this was in Kimberly. And it was there that I realised that . . . I liked men. Of course, there was no one to talk to, so it stayed a secret apart from one, no, actually two men who I could be very open with. [*Slight pause.*] The first was . . . [*Laughs.*] . . . the gym teacher. And where did it start? [*Mimes showering. Laughs again.*] And then around the same time there was the handyman, in those days, the handyboy. Yes, the two of them, a good South African combination. [*Slight pause.*] And needless to say, the latter introduced me to ganja. Ja, it was as typical and obvious as that. [*Slight pause.*] Hey, stick around – I'll roll you one later.

VISH: There was a funny incident at the NGO that made me leave. Some cash went missing. Not a hellava lot but enough for one of our biggest overseas funders to get pissed off. And when we went through the paper trail, all fingers pointed in one direction. But Stannie, who was the head honcho at the time, didn't want to make a case of it, so the whole thing was dropped. Maybe I'm wrong but it seemed like a fucking cover. [*Slight pause.*] The cash was gone and no prizes for guessing who was responsible. You hear me? No bloody prizes.

MNCEDISI: My father was a miner. You know, one of those men who left his village to go and work in the old Transvaal gold mines and came back once a year and didn't recognise his own kids because we'd grown and how the hell could he recognise me when I was shooting up like a mielie on Red Bull. My mother was a . . . yes, a maid, in East London for a Jewish family. We got the clothes their kids couldn't wear and chocolates that were too hard to eat. [*Laughs.*] Ja, there were five of us, only my brothers are still alive and one of them was crippled in a car accident. My eldest sister died of TB and the middle one was shot by a jealous boy-friend. And what do you know? They left behind kids, plenty kids. Sound like a story, a bad story? So I had to help out, had to find the extra bucks. And sometimes take a few chances. Yes, but I'm ready to go on. [*Slight pause.*] I'm still ready to struggle.

STANTON: At the time the three of us were working together, we actually believed people, all people, but especially the poor, can work together for the common good. [*Slight pause.*] Ah, "the common good. "Just be a good boereseun, my seun. And don't talk about everyone having rights. And why don't you play rugby instead of chess? And why don't you take sweet little Hester out, she's such a beautiful girl and her family has five farms?" [*Slight pause.*] Why can't people deal with reality? Take Mbeki's refusal to provide anti-retrovirals. Hundreds of thousands of people . . . If Mbeki had been white he would have been accused of genocide. But to defend what he called 'black pride' and prove that Blacks aren't sex maniacs, he thought he had to take the view that HIV isn't transmitted by . . . [*Makes the indecent sign of fucking.*] . . . and that these drugs are a fraud, a western conspiracy. [*Slight pause.*] But I was saved. I was saved because I had the money to pay for ARVs. I was saved because I was privileged.

CORNELIA: You know, we *Kullids*, a lot of the time we've been caught between blacks and whites, and depending which way the wind was blowing, we've changed sides. Hell, that has caused some problems. As for the new Khoisan movement, well, it's important but how do we revive dead languages and an ancient way of living that right now doesn't apply to ninety-nine percent of us? Apart from that, there are so many different dialects and shades of coloured. But I teach in a very mixed school and my friends swing all ways. Underneath the tans and the false eyelashes and the weaves, we're all relatives of the same chimpanzee. So don't get clever, brother. It's the luck of the draw. Having said that, I'm not here to give you a first year lecture on the do's and don'ts of racial togetherness, so I won't pretend it's not sometimes difficult. The old ways are still stuck in our heads although the reasons for any retreat into the tribe, or whatever you want to call it, are all too clear and, quite frankly, bloody pathetic. [*Slight pause.*] Ja, Stanton. Am I supposed to give him hope?

MNCEDISI: When I look around and see the buildings and the telephone poles and the electricity lines and the cars and shops and all the stuff that makes this a city, I feel more and more cut off, and at the same time totally trapped, like I've been kidnapped and thrown into a bubble on another planet. Ja, this white city our people were forced to build but those who designed it wanted to make it look like the cities they'd left in Europe. They stole our gold, our diamonds, to pay for everything. So how can I belong here? People running past each other: no time to greet, no time to look deep into the eyes, no respect, just boom-boom, using and abusing each other. [*Slight pause.*] And for what?

STANTON: Sure, I was involved but I don't want to give the impression that I was a hero. During the Second State of Emergency, the Boers cast the net wide, they took in thousands of people. I certainly wasn't involved in anything underground in a military sense and I don't think Julius or Vish were either. Ja, that was an experience. Being held at John Vorster. We'd been close, a good team, but those two weeks inside really strengthened our bond. [*Slight pause.*] Relationships. I've been involved in quite a number over the years but only lived with four of those guys. Take the last. Andile and I were together for seven years. It ended about six months ago. I miss him terribly but I know we can't work it out. He's just too . . . what can I say . . . adventurous? Thing is I'm past all the clubbing, the parties, so it's not so easy to meet people. Tonight I just want to see some familiar faces, bring in a few new ones . . . talk, drink, think. Just hang out, with intelligent folk. [*Slight pause.*] You get it?

CORNELIA: I love reading. Since I was a kid. And I've got my mom to thank for that. She always made me aware of the power of imagination and the need to learn. Especially when your circumstances are pretty shit. After all, it's up to each of us to decide what we want to believe. She was growing up in Cape Town and went through all the forced removals and being dumped in nomansland. And she was the youngest and brightest but she wasn't able to finish school 'cause they all had to go out and work, the whole bloody lot of them. For years she was a machinist in a clothes factory until something happened, something that changed her life big time. [*Slight pause.*] The neighbour's son.

MNCEDISI: They say we should go back to the bush if we don't like it, as if we never had villages and towns. They say we must be grateful for their civiliza-tion. [*Laughs.*] Hitler, Stalin, Hiroshima, the the Crusades, the Hundred Years War, the not-so holy Roman Empire . . . have I left anything out? Our masters . . . we had so much before they came. So many languages and so many stories; so many medicines, so many foods, so many drinks; so many tools and materials; so many ways to count the stars and predict the rain. [*Slight pause.*] But now I'm walking in their city and I turn round and go home, and pour myself a beer, and pick up my old guitar and write a love song, a good old love song to good old . . . Mama Afrika.

CORNELIA: He was a student and he started to give her all sorts of things to read – novels, poetry and then political stuff which really got her going. And soon she was invited to join his study group, that's how these Marxist groups operate. And she found it tough at first, all that fancy language but she didn't give up and after a while it started to make sense. And when they formally recruited her, she was ready for action. Fuck, she was the star of that group. Always the first to volunteer for placing pamphlet bombs and then the real thing. But not too much of that. She said she was scared shitless of the grenades. And she didn't want to admit she was frightened. Apart from that she couldn't take the home situation. Like her dad was unemployed and expecting the girls to do everything. It was driving her crazy so she came to Joburg. Her mom's sister was up here, in Riverlea, and that's where she's stayed ever since. Except for that time in Yeoville. With these guys. [*Slight pause.*] So books saved her life. And they're saving mine. Better than the nonsense the laaities are using to run away from themselves.

VISH: Sex! Sex is a sensitive subject: we either have an obsession and overdo it or we stay starved of it. The thing about feminists is that they won't accept certain biological imperatives. [*Mimes these actions.*] Hunt, hunt – gather, gather! [*Stops.*] You were expecting me to come up with that facile shit? [*Slight pause.*] The real reasons why men struggle with monogamy are as follows. [*Whispers conspiratorially.*] "a. With our small brains we get easily bored and crave constant stimulation. [*Sexily.*] b. We're susceptible to most women who will make themselves available. [*Lecturing tone.*] c. We're democratic and don't believe in not giving everyone a chance to enjoy it to the hilt. All the way, baby, all the way." [*Coughs.*] Now this tool called rationality, it's a new thing. We're struggling. And that's why for the foreseeable future, `there's only . . . the Master's way to enlightenment . . . [*Sways his hips, belly-dance style.*] . . . Kundalini, my bra, that shivering down the spine.

STANTON: Yes, it's true. My consultancy is starting to go down. Things are looking quite tight and I may have to sell this house. The department of Public Works is so shambolic that nothing gets done and you have to fight like crazy to get paid, never mind being paid on time. I draw up plans, check the costings, have dozens of site meetings, consultations with communities but to get authorization for anything to actually happen . . . And then there's all the black/white niggle. That's why I left the NGOs. At the last one there was this one guy, very ambitious, who wanted me out. So he came up with this story about my insulting black culture. When I asked him to prove this, he said I never went to funerals, the funerals of family members of staff, sometimes even of staff themselves. I told him that was because I thought funerals were a sentimental luxury, people were spending fortunes on the dead when there was so little for the living. [*Slight pause.*] After he organised his coup, the organisation became his private business. He brought in his girl-friend and other family members. He killed off projects we had fought so hard to make happen. Gone. All gone because of the Baas with a black skin. [*Slight pause.*] But you know something. He had a point regarding the funerals. [*Slight pause.*] He had a point. [*Slight pause.*] Was I being racist or . . . was I just being plain fucking stupid?

MNCEDISI: Vish left first. He said the Struggle was dead, nothing much was going to change. After Stanton also bailed out, I decided to make a break. I didn't really know what I wanted to do so I left Jozi, went to my cousin's place. She had a small run-down house in Cala that needed fixing. I cut myself off from everybody. Sometimes I wouldn't even get out of bed. I would just lay there half dead with depression. And then, by total chance, I found a book, a history of the Eastern Cape. It was all about the Frontier Wars. And I was reminded how much 'divide and rule' destroyed us – as much as superstition. I mean how could the elders have thought that sacrificing our cattle would help the ancestors give us the power to destroy the enemy? [*Slight pause.*] But aren't I blaming the victim rather than the conqueror? [*Laughs.*] To be fair, I must admit that what Shaka did to his neighbours wasn't very neighbourly either.

CORNELIA: Two days ago while I was driving home after work I got a message. The school was broken into, they went straight for the computer centre . . . everything was taken, every single damn computer, every single last computer the kids need so desperately. And you know what? It must have been an inside job – no doors broken, no windows smashed. The thieves had the keys to the main gate and to all the doors that led to the computer centre. [*Slight pause.*] And tomorrow at school assembly when the principal makes the announcement, the person who gave them the keys will be there and he or she will be shaking his or her head and crying krokodil trane, and saying what I'm saying now: that the bastards should be shot.

MNCEDISI: Almost to the end of high school I still didn't really know how to read English. I had the basics but I didn't have the patience to start and finish a book. I mean, school was damn boring. I wasn't in the Struggle then so there wasn't anything else to do except skip class and hide in the toilets and smoke zol. Now we weren't given real toilet paper, just scraps of old newspaper. So to pass the time I used to sit there and read the toilet paper, I mean the newspaper. And that's how I got into it – I got into reading the shit.

STANTON: Wragtig, liefie? Just look at us. Whatever he's become, he did some good work at that time. God, he was thin. And he had quite a scar under his bottom lip. Old knife wound. Bloody lucky not to have had his whole jaw sliced. Not that he was the violent type. But why I am saying this? Maybe because Julius was always a fierce arguer, the type of person who once he started a discussion was never going to leave you the last word. Though I must say he backed up what he said with some solid reading. We understood what we were fighting for. [*Slight pause.*] Speaking of which, I made an avocado salad this afternoon with onion. You spice it with a touch of mayonnaise, lemon, salt and pepper. I sometimes cut in a boiled egg though today I didn't. When we three lived together we also ate a lot of pilchards. Julius liked them in chilli tomato sauce, I liked the plain, so there had to be a compromise. At first, neither of us was very happy. But after a while we found the blend so tasty we didn't want it any other way. [*Slight pause.*] Can it still work today?

CORNELIA: That's a good question. [*Takes a journal out of her bag.*] Listen to this. It's from someone's journal. [*Starts reading.*] "I want a world of open borders, of open minds, of horizons that are never clouded. I want to be able to eat biltong in Beijing and sushi in Somalia, mopane worms in Mumbai and lasagne in Lagos. I want to walk alone at night and feel no fear. I want to choose any path and try it without being told I'm too weak or brainless or don't have the right. I want love to be the natural expression of the soul and not an emotion for sale. And I want what I want for everyone." [*Slight pause.*] Quite a mouthful, hey? Almost religious. And does it matter who wrote it? Is the writer's age important? Do we only reach understanding of the world after a lifetime of experience? Well, let me tell you, it was a sixteen year old girl who wrote this passage. And it wasn't for a competition, it wasn't an assignment. It was an ideal, a pledge made to herself. Now has she achieved this? Has she remained true to her vision? You'll have a chance to answer that question this evening because that girl was . . . [*Smiles.*]

The song, No VIPs, plays. CORNELIA dances. Black out. Music fades. They all exit.

ACT 2

VISH enters. Using his smart-phone as a torch, he walks around, examining the pot plants.

STANTON: [OFF.] I won't be long, Vish. Make yourself at home.

VISH: [*In a loud voice which is sustained every time he answers STANTON.*] Don't worry, pal. I'll find the perfect spot. [*Takes off his jacket.*] Hell, you've always been cheap. I've brought my own booze. [*Takes out a hip flask and swigs. Starts walking around again examining the plants.*] You know, I'm a great admirer of this type of grill work, the little side corners, the mass of plants.

STANTON: [OFF.] But, darling, that's because it isn't a *veranda*. [*Sticks his head out.*] It's a high class *patio*.

VISH: *Patio?* No, man, it's a good old *South Effrican* stoep which looks out onto the last dagga plantation of a doomed white man.

STANTON: [*Half his body visible. Wears a head torch.*] Are you sure you want coffee? Not a beer.

VISH: Black coffee. Strong. And bring some candles.

STANTON: Ok. [*Withdraws off stage.*] This last week we've been load-shed three times. [*Enters. Places a tray with the coffee and some other drinks on the table.*] Here we are. I hope there's enough sugar. [*VISH opens the hip flask and pours into the coffee.*] Ooh, stylish! That flask must have cost a packet.

VISH: It did. As to what's in it, I don't stint either.

STANTON: Nonsense– since when do churrahs drink *expensive* whiskey?

VISH: We have to thank the bloody Brits for this most excellent habit. [*In a 'posh' English accent.*] On the other hand, when it comes to genius, we lot came up with something even more important – the world's first, most exact and most comprehensive . . . sex manual . . . le *karma sutra*.

STANTON: If you spent half the money you throw at women on shrinks, maybe you'd get somewhere. [*Rising.*] Let's face it, Vish, you're a very *horny* and very *pushy* dealer who underneath it all is still fucking BC.

VISH: You want the truth? [*Shakes his head.*] The first two – it's not happening like it used to, my brother. As for the BC label, I'll leave that to Julius.

STANTON: Julius? He wasn't that hard core.

VISH: [*Slight pause.*] To be honest, I'm not sure I'm looking forward to seeing him again. He was a real bull-shitter, always looking for the limelight.

The lights come on.

STANTON: Hallelujah! But isn't that the way to become a successful brand? [*Sits again.*] No, he was committed.

VISH: [*Sips his coffee. Makes a face.*] Shit, where's the sugar? [*Starts to rise.*]

STANTON: On the side board. [*VISH exits.*] He was better than me at most things.

VISH: [OFF.] True.

STANTON: And from the sound of it he's still a reader. And to prove it, when I spoke to him on the phone about the book club, he said he's long had enough of his *slave* name. He now insists on being called *Mnce…Mn…Mn…* [*Mangles the correct isiXhosa pronounciation.*] … Damn, I just can't get it.

VISH: [*Enters.*] Hey, shape up, bru. It's *Mncedisi* [*Uses the correct pronounciation.*] But he was so proud to be called after Nyerere. Slave name or not, to me he'll always be Julius. [*Sits.*] I bet he's in one of those *really* small Africanist groups that's constantly splitting.

STANTON: He mustn't bring that nonsense into my house. [*Drains his beer.*] Ag, don't ride him too hard. He's apparently running some quite successful Youth Fund, one of those private/public job creation projects.

VISH: And no doubt also gives *motivational* courses.

STANTON: Don't be so cynical.

VISH: Why not? It's just *identity* politics. NGO's sponging off guilt-ridden funders. [*Stands. Looks at his smart-phone.*] What! Nine o'clock! Where the hell are they, comrade? What's up with your miserable list of *bookworms*? [*Yawns. Takes another hit from the hip flask.*] I'm getting bored and dozy.

STANTON: That's what comes from potting since you've arrived. And, if I'm not mistaken, potting *before* you arrived. [*Standing.*] Let me put something in your stomach before you pass out. [*He takes out his cellphone to check a message.*] Now, who's this from? [*Exits. OFF*] Oh, no! He may not make it!

VISH: What's that?

STANTON: [OFF.] Julius! He's in a meeting. He may not make it.

VISH: I'll guarantee it's not *work* that's holding him up. [*Begins to walk around examining the plants.*]

STANTON: [OFF.] Can't hear you.

VISH: He can't make it because he's busy trying to pick up some juicy under-age *number*.

STANTON: [OFF.] Ha, ha. Who doesn't want to enjoy fruit with firm flesh? [*Returns with a bowl.*] Here some nuts to nibble. The *real* snacks are in the oven. I never put samooses in the microwave. They get soggy. [*Sits.*] It's been lekker to see you these last few months.

VISH: Enjoy it while it lasts, brother.

STANTON: Now give me one of your famous back rubs. The memory of the bliss they leave is indelibly indented in my shoulder blades. [*Squats down next to Vish. Indicates his back.*] Come on, just here. Dig those fingers deep.

VISH: [*Touching STANTON'S shoulders.*] Hell, you *are* tense. [*Starts massaging his back.*] But you've always been a manic type.

STANTON: Ouch! Don't rub it in. Not so hard!

VISH: [*In an Afrikaans accent.*] Of course, not! Ons sal things nice and soft let bly. Won't we, skatie? [*Continues massaging.*] You'd think you wouldn't have to deal with much stress in that cushy job of yours.

STANTON: Cushy?

VISH: Didn't the government spend thirty-four fucking billion rand on consultants?

STANTON: Not all on me!

VISH: Come on – you got your fair share, right? [*Stops massaging. Looks at his cellphone.*] Yo, I've got to split. I really must. [*Slight pause.*] Business, pal.

STANTON: Don't talk nonsense.

VISH: 'Strues God.

STANTON: What business?

VISH: With some guy . . . from Saudi.

STANTON: A bloody *Saudi prince* . . .

VISH: Just because they're homophobic, misogynistic, corrupt, hypocrite bastards doesn't mean . . .

STANTON: [*In an Afrikaans accent.*] You can't do business with these people.

VISH: I really must leave.

STANTON: But everyone's on their way. [*Slight pause.*] Except for . . . Cornelia. She was supposed to be a surprise. But she'll come to the next one.

VISH: Who the hell is Cornelia?

STANTON: Ah, she's . . . Nettie's daughter.

VISH: Nettie? Nettie Hendricks! I don't believe it!

STANTON: She's a teacher, history *and* science, and very dedicated.

VISH: Tell me more about Nettie.

STANTON: I know as much as you do. I met Cornelia by chance.

VISH: Well, if she's anything like Nettie I hope she'll give me a chance. Ha, ha.

STANTON: [*Laughing.*] From what I've seen she's just a little bit too independent for the likes of Vish Naidoo.

VISH: [*Slight pause.*] Who else is supposed to be coming?

STANTON: Just relax. There are quite a few people . . .

VISH: And the few are few and far between. [*Takes another shot from his hip-flask. Puts on his jacket.*] No, man, I've done my time on *colonial* patios.

STANTON: [*Holds out his hand to VISH.*] Please, Vish, just another half an hour. I suppose I could have organised it a bit better but, you know how . . .

VISH: You've always been *totally* fucking deurmekaar.

STANTON: See your Saudi tomorrow! How's the flask doing? I'll bring some Red Label. Just sit down and chill. [*His cellphone rings.*] At last! And *I'll bet* this is . . . yes, it's got to be . . . [*Answering the phone.*] Julius! [*Slight pause.*] Julius, is that you? [*Shocked.*] Cornelia! [*Slight pause.*] No, just surprised. I'm *really* sorry you can't make it. We're having such a lovely . . . [*Slight pause.*] No, no, you're not too late.

VISH: [*Calling out.*] Come on in, baby. Come rollin' in.

STANTON: [*To CORNELIA.*] Yes, things *are* getting a little rowdy. [*Slight pause.*] You're five minutes away! That's wonderful! [*To VISH.*] You see! I knew things were going to pick up. [*To CORNELIA.*] I'm so excited! See you now-now. [*To VISH.*] Let me check on those snacks. [*Exits.*]

VISH: Jesus. Nettie's daughter . [*In a self-mocking voice.*] No, we're *not* drunk and we're *not* high. [*Blackout.*] Oh, damn! Not again! [*Calls out.*] Hey, Stannie, don't forget to bring candles. [*Phone rings. Answers.*] Hello, hello . . . [*Slight pause.*] Ah, Mr Feisal! I was just about to phone you. I've got good news. My other appointment's already over. [*Slight pause.*] I can be with you in twenty minutes. [*Very disappointed.*] Oh, I see. [*Slight pause.*] I'm sorry to hear that.

STANTON: [*Running in.*] God, I'm so please she's made it, and you won't believe it . . .

VISH: [*Gesticulates to STANTON to keep quiet.*] Sorry, say that again Mr Feisal . . .

STANTON: Julius has just phoned. He's also . . . on the way.

VISH: [*Still on the phone.*] But it won't take long. There just a few things to wrap up. Can we not possibly . . .

STANTON: Did you hear me?

VISH: [*Covers the phone. To STANTON.*] Shut the fuck up! [*Waves STANTON away.*] Not at all? [*STANTON exits.*] Not even for half an hour? [*Slight pause.*] You leave first thing in the morning? [*Slight pause.*] You really don't have any . . . [*Slight pause.*] It's been a pleasure. I understand, Mr Feisal. I understand. [*Slight pause.*] Yes, have a safe trip. [*Puts the phone back in his pocket.*] Have a safe fucking trip.

STANTON: [*Enters with a tray of snacks. Puts them down. The lights come on.*] Thank God!

VISH: Don't you know when to shut up? Fuck you, Stanton! If I hadn't come here first I could have met him earlier and sealed the deal. [*Slight pause.*] He's going back to Saudi tonight.

STANTON: [*Puts an arm round VISH.*] Don't give up, man! Drive out to the airport. Make a bloody commotion.

VISH: [*Mockingly.*] In front of the twenty armed guards doing laps round his private jet. [*Slight pause.*] Actually, he did sound quite . . . stressed.

STANTON: I'm sorry, Vish. [*Puts an arm round him.*] Could it be that . . . his favourite wife's escaped the harem and he's personally taking charge of the search. But as we speak, Princess Fatima, dressed in a zebra skin bikini is about to join Sheikh Feisal's half-brother in his palace on the Island of Jozi . . .

CORNELIA: [*Enters.*] Hello!

STANTON: And here she is!

CORNELIA: So sorry I'm late but I had a mountain of marking, it was crazy.

STANTON: Say no more, my darling! You're here – that's all that counts [*Kisses her.*] This is absolutely historic! But how rude of me! Cornelia, Vish, my old buddy, Vish. Your mom also . . .

CORNELIA: Yes, I've heard a lot about you.

VISH: You have? From Stannie? [*Takes off his jacket.*]

CORNELIA: No, from my . . .

STANTON: Vish knows lots about your mom. We were just talking about her.

VISH: Nettie – what a woman! [*Stands up, extends a hand.*] Lovely to meet you. You're her spitting image.

CORNELIA: [*She thrusts a bottle of wine into his hand – giving the impression that she doesn't want to make physical contact with him. STANTON takes her bag. Sits her down.*] Oh, thanks. [*To VISH.*] My mom says that apart from your *Struggle* reputation you have an artistic side. And in recruiting me, *Oom* Stanton told me you're very well read.

VISH: No, not at all. Oom Stannie is the big reader. I concentrate on other things. But . . . God, your mom was a beauty . . . how come you're here?

CORNELIA: Why? You think I'm not up to your intellectual standard?

VISH: It's just that Stannie told me you'd cancelled.

CORNELIA: What nonsense! I've been looking forward to this evening the whole month.

STANTON: [*Light-heartedly.*] Liar! You said you couldn't make it tonight. But then you swore on your *Maiden's Honour* you'd make the next one.

CORNELIA: Oh, I've had to swear on *other* things for quite a while now.

VISH: Wonderful how the apple doesn't fall far from the tree.

STANTON: Hey, Vishnu, behave.

VISH: [*To CORNELIA.*] But don't worry, my dear. I'll protect you from myself *by myself*.

CORNELIA: Why, thank you Mr Naidoo. It's lucky I do a good job all on my own. Anyway, here I am and I've got these *amazing* books to tell you about. [*To

STANTON.] You said two very different books, right? And never the twain shall meet ... though of course they usually do in one way or another.

VISH: That sounds too much like *reconciliation*.

CORNELIA: Don't worry. I'll give you in depth *contestation* if that's what you want.

VISH: With or without agendas?

CORNELIA: [*Pointing at STANTON.*] Well, our host here is setting the agenda and from what he's told me he's a believer in the psychological interpretation of history, or should I say *herstory*. People *always* have agendas.

STANTON: Exactly. Strip away the rhetoric and what do you find?

CORNELIA: Men fighting over the biggest bone and ... *the sexiest bitch*?

VISH: Oh, very insightful for one so young.

STANTON: [*Laughs.*] You should publish a collection of wise sayings.

VISH: Wait a minute – getting published isn't be an easy thing. It's hard work to entice a complete stranger to fork out thousands to put your genius onto the market.

CORNELIA: [*Sarcastically.*] Is that what stopped you?

STANTON: Oh, no. Monsieur Naidoo here, as you know, is an authentic if *self*-published author who has never compromised his ideal of writing books for people who never read books.

CORNELIA: [*To VISH.*] What did you publish?

STANTON: Don't be modest, Vish. You've published two collections.

CORNELIA: But that's cool.

STANTON: It was ... very *cool*. That is – the reception.

CORNELIA: And what were the poems about?

VISH: That long distant time before the ink dried on the arms deal ... and a few other ... minor Mzansi 'wink-winks'.

CORNELIA: Meaning?

VISH: Forget it. I really am embarrassed.

CORNELIA: Were they that bad?

STANTON: No, they were very eloquent celebrations of the revolution ... -to-be.

CORNELIA: And Madiba was the hero or the sell out?

VISH: [*Crossing himself.*] Saint Nelson, Father of the Fading Rainbow. Together with quite a few real *kommunists*, 'blink-blink'. And other banker gangsters. As for how they got away with the sell-out, well, there are very clear explanations.

CORNELIA: And that's why you've stopped working together and have . . .

STANTON: Yes, moved on and now recognise that . . .

CORNELIA: Only the rich have any brains and that the *bigger* the wage gap the more advanced a country is. What would we youngsters do without such penetrating analyses?

STANTON: Ja, we have failed you.

VISH: Go to hell, I've haven't failed nobody.

STANTON: We've fucked up, Vish. We all know the country's in trouble.

VISH: Well, here's more trouble! [*Holds his empty glass upside down.*] This here is too damn empty. Mister *Betrayal* wants more damn *fire* water.

STANTON: [*Fake posh English accent.*] A double, on the double, sir! But any refill on my part won't be up to the standard of your usual spirits. [*Fills his glass.*]

CORNELIA: [*To VISH.*] From here you smell of home brew.

VISH: Don't be too *clever*, my darling. In a short while we'll see how you handle someone who's a hundred percent proof. He's classy. His name is . . .

CORNELIA: *Julius* . . .

VISH: [*Picks up a glass from the table.*] To *Julius*!

Blackout.

STANTON: Oh, fuck, not again. [*Starts Singing.*] "We love you, Eishkom, oh yes we do . . . we love you, Eishkom, we're black and blue . . ." [*Exits.*]

CORNELIA: [*Switches on her cellphone torch. Shines it in his face interrogation style.*] Why do you disown your poems?

VISH: I don't disown them – they disowned *me*.

CORNELIA: Because you got married and had a family and had to get some *standards*?

VISH: My ex certainly wanted *standards*. She insisted on leaving Yeoville. What could I do?

CORNELIA: Beat her. Bribe her.

VISH: Believe me I tried. I doubled her plastic surgery allowance.

STANTON: [*Entering with a lit candle on a tray and several others candles ready to be lit.*] Sorry about that. I couldn't find all the candle holders but a boer will make a plan.

CORNELIA: Let me help. Only a *klonkie* can get the *boer's plan* to work.

STANTON: No, don't worry. I always find the right place in the dark. [*Sniggers. Starts setting the candles up around the patio. CORNELIA walks behind him and lights them.*] And how did the two of *you* pass the time?

CORNELIA: We were talking about how men get rid of unwanted *wives*. Or should I say . . . *side-chicks*

VISH: You get the nyaope boys to do that shit.

STANTON: Nyaope? What do you know about the neighbourhood favourite? Wait a sec, I can smell burning! [*Exits.*]

VISH: Where do you live?

CORNELIA: In Riverlea.

VISH: With your family?

CORNELIA: With my mom and her sister.

VISH: You're not married?

CORNELIA: No.

VISH: Why not?

CORNELIA: There must be about two thousand reasons.

VISH: So you're not looking for a boy-friend?

CORNELIA: No. I'm not looking for a *boy*-friend.

VISH: Are you looking for a *girl-friend*?

CORNELIA: No, I'm not looking for a *girl*-friend.

VISH: Then what the hell are you looking for?

STANTON: [OFF] For God's sake, give the lady a break, Vish.

VISH: Why, she's enjoying this. [*To CORNELIA.*] And no kids, I take it.

CORNELIA: [*Shakes her head.*] I have more than enough of them in the classroom.

VISH: Ok, forget the kids. But let's talk about your mom. She was a lovely woman.

CORNELIA: She still is.

VISH: I'm sure she hasn't forgotten.

CORNELIA: What you did to her?

VISH: Of course not! I treated her very, very well.

CORNELIA: Like you do everyone.

Lights come on.

STANTON: [*Enters with some eats.*] Looks like it's going to be one of those bloody nights. [*Fusses, arranging the bowls.*] Riverlea! God, I haven't been there in years.

VISH: [*To CORNELIA.*] Has the grand *liberation* changed your lives?

CORNELIA: You really want to know? [*Slight pause.*] There have been some changes. Some new housing, a new school, more tarred roads, there's a new light industrial zone nearby so there a few more jobs ...

VISH: But mostly there's the usual stuff. You know, like ... eh. ... child *abuse*, drug *abuse*, alcohol *abuse*, dog *abuse*, plant *abuse* ...

STANTON's phone rings.

STANTON: [*Answering the phone.*] Hello. Julius? Hello. [*Slight pause.*] Wrong number. I wonder where he is. [*Puts the phone back in his pocket.*] But let me get the cocktail sausages before you burn the house down.

VISH: Wait! Quick question. [*To CORNELIA.*] Do you eat pork sausages?

CORNELIA: No.

VISH: I thought so. Your mom wasn't very observant. But she did keep halaal.

CORNELIA: We still do.

VISH: Good. I don't touch pork myself. [*Slight pause.*] And what about your dad?

CORNELIA: I don't know.

VISH: You don't know what?

CORNELIA: If he liked pork cocktail sausages.

VISH: Why? Did he leave before you were born? But of course you've met him since?

CORNELIA: No ...

STANTON: [*Laughs.*] For real?

VISH: [*Sniggering.*] Do you know who he was?

CORNELIA: [*Sarcastically.*] Is it important?

STANTON: Didn't your mom tell you?

CORNELIA: [*Sarcastically.*] She just *found* herself pregnant. As you well know, she was a little *wild* at a certain point.

STANTON: But ... she was a very valuable comrade.

CORNELIA: [*Cuttingly.*] Yes, someone had to make food for the heroes and provide comfort when nights were cold.

VISH: But she wasn't a mattress, sweetie. No, no, not Nettie. She was a ... blanket, a nice warm blanket.

STANTON: Jesus, Vish!

VISH: [*Drunkenly.*] 'Cause you know what, sweetie, we had a serious fucking system to overthrow and your mom seemed quite happy with her contribution. [*Walks towards her.*] My, my, you've got her forehead. And maybe her hips ... [*Tries to touch her hips.*]

CORNELIA: How dare you!

VISH: You've definitely got her chin. Ja. Fortress chin with the faintest hint of her dimple. As a matter of fact ... [*Opens his arms as if to hug her. She pushes him away.*] Wait, this is stupid. Let's not fight. This is really an occasion. Why've I been so rude?

CORNELIA: Because this is your normal way of behaviour.

STANTON: [*Slaps VISH on the back.*] Especially after a few ... [*Makes as if he is downing a drink.*]

VISH: [*To CORNELIA.*] What's she doing these days? I must get in touch.

CORNELIA: I wonder what's kept you away for twenty-five years.

STANTON: Whoa, comrades! Cease fire! [*To CORNELIA.*] Forgive him, my darling. Just see this as an *initiation*.

CORNELIA: [*To VISH.*] Keep your hands to yourself.

VISH: Hey, I said I'm sorry. Now get the halaal eats, Stannie. My stomach is voicing its utmost concern. [*Looks at his watch.*] And no wonder – it's already fucking ten o'clock. And bring another bottle. No water, no rocks. Just fucking straight.

STANTON: As always, sahib. Only the bent can procure. [*Bows. To Cornelia, in a staged whisper.*] Don't worry. He'll get no more booze from me tonight. [*His phone rings. He answers.*] Julius? [*Slight pause.*] Oh, my God, at last! I'll buzz you in. [*Whispers theatrically to VISH and CORNELIA.*] Isn't this amazing! He's here! [*Pushes CORNELIA down on her seat.*] Let me go get him. [*Exits.*]

CORNELIA: [*Slight pause.*] I'll give you one more chance.

VISH: [*Bows.*] Best behaviour. [*Smiling.*] You haven't known Stanton long, right?

CORNELIA: Just a few weeks.

VISH: Where did you meet?

CORNELIA: Where else but in a bookshop.

VISH: In the kiddies section.

CORNELIA: No, it was the *drama* . . .

STANTON: [*Running in.*] Oh, my God, there's blood all over his shirt!

VISH: Blood?

STANTON: All over his shirt. He ran in like a madman. He's in the bathroom.

CORNELIA: Does he need help?

STANTON: I don't know. He wouldn't let me get close.

MNCEDISI: [*Shouts.*] This country is totally insane! [*Entering.*] Hello! Hello, every-one! Greetings! [*Bows and starts declaiming.*]

Another day in RSA
eat your pap and eat your cake
it's make or break
secure your stake in RSA
shoot first, that's the safest way
or criminals will make you pay
it's old and new taking what they think's their due
the colour's green no matter the dream
take it quick and take it neat
be the Chivas guy on your street

that's the way we play
that's the way the very cool play in RSA
[They all clap.]

STANTON: *[Imitating MNCEDISI.]* "From the moment I woke up I knew there was going to be hell to pay."

CORNELIA: That was wonderful. Did you write it yourself?

VISH: Him! You want to hear a real poem, listen to this. *[Starts declaiming in an exaggerated manner.]* "*They came from the West sailing to the East with hatred and disease flowing from their flesh and a burden to harden our lives. They claimed to be friends when they found us friendly, and when foreigner met foreigner they fought for the reign, exploiters of Africa.*"

CORNELIA: Not even a clown can destroy a classic.

VISH: Hey, lady, I told you to watch that little tongue of yours.

STANTON: Peace, peace! You're all magnificent! *[Trying to embrace MNCEDISI.]* Give me a hug. But . . . what the hell happened? Let me get you another shirt.

MNCEDISI: No, not yet, Stannie. Let me first see who's here. *[To VISH.]* Well, I'll be damned, the all-powerful one who cools the hottest curry with his whisky breath. *[Holds out his hand.]* Looking good, my friend. Not too much flab.

VISH: *[Taking his hand.]* Ja, keeping fit.

MNCEDISI: Fit for what? Fit for what? *[Continues pumping VISH's hand aggressively.]*

CORNELIA: *[To the audience.]* Mister Naidoo, as I've heard from his very own mouth, is very, very fit. And he keeps so fit just by wagging his tongue. *[Laughs.]* He's been telling me all about survival in the jungle. Especially how to survive bee stings. As in B.E.E.

MNCEDISI: And you don't support that idea?

CORNELIA: How could I? I'm Nettie Hendrick's daughter.

MNCEDISI: Nettie's daughter! How's your mama? I hope she's still a comrade.

CORNELIA: We fight a bit about that. I know she did a lot in the day but right now it's not enough to just have opinions. Ag, and I don't want to change the subject but seeing you're all here now, and I don't want to be rude, but from what I've heard, your famous NGO fell apart. Was that because of a lack of commitment? Or did you run out of money?

STANTON: A bit of both. Everything was changing.

MNCEDISI: The door we opened was shut in our faces.

CORNELIA: I heard *Comrade* Slovo, in his wisdom, was one of the gatekeepers. But he wasn't alone, hey. There plenty more of them to keep up the tradition. Take *Msholozi* – is he a comrade *enemy* or an enemy *comrade*?

VISH: [*TO MNCEDISI.*] Never mind him. You're the one who always want to make an impression.

MNCEDISI: So these are . . . [*Points to the bloody marks on his shirt.*] . . . just for show?

VISH: No, no, man. I'm referring to your *poem*, Julius. You're dead bloody right. RSA. It's either the 'bullet or the bribe'. And that shirt of yours – it's the blood of workers making a red flag. [*To CORNELIA.*] You see, he's just come from moering a bunch of scabs. It was on CNN. Our bra here is going viral.

MNCEDISI: You've got quite a reputation yourself.

STANTON: For what?

MNCEDISI: Oh, you know, a bit of this and bit of that . . . [*To STANTON.*] And you aren't far behind.

STANTON: Seriously, Julius, what happened? Let me get you a clean shirt. [*Is about to exit.*]

MNCEDISI: Wait, don't go. You'll enjoy this story. [*Slight pause.*] Like I'm coming off the highway at Empire Rd . . . and this fucking idiot tailgates me all the way to the robots. There's a red light. I stop. He pulls up next to me and starts shouting that I cut him off, you know, like I was switching lanes and almost forced him off the road. And then . . . before I know it, he's at my window, and he's got a fucking iron pipe in his hand, a fucking metre long iron pipe and he's swinging it around, screaming he's going to kill to me.

STANTON: Jesus!

MNCEDISI: [*Shouts out in a thick Boere accent.*] "I'll teach you a lesson, you foking baboon! Where did you buy your licence? Go back to your foking township and stay there till you learn how to drive!"

VISH: You sure you didn't cut him off?

MNCEDISI: I didn't see this guy until he was up my arse on the off ramp.

VISH: Maybe he was in your blind spot?

MNCEDISI: You think I'm making this up?

VISH: It's just that I remember how shit a driver you used to be. [*To CORNELIA.*] Like that time he went to Kimberley and he had more than one *regmaker* for breakfast and . . . [*To MNCEDISI.*] . . . you almost rolled the car at fucking ten in the morning.

STANTON: Cool it, Vish! This sounds serious.

CORNELIA: Yes, it certainly does.

MNCEDISI: He nearly took my head off!

VISH: Maybe he was drunk.

MNCEDISI: Does that excuse him?

VISH: If it was a state of *diminished responsibility* then . . .

CORNELIA: Quiet! Let him finish.

MNCEDISI: If I hadn't put my foot down he would have killed me.

VISH: Did you go through a red light?

MNCEDISI: I would have gone through anything.

STANTON: [*Embracing MNCEDISI.*] Thank God you're ok.

MNCEDISI: I don't remember seeing the guy at all.

VISH: What do you expect when you're wearing shades at night?

CORNELIA: God, stop making light of this.

MNCEDISI: [*Laughing.*] Get me a whiskey, Stan.

STANTON: Now we talking! Don't let crazies knock you off your stride.

MNCEDISI: Pour the whole bottle, boertjie. Pay your fucking reparations. [*Slight pause.*] Luckily after he smashed the mirror a few people started shouting at him.

CORNELIA: Only shouting? No one came to help you?

MNCEDISI: Actually one guy got out of his car and ran towards him.

VISH: I thought you said you pulled off straight after the mirror was smashed?

MNCEDISI: I did.

VISH: Then how do you know another guy got out of his car?

MNCEDISI: I saw him just as I was pulling off.

VISH: So just before you decided to burn your tires, you casually checked out the scene.

MNCEDISI: What are you getting at?

VISH: Nothing, just that by getting out, the dude confused the Boer so you could get away.

MNCEDISI: And suppose he did?

VISH: *Suppose, suppose* . . . he fucking saved you, bro.

STANTON: Hey, Vish what's the point of all this?

MNCEDISI: The main thing was that I got out of there.

CORNELIA: And not a moment too soon.

VISH: I hope your rescuer was another *wit ou*.

STANTON: [*Loudly.*] Enough! Comrades, where are your books? Let me make some room on this table.

VISH: Don't distract us from our *contestation* over a little *situation*. [*To MNCEDISI.*] *Umlungu saves darkie from umlungu.*

STANTON: Here are mine. [*He places two books on the table. To VISH.*] Hey, where yours? We've got work to do.

VISH: It's hard labour finding the potjie at the end of the rainbow. [*Takes two books out of his jacket pockets. Waves them in the air. Lays them on the table. To MNCEDISI.*] And where are *your* books, bro? Did you manage to bring something other than your usual *"Wretched of the Earth"*?

MNCEDISI: Back off, Vishnu. Otherwise there'll be more blood on my shirt.

VISH: Yours or mine?

STANTON: Oh, come on, guys! [*Putting an arm round MNCEDISI.*] You really can't sit here like that. [*Points to his shirt. Starts to exit.*] I'll fetch you something. Then we'll start. [*Exits.*]

VISH: [*To CORNELIA.*] And you, Cornelia. What are you reading?

CORNELIA: [*Very cool and ironic.*] I'm also reading *"Wretched of the Earth."*

Blackout – strobe effect for just a few seconds.

VISH: Ah! Just what we need – a power surge!

STANTON: [*Running in.*] Here you are! Nice and fresh and chosen with care. [*Dis-*

plays the t-shirt; it bears Bob Marley's face.] Your poem wasn't quite rasta but I if I remember you loved the man's music. [*Hands MNCEDISI the T-shirt. Clears his throat.*] Comrades . . .

CORNELIA: God, how you love the word!

STANTON: How I love the word . . . As you know I've wanted to get this off the ground for quite a while and it's overwhelming that it's finally happening. And by way of opening, I'd like to raise a few observations that came to me while I was reading a fabulous novel, a relatively old one, as it is. Well, I picked it *up* and I must say I haven't put it *down* for the past three days. It's . . . well . . . *'Picture This'*. [*Holds up the book.*] By Joseph Heller – you know the guy who wrote 'Catch 22'. Well, this one's about Rembrandt painting Aristotle while Aristotle's contemplating a bust of Homer. And all the while he reminisces about Plato talking about Socrates.

CORNELIA: Socrates was put to death, right?

STANTON: Ja, for corrupting the youth.

CORNELIA: [*To the audience.*] And they were right – it *is* corrupting to teach the young to think for themselves.

VISH: But they were reasonable in those days. They didn't necklace him. They gave him the choice of exile.

MNCEDISI: That's where you should go, my brother.

CORNELIA: A nice long *lekker* exile . . . maybe in . . . *Orania*?

STANTON: Listen! "Socrates did not like books, something that should have upset Plato who wrote so many. And he had a low regard for people who read them. He mistrusted books because, as he said, they neither ask nor answer questions and are apt to be swallowed whole. He said that readers of books read much and learn nothing, that they appear full of knowledge, but for the most part are without it, and have the show of wisdom without its reality."

MNCEDISI: [*To VISH.*] Vish, that shouldn't bother you. You don't read. You never used to.

VISH: And you, *my bra*? You're were so busy reading you forgot how to fight back? Why did you just drive off?

CORNELIA: You expect him to take a chance with a drunken Boer?

VISH: I don't remember him saying the guy was drunk.

CORNELIA: They usually are.

STANTON: [To CORNELIA.] Don't get Vish wrong. Mr Action *walks the talk*.

MNCEDISI: [To VISH. Sneering.] Yeah, like in *those days*. [To STANTON.] And you? What are *you* doing that's so *involved*?

STANTON: I didn't say I was involved.

MNCEDISI: Of course you aren't. How can you be? You always have it easy.

STANTON: What do you mean?

MNCEDISI: Even in detention. But I can't blame you, can I?

VISH: No, you can't blame him. This . . . [Rubs STANTON's arm, referencing his white skin.] . . . gives them better chow, clean clothes and less of the *nasty stuff*. [Grabs his throat and pretends to be hitting himself.]

MNCEDISI: [To STANTON.] You got out after only one week. How did you manage that?

STANTON: I didn't decide when to release myself.

MNCEDISI: Why was I stuck in that shithole for almost three months?

STANTON: How am I supposed to know?

MNCEDISI: You're all hypocrites.

STANTON: This is unfair. I did what I could. I want to be free of all the kak as much as you.

VISH: Then learn *isiXhosa*, man. No, learn *Sepedi*, it's much easier. Yeah, Sepedi, man, that's one helleva language. But what about *Swahili*? Jumbo! Even the fucking Black Panthers were learning Swahili. Why don't you be cool?

CORNELIA: Can I answer for him?

STANTON: That's not allowed.

CORNELIA: Why not?

VISH: [In a mocking voice.] I suppose with your *psychological* training, you know this moffie better than he knows himself. [Blows her a kiss.] Our little Ms Socrates.

CORNELIA: [To VISH.] I don't envy you.

VISH: [Points at STANTON.] Don't envy him either, sweetheart. [Points at MNCEDISI.] Or him.

MNCEDISI: There you are being Vishnu again. [*Looks suggestively at CORNELIA.*] Life's worth living so long there's an *Angela Davis* around. Let's drink to a beautiful black sistah. [*Knocks back a shot.*]

VISH: Yeah, let's get down to *basics*.

CORNELIA: [*To MNCEDISI.*] You also want to get down to *basics*?

MNCEDISI: And why not? Let me tell you another story. [*Dramatically.*] It was hot like tonight. We'd been drinking. I fell asleep in my bedroom. I woke up. It was dark. [*Redout.*] I just felt this hand moving up and down my body. It was so relaxing, I felt myself getting all . . . I closed my eyes then I felt a hand taking mine, and then I was touching something, this hard thing, and just before I . . . I realised I was fucking holding a stiff bloody cock in my hand and the man next to me was holding mine and it was . . . just . . . I felt so . . . [*Slight pause.*] And then I remembered who I was with, who had been with me in my bedroom before I'd gone to sleep. [*Lights.*] It was . . . .

VISH: [*Looks from MNCEDISI to STANTON.*] I knew there was something going on between the two of you.

MNCEDISI: I didn't let him near me again. [*To STANTON.*] Isn't that so?

STANTON: Stop talking nonsense, Julius. I never touched you.

VISH: You're lying.

STANTON: I did not.

MNCEDISI: Come now, *Stannie*, if you don't have your hands on the *levers*, you don't control production. And we blacks are here to give *everyone* pleasure. [*Turns to VISH.*] And you guys, you're getting rich like the Jews. You and your families.

VISH: Rich? My family?

MNCEDISI: And who else? Corrupt bastard.

STANTON: Leave this, Julius. This is totally unnecessary.

MNCEDISI: [*To VISH.*] You've come a long way from when me and Stannie found you in that pathetic clothes shop and gave you a *real* job . . . that you left.

VISH: Yes, I did. And you remember why?

MNCEDISI: What are you suggesting?

VISH: Anything on your *conscience*?

MNCEDISI: What would be on my *conscience*? [*Moves towards VISH.*] Shut up already!

STANTON: [*Coming between them.*] Please, guys! Please!

VISH: You aren't on the *winning* side of any government grants, are you now, my bra?

MNCEDISI: Why shouldn't I take government funding?

CORNELIA: [*To VISH.*] Don't *you* have dealings with government?

VISH: I didn't win any tenders.

CORNELIA: Because you're *Indian*?

VISH: No, because I wouldn't pay bribes.

MNCEDISI: Unlike Mr Shaik, and Mr Gupta and Mr Reddy and Mr . . .

STANTON: You serious, Vish? You wouldn't pay anyone?

VISH: No, I wouldn't.

CORNELIA: I'm sure he wouldn't.

MNCEDISI: [*To STANTON.*] Is that too good to be true?

STANTON: Oh, Vish has a hot deal going with a *Saudi* – not a *Zulu* prince.

CORNELIA: A big, fat deal. Could his name be . . . Khulubuse?

VISH: Damn, you, Stannie.

STANTON: Yes, Sheik Khulubuse. You hear that, Julius. I mean, *Minisi . . . minisi . . .*

MNCEDISI: Come on, say it.

VISH: Give him a break – he can't pronounce these fucking . . .

MNCEDISI: Well, the least he can do is give me another shot. [*Holds out his glass and STANTON pours.*] Fill it up, Mister Lazy Tongue. Or should I say, Mister Forked Tongue. [*Swallows the whiskey. Laughs.*] Good. One more kick for the road. One more fucking kick. You lahnies must wake up.

STANTON: Let me finish what I had to say about Plato.

MNCEDISI: Yeah, finish with those Greeks. Then I'll go fetch my books from the car.

VISH: Hope they don't include . . . [*Mockingly.*] . . . "*I write what I like*"?

MNCEDISI: No. It's I *mic* what I like. [*To STANTON.*] As for your Socrates, he had a lot of interesting things to say and a clever way of going about it – pity he was a slave owner like the rest of you.

STANTON: Small scale, bro, only two or three to help round the house.

MNCEDISI: Only a maid, a gardener, a trainee or two . . .

CORNELIA: [*Laughs.*] What do you expect? While half the country is telling baas to fuck off, the other half is begging him for a job.

STANTON: [*To audience.*] God, I'm so sorry. I didn't think it would turn out like this.

CORNELIA: There's nothing like perfecting the art of listening. So listen up! I'll guarantee none of you have read *my* first book though you've probably heard about its author. [*Holds up a book.*]

VISH: The Marquis de Sade? Quite tame stuff actually. Just a little whipping and cutting.

CORNELIA: Which he did to young women workers whom he kidnapped.

VISH: [*In a high-pitched voice.*] He and/or she who is about to sell his/her body should first do a security check before going off with a client.

STANTON: You're drunker than I thought, Vish.

VISH: What's the book called?

CORNELIA: Justine.

VISH: What a coincidence! That's my ex-wife's sister's name. She's certainly a whore.

CORNELIA: You know, I've waited a long time to meet you. I've heard so many stories. My mother really loved you. But what did you do with that love? You trashed it. And the stupid woman allowed you to walk all over her. No, you didn't blush. Even when you called it off and then after a few months demand- ed that she come back and *serve* you! Serve your screwed up ego, and your sexual . . .

VISH: Nonsense! I've never abused any woman. Least of all your mother.

MNCEDISI: [*Confronts VISH with a physically threatening gesture.*] Don't lie, Vishnu. You played games with Nettie. We all saw it.

VISH: Games? How many women did you dump with kids? [*Laughs nastily.*]

MNCEDISI: [*Grabs VISH.*] I'll give you something to really laugh about.

STANTON: No, stop. Stop! Please, leave him. He doesn't know what he's saying.

MNCEDISI: Nothing new about that. Make *him* stop!

CORNELIA: That's right – stop his nonsense.

MNCEDISI twists his arm.

STANTON: Don't hurt him!

CORNELIA: Why the hell not?

VISH: [*Shouting.*] Let go of me! Are we already like every other fucking African country?

CORNELIA: Don't make things worse!

VISH: Worse? I can't make it worse. [*Points at MNCEDISI.*] That's their job.

MNCEDISI: Now I'll really . . . [*Pushes Vish violently so he falls.*]

STANTON: [*Coming between them.*] Please, guys!

MNCEDISI: [*Putting his foot on VISH's chest.*] He must fuck off before I break his neck.

CORNELIA: [*To STANTON.*] Get him out of here. It's not just that he's drunk.

STANTON: It's the divorce. He's all bloody twisted . . .

VISH suddenly goes into a spasm at the end of which his head rolls to one side; his mouth remain half open.

STANTON: Oh, my God? [*Rushes to VISH.*] Vish! [*VISH doesn't respond.*] Vish! [*To MNCEDISI and CORNELIA.*] I'll get some water.

CORNELIA: He's too far gone. You won't sober him up.

STANTON: Vish! Can you stand? [*Struggling to lift him.*] Damn, you've caused enough trouble. [*To MNCEDISI and CORNELIA.*] I can't move him alone.

MNCEDISI: I'm not touching the bastard. Get him out of here.

CORNELIA: Yes, throw him out.

STANTON: I don't know how he could have . . . slipped up like this. [*Exits, dragging VISH along.*]

MNCEDISI: [*Shouts out.*] Another little *slip* of the tongue and I'll . . . [*Pause. To COR-NELIA.*] Let's get out of here. You want to go for a drink?

CORNELIA: Thanks but I've still got lots of marking to do.

MNCEDISI: This late?

CORNELIA: I take my kids seriously.

MNCEDISI: I'm just too wired. Come, a quick night cap.

CORNELIA: No, I'll pass. You're a dangerous bunch.

STANTON: [ENTERS.] I've never seen him like this before.

CORNELIA: Ja, it was a once-in-a-lifetime performance.

STANTON: It's just that he lost out on some mega deal tonight.

MNCEDISI: Is he in the shower?

STANTON: No, sleeping on the couch.

MNCEDISI: Why did you defend him?

STANTON: I didn't.

CORNELIA: Yes, you did.

STANTON: [To MNCEDISI.] Don't tell me you've ever seen him like this before. Not like this.

MNCEDISI: You're lucky I didn't sort him out earlier the way I klapped that Boer on the highway.

STANTON: You klapped the Boer?

MNCEDISI: Ja, I got back at that drunken bastard. It took just one shot and he was in no position to say another word.

CORNELIA: You shot him?

MNCEDISI: He got what he asked for. [Slight pause.] No, I didn't shoot him. Just fucking smashed him in the face. If they can't behave, we have to teach them a lesson.

STANTON: So that blood on your shirt was his – not yours?

CORNELIA: He didn't attack you?

MNCEDISI: What do you call cutting me off and calling me a kaffir?

STANTON: But he didn't actually hit you?

MNCEDISI: You should have heard the filth that came out of his mouth. Let him be too fucking scared to insult a black man again.

STANTON: But there could be a charge.

MNCEDISI: So what! Even the *whitest* judge will understand it was *self-defence*.

VISH: [*Runs in half naked; grabs MNCEDISI's hand and lifts it up.*] Bravo! Well done, my brother. That's the only language they understand. You did what you had to do. Amandla! [*Takes his hand.*] Man, I'm sorry about . . . I was *way* out of line but . . .

MNCEDISI: Get out of here.

VISH: Truly, bro, my apologies, big-big apologies. [*Bows, indicating humility.*] The last few months have been a nightmare.

CORNELIA: And you haven't woken up yet. [*To STANTON.*] I'm going to have to leave now. Got work to finish.

STANTON: But you will come again?

VISH: Yes, you must. I swear I won't . . . Hey, we've all taken strain. And those who claim to know better, don't always *act* better.

CORNELIA: Write a *better* script, Mr Naidoo.

MNCEDISI: [*To VISH.*] You looking for amnesty?

VISH: [*Pause.*] Kind of.

CORNELIA: [*To STANTON.*] If I come again will I find you sticking to your original agenda?

STANTON: What do you think, my darling? I just want to spend time with some intelligent people and a few of these . . . [*Lifts up a book.*] . . . and try and under-stand this current . . . *dispensation*. And like tonight, membership of Stanton de Villier's book club will be free though there may be a price. [*MNCEDISI and CORNELIA start exiting.*] Wait! Before you leave, I want to give you all something. [*Takes three book marks out of his pocket. Holding two of them in one hand, one in the other, waves them around.*] Here. Let them travel with you through *many* reads down many roads. [*Slight pause.*] For you. [*Offers one to CORNELIA. After some hesitation, she accepts it.*] And one for you . . . [*Offers one to MNCEDISI.*] . . . sir. [*MNCEDISI also hesitates but ultimately accepts.*] They were all done by an artist from Ghana. She lives next door. [*To VISH.*] And for you. [*Offers one to VISH who takes it with alacrity.*]

CORNELIA: [*To Vish.*] You'll certainly need one, *comrade*. You're lucky *oom* Stannie's the generous type. It's *so* easy to lose your place.

They all freeze. Fade as song "The Revolution Needs Revolutionaries" plays out.

END

Glossary

The Pump Room

The play is set in Cape Town. A good deal of the dialogue, particularly involving the Coloured characters, employs Afrikaans terms and expressions. The glossary essentially features their slang and colloquialisms. Afrikaans was once maligned as 'Kitchen Dutch' because it originated as the language of Khoisan and Malay slaves and indentured servants. It was only in 1929 that Afrikaans was recognised by the Union of South Africa (then dominated by English) as an official language.

Bangbroek – 'scaredy pants'

Bietjie – a little

Boep – paunch

Boertjie – little Boer (pejorative for Afrikaner)

Boeta – (slang) brother

Boom – dagga (marijuana)

Bossies – small bushes

Broederbonder – member of the Afrikaner secret society that controlled the Apartheid government

Broer – brother

Bushie – pejorative derived from "Bushman'; applied to Coloured people particularly of Khoisan origin

Dief – thief

Dik – thick (stupid)

Dof – deaf (stupid)

Dom – stupid

Domkop – dunderhead (idiot)

Donder – thunder (in this instance 'you dunderhead')

Doos – cunt

Dop – drink (alcohol)

Dorp – small town

Dronkgat – drunkard

Foking – fucking

Gemors – mess, chaos

Goeters – things (in this instance, drugs)

Groot bek – big mouth

Hardegat – stubborn

Hoer – whore

Hokkie – hole (tiny room)

Hotnot – pejorative for Khoi-Khoi people (derived from Hottentot)

Impimpi – (isiZulu) informer

Joint – marijuana cigarette

Joling – partying

Kak – shit

Klonkie – (pejorative) Coloured person

Koeksusters – traditional sweet pastry (in this instance an image for prostitutes – play on koek as cookie viz vagina)

Lekker – nice, lovely

Liefling – darling

Lus – lustfull (sexually 'worked up')

Maak oop – open up

Mal – mad

Mampara – fool, idiot

Mannetjie – (pejorative) small man

Meneer – mister

Mense – people

Moered – murdered

Moerse – (slang) massive

Naai – fuck

Nogal – and in addition (ironic)

Oom – uncle

Ouens/ous – people, guys

Piepie – penis

Pomping – fucking

Pondoks – shacks

Pop/poppie – doll

Skat – treasure (term of endearment)

Skeef – skew

Skeem – think, imagine

Skollies – gangsters

Skop – kick

Skyf – smoke

Slag – kill

Slang – snake (penis)

Slap – sloppy

Sluk – sip

Smaak – to like

Steeked – stabbed

Stuk – nice 'piece' (attractive woman)

Suiping – drinking alcohol

The Island – Robben Island (where political prisoners like Mandela were imprisoned)

Totsiens – abientot (till we see each other again)

Tunes – tells

Uitgesuip – very drunk

Vark – pig

Voeltjie – little bird

Voetsek – go away!

Vrek – dead

Vuilgat – dirty hole (arse hole)

Woes – angry

Comrade Babble

Abasebenzi – (isiZulu) workers

AmaChina – (slang - pejorative) Chinese people

Amagents – (gangster slang) gents (men)

AmaKhulu – (slang - pejorative) Indian people

Baba – (isiZulu) father

Bantwana – (isiZulu) girls (in this instance used contemptuously)

Bedonnerd – crazy

Doos – (slang) cunt, idiot

Gat – (slang) gun

Gees – spirit

Goofed – stoned

Gooi – throw

Ikasi – (slang) black township

Izwelethu – (isiZulu) 'the land is ours'

Kif – hashish

Laaities – (slang) youngsters

Lahnies – (slang) masters, bosses

Madiba – clan name for Nelson Mandela

Majita – (gangster slang) a guy

Maqabane – (isiZulu) comrades

Mpundus – (isiZulu) buttocks

Mzansi – (slang) south (short for South Africa)

Ngwenya – (isiZulu) crocodile

Nyaope – cheap, highly addictive drug that often leads users to anti-social behaviour

Pozzie – (slang) house, place

Rand Club – club formed in Johannesburg in the 1920s by mining magnates

Tjoekie – (slang) jail

Umlungus – (isiZulu) whites (over the last two decades has become a pejorative)

ZCC – Zionist Christian Church (a South African church that combines Christian and traditional African practices and articles of faith)

Boykie and Girlie

Mbongolo – (isiZulu) donkey

Book Marks

Bra – (slang) brother

Amandla – (isiZulu) revolutionary cry/slogan much used in the anti-Apartheid struggle; literally 'power', as in 'power to the people!'

Arms deal – the massive and notorious arms deal entered into by the ANC government in the 1990's that left a trail of corruption and scandal in its wake

BC – Black Consciousness philosophy

B.E.E – (acronym) Black Economic Empowerment (ANC policy to advance black stake in the economy)

Baas – boss

Biltong – dry meat

Chivas – brand name of a high quality, expensive whiskey

Deurmekaar – upside-down (disorganised)

Eishkom – play on the name Eskom (South Africa's state owned electricity utility); 'eish' – slang expression denoting unhappiness, dissatisfaction, sorrow etc

isiXhosa – the Xhosa language

John Vorster – former prime mister of South Africa (1966 to 1978); thereafter president of the republic (1978-79); name of police head quarters in Johannesburg during the Apartheid era

Khulubuse – Khulubuse Zuma, obese nephew of Jacob Zuma; notorious for corrupt business deals and exploitation of workers

Klapped – hit, struck

Krokodil trane – (Afrikaans) crocodile tears

Kullids – (slang) Coloured people

Mr Shaik, Mr Gupta, Mr Reddy . . . – Names of well-known millionaires of Indian origin who have been found guilty of corrupting Jacob Zuma and other black African leaders

Msholozi – clan name for Jacob Zuma (current ANC president of South Africa)

Necklace – (slang) township practice during the anti-Apartheid struggle of burning suspected informers (impimpis) alive by placing a tyre round the neck, dousing the suspect with petrol and then setting him/her alight

'Ons sal things nice and soft let bly' – (Afrikaans) we'll let things stay nice and easy

Orania – whites-only, Afrikaner village in the Northern Cape of South Africa

Potjie – cooking pot

Potting – drinking (alcohol)

Regmaker – (Afrikaans) morning drink to dispel a hangover (literally to 'make right')

RSA – (acronym) Republic of South Africa

Slovo – Joe Slovo (general secretary of the South African Communist Party (1984 – 1991)

'Wat is 'n volk sonder land?' – (Afrikaans) what is a nation without land?

Wit ou – (Afrikaans) white guy

Zol – (slang) dagga (marijuana)

Other books by the author

POETRY

Call from the Free State
We Jive like This (with the Botsotso Jesters)
Dirty Washing (with the Botsotso Jesters)
Greetings Emsawawa (with the Botsotso Jesters)
Saving Water
There are Two Birds at My Window
The Colours of Our Flag

SHORT FICTION

Un/common Ground
Out of the Wreckage
Meditations of a Non-White White

CHILDRENS BOOK

Blue Wings

MUSIC (ALBUMS) – under the name 'All Clear'

No VIPs
Faster than Light
Look in the Mirror

ALLAN KOLSKI HORWITZ was born in 1952 in Vryburg, South Africa but grew up in Cape Town. Between 1974 and 1985 he lived in the Middle East, Europe and North America, returning to live in Johannesburg in 1986. Since then he has worked as an organiser and educator in the trade union and social housing movements. He is a writer in various genres as well as being a songwriter and singer. Since leaving full-time employment in the trade unions in 2009, he continues on an ad hoc with his work as an educator and activist. He is a member of the Botsotso Jesters poetry performance group and of the Botsotso Publishing editorial board.

Printed in the United States
By Bookmasters